SEARCHING FOR YELLOWSTONE

"There is no such thing as the true West anymore. It's a dead issue."

(SHEPARD 1981, 19)

"To write history therefore means to quote history back to itself."

(BENJAMIN 1983, 24; ALSO QUOTED BY ULMER 1989, 211)

"Red Lodge is the center of a triangle formed by Billings, Montana;
Cody, Wyoming; and Yellowstone Park, each about 65 miles apart."

(RED LODGE CHAMBER OF COMMERCE BROCHURE 1996, 1)

"One cannot be pessimistic about the West. This is the native home of hope."

(STEGNER 1980, 38)

SEARCHING FOR YELLOWSTONE

Race, Gender, Family, and Memory in the Postmodern West

NORMAN K. DENZIN

Left Coast
Press Inc.

Walnut Creek, California

LEFT COAST PRESS, INC.
1630 North Main Street, #400
Walnut Creek, CA 94596
http://www.LCoastPress.com

Left Coast Press inc.

This book is a product of my ethnographic imagination. Names, characters, places, events, and incidents are used fictitiously. Any resemblance to actual events, locales, or persons, living or dead, is at least partially coincidental.

ISBN 978-1-59874-319-7 hardcover
ISBN 978-1-59874-320-3 paperback

Library of Congress Cataloging-in-Publication Data

Denzin, Norman K.
   Searching for Yellowstone : race, gender, family, and memory in the postmodern West / Norman K. Denzin.
      p.   cm.
   Includes bibliographical references and index.
   ISBN 978-1-59874-319-7 (hardback : alk. paper)
   ISBN 978-1-59874-320-3 (pbk. : alk. paper)
1. West (U.S.)—Race relations.   2. West (U.S.)—Social conditions.   3. Indians of North America—West (U.S.)—History.   4. Sex role—West (U.S.)—History.   5. Stereotypes (Social psychology)—West (U.S.)—History.   6. Family—West (U.S.)—History.   7. Memory—Social aspects—West (U.S.)—History.   8. Indians of North America—Yellowstone National Park—History.   9. Yellowstone National Park—In popular culture.   10. Historical reenactments—Yellowstone National Park.   I. Title.
F596.2.D46 2008
305.800978—dc22   2008003535

Printed in the United States of America

∞™ The paper used in this publication meets the minimum requirements of American National Standard for Information Sciences—Permanence of Paper for Printed Library Materials, ANSI/NISO Z39.48–1992.

08 09 10 11 12   5 4 3 2 1

Designed by Detta Penna
Copyedited by Sandra Craig
Indexed by Joan D. Dickey

CONTENTS

green press

INITIATIVE

Left Coast Press is committed to preserving ancient forests and natural resources. We elected to print this title on 30% post consumer recycled paper, processed chlorine free. As a result, for this printing, we have saved:

3 Trees (40' tall and 6-8" diameter)
1,159 Gallons of Wastewater
2 million BTU's of Total Energy
149 Pounds of Solid Waste
279 Pounds of Greenhouse Gases

Left Coast Press made this paper choice because our printer, Thomson-Shore, Inc., is a member of Green Press Initiative, a nonprofit program dedicated to supporting authors, publishers, and suppliers in their efforts to reduce their use of fiber obtained from endangered forests.

For more information, visit www.greenpressinitiative.org

Environmental impact estimates were made using the Environmental Defense Paper Calculator. For more information visit: www.papercalculator.org.

ACKNOWLEDGMENTS

I would like to thank Mitch Allen, Katherine E. Ryan, Nathan Summers, Yvonna S. Lincoln, Art Bochner, and Carolyn Ellis for their quick and early support of this project. Mitch Allen is the editor of all editors—his vision and fingerprints are all over this book. I cannot thank him enough. Laurel Richardson gave me a careful and very helpful and challenging reading. An unnamed postmodern archaeologist inflicted pain and forced me to rethink the entire project and my place in it. My interactions in the Unit for Criticism and Interpretive Theory, the International Institute of Qualitative Inquiry, and the Program in Cultural Studies and Interpretive Research at the University of Illinois, and conversations with Heidi Summers, Richard Bradley, Johanna Bradley, Mike and Rachel Maehr, Michael Giardina, Mary Weems, Patricia Clough, Michal McCall, Andy Fontana, Kathy Charmaz, Jack Bratich, Kevin Dolan, James Salvo, David Monje, Aisha Durham, Shoshana Magnet, Lawrence Loendorf, Peter Nabokov, Bob Moran, Lee Whittlesey, Doug Foley, Joni Kinsey, Sara Delamont, Paul Atkinson, and Ed Bruner helped to clarify my arguments.

For assistance in securing permission to reproduce many of the images in this book I thank Marguerite House (Buffalo Bill Historical Center), Bridgette Guild and Colleen Cury (Yellowstone National Park), Lory Morrow (Montana Historical Society), Richard Sorenson (Smithsonian), Carter Gowl, Harry Jackson, and Lew Hansen. I wish to thank Detta Penna for her careful assistance during production, Sandra Craig for her meticulous copyediting, and Joan Dickey for her proofreading of the page proofs and the creation of the index.

This project would not have been completed without the assistance, patience, and talents of James Salvo. I also thank the students at the University of Illinois, who patiently sat through formal and informal seminars, listening to earlier versions of my arguments about performance ethnography, cultural studies, politics, and pedagogy. I especially thank Kathy Charmaz, editor of *Symbolic Interaction*, and Paul Atkinson and Sara Delamont, editors of *Qualitative Research*, who published early versions of several of the more experimental chapters that appear in revised form in this book.

Finally, I gratefully acknowledge the moral, intellectual, and financial support given to this project by the late Dean Kim Rotzoll, of the College of Communication; by Paula Treichler, former director, and Cliff Christians, current director, of the Institute of Communications Research; and by Cinda Robbins Cornstubble, Janette Bradley Wright, and Robin Price in the Department of Advertising and Consumer Studies, for their unfailing support at all levels of this and related projects.

Portions of the materials in Chapter 2 appeared in Norman K. Denzin 2002a; portions of Chapter 3 appeared in Norman K. Denzin 2005b; portions of Chapter 4 appeared in Norman K. Denzin 2004; portions of Chapter 5 appeared in Norman K. Denzin 2007; a condensed version of Chapter 6 will appear in Norman K. Denzin 2008; portions of Chapter 8 appeared in Norman K. Denzin 2003; portions of an earlier version of Chapter 9 appeared in Norman K. Denzin 2000b.

Photo Credits

and sister, Lilly, age 5, taken in front of Harry Jackson's monumental sculpture *Sacagawea* in the BBHC's Cashman Greever Garden." Gift of Mr. and Mrs. Richard Cashman. BBHC photo by Chris Gimmeson.

Plate 2. Photograph, "Chief Illiniwek: The Last Dance." Reprinted with permission of the University of Illinois Allumni Association and Mark Jones, photographer, illiniphoto.com.

Plate 3. Photograph, Chief Plenty Coups statue, *Red Lodge Magazine*.

Plate 4. Photograph, William Henry Jackson, *Setting the Record Straight*, 1871, Catalog #YELL 37737, courtesy of the National Park Service, Yellowstone National Park.

Photo Montage 2

Plate 5. Postcard, Old Faithful, Yellowstone National Park.

Plate 6. Cover, *Haynes Guide: Yellowstone National Park*, 1953 (photograph of Old Faithful by Frank J. Haynes), courtesy of Montana Historical Society.

Plate 7. Map, the Grand Canyon of the Yellowstone, 1953 *Haynes Guide: Yellowstone National Park*, courtesy of Montana Historical Society.

Plates 8, 9. Painting, Thomas Moran, *Grand Canyon of the Yellowstone*, 1872, and detail. Oil on canvas, 84 × 144¼ in. (213 × 266.3 cm). National Museum of American Art, Smithsonian Institution.

Plate 10. Travel brochure showing Old Faithful, Northern Pacific Railroad, 1933, *Yellowstone Journal*, fall 2006: 12.

Plate 11. Book cover, *Along the Trail with Lewis and Clark*, courtesy of Farcountry Press, (800) 821-3874.

Plate 12. Brochure, *Drawn to Yellowstone*, 2005, courtesy of Buffalo Bill Historical Center, Cody, Wyoming.

Plates 13, 14. Front and back cover images, Lindblad Expedition brochure "In the Wake of Lewis and Clark, 2006."

Plate 15. Crazy Mule's map #1, courtesy of Joslyn Art Museum, Omaha, Nebraska.

Plate 16. Map, Yellowstone National Park highway system, from 1953 *Haynes Guide*: *Yellowstone National Park*, courtesy of Montana Historical Society.

Photo Montage 3

Plate 17. Photograph, Nez Perce mother in native dress and son in everyday dress, on horseback, from *Yellowstone Discovery* 20 (spring 2005): 1. Photo: National Park Service.

Plate 18. Gallery ad, *Midday at the Oasis*, by Dennis Ziemienski. Mark Sublette Medicine Man Gallery, Inc., Tucson and Santa Fe, medicinemangallery.com.

Plate 19. Cover ad, *The Virginian* by Owen Wister, illustration by Thom Ross. Buffalo Bill Historical Center.

Plates 20–28. Author family photos.

Photo Montage 1

❀

MYTHIC NATIVE AMERICANS AND THE NEW/OLD WEST

The first three photographs in Montage 1 represent white Americans' mythic views of Native American women and men, from Sacagawea to Chief Plenty Coups and Chief Illiniwek. These images circulate in the New West in the present. But they are meant to be timeless, existing in a continuous time frame from the past to the present.

Harry Jackson's famous bronze statue of Sacagawea (Plate 1) stands in the Cusman Greever Garden at the Buffalo Bill Historical Center, Cody, Wyoming (Chapter 5). Chief Illiniwek (Plate 2) is an invented college mascot who has had a troubled history at the University of Illinois, Champaign-Urbana (Chapter 8). Some believe he danced for the last time at a halftime ceremony during an Illini basketball game in February 2007. The statue of Chief Plenty Coups (Plate 3), the last chief of the Crow Indians, greets visitors as they enter Red Lodge, Montana. Chief Plenty Coups State Park is 35 miles south of Billings, Montana.

The five Bannock Native Americans in *Setting the Record Straight* (Plate 4) were photographed by William Henry Jackson in 1871. This staged photo represents the classic nineteenth-century museum view of Native Americans. The photographer has the subjects dress in native or ritual garb, has them pose, and then claims that the photograph is a realistic representation of male or female Native Americans. Whose record is being set straight?

Plate 1. Harry Jackson's statue of Sacagawea, Buffalo Bill Historical Center.

Plate 2. Chief Illiniwek, "The Last Dance."

Plate 3. Chief Plenty Coups, Red Lodge, Montana.

Plate 4. William Henry Jackson, *Setting the Record Straight*, 1871.

SEARCHING FOR YELLOWSTONE I

"If we do a census of the population in our collective imagination, imaginary Indians are one of the largest demographic groups. They dance, they drum; they go on the warpath; they are always young men who wear trailing feather bonnets. Symbolic servants, they serve as mascots, metaphors. We rely on these images to anchor us to the land and verify our account of our own past. But these Indians exist only in our imaginations."

(SPINDEL 2000, 8)

"We say that Yellowstone National Park was established on 1 March 1872, but in fact we have never stopped establishing Yellowstone. Whether as first-time visitors or as world-famous biologists, we continue to discover and explore it, and we also continue to create it. That is why I have called this book *Searching for Yellowstone*; ... indeed, the search for Yellowstone is a search for ourselves."

(SCHULLERY 1997, 2–3, 5, 261–62)

In 1994 my wife and I bought a small cabin on Rock Creek, 4 miles outside Red Lodge, Montana, 20 miles from the Wyoming border, 69 miles over the Beartooth Mountains into Yellowstone Park.[1] Red Lodge is at the center of a triangle formed by Billings, Montana; Cody, Wyoming, with its famous Buffalo Bill Historical Center (Bartlett 1992); and the park itself, each about 65 miles apart. We have become cultural tourists in the New West (Limerick 2000), "seasonals" traveling back and forth between Champaign and Urbana, Illinois, and Billings and on to Red Lodge—and to many of the small cities and towns between Red Lodge and the park, including Big Timber, Cody, Cooke City, Gardiner, Livingston, Mammoth Hot Springs, Silver Gate, and, in the park, Tower Junction, Lamar Valley, Roosevelt Lodge, Canyon Village, Yellowstone Lake, and Old Faithful.

THIS BOOK

This book—part memoir, part ethnography, part performance text—comes out of experiences in this complex triangular space. In this tiny slice of the postmodern West, cowboys, Native Americans, park rangers, and cultural tourists collide. In the summers of 2004–2006 the Lewis and Clark Expedition of 1804–1806 was reenacted. Suddenly our corner of Montana was filled with Native Americans, some dressed as Sacagawea, others as fancy dancers. White males dressed as mountain men reenacted the Lewis and Clark journey. Sacagawea cookbooks sold out at Red Lodge Books. It was as if time had stood still.

In each chapter I encounter these idealized Native Americans and their representations (Huhndorf 2001; Hoxie 2006). These images invoke the idealized authentic, prewhite, historical Native American or the Native American assimilated to white culture, as in the case of Sacagawea. I find myself embedded in these representations, in these narratives: Indians playing cowboys, cowboys playing Indians, twenty-first-century Native Americans playing nineteenth-century Indians, and little white boys playing Indians (Deloria 1998).

I interrogate the emotions, the identities, and the memories that accompany these collisions among white, Native American, and contemporary western popular culture (Lear 2006). These stories connect to my childhood and the movies about the West that I watched with my grandfather. They show how my childhood and family experiences continue to shape what I write about today.

Chapter 2, an autoethnographic performance text, folds family memories into reflections occasioned while watching Crow Indians performing fancy dances for white tourists in Red Lodge. Chapter 3, a four-act play, focuses on the disappearance and reappearance of Native Americans in Yellowstone (see also Christofferson 2007; Nabokov and Loendorf 2004). The three-act play in Chapter 4 interrogates the place of Hudson's Bay blankets in the Lewis and Clark Expedition. I connect these same blankets, metaphorically, to my family, where they function as gifts that connect one generation to the next.

The play "Sacagawea's Nickname, or the Sacagawea Problem" (Chapter 5) dramatically explores the sexualized representations of Sacagawea and Native American women in the Lewis and Clark journals as well as in Montana's foundational novel, *The Big Sky*, by A. B. Guthrie Jr. (1947). Chapter 6 consists of a historical drama which reenacts the creation of the most famous painting of the park, Thomas Moran's *Grand Canyon of the*

Yellowstone. A Native American male is buried in the center of Moran's panting. The meanings of this presence are debated in the play.

Chapter 7 offers a more traditional narrative reading of the only known Native American representation of Yellowstone Park, Crazy Mule's map. Chapter 8, another three-act play, examines the conflicts surrounding racial performances of idealized Native Americans in Red Lodge, Montana, and Urbana, Illinois. Chapter 9 takes up another version of my search for Yellowstone. I work my way back through another set of family memories as well as more recent encounters with postmodern western performances on Rock Creek. The Coda (Chapter 10) comes full circle, locating these stories and performances in the current historical moment.

In each chapter I examine the social and historical circumstances that reproduce racial and gender stereotyping in the contemporary West. At a deep level I write about a search for more realistic utopias, more just and more radically democratic social worlds for the twenty-first century, a search for self in troubling times. I hope to chart a course of action that acknowledges complicities with past atrocities, while outlining new myths that are more inclusive and not just "Indians first, and then us."[2]

So I borrow my title from Schullery (1997). Like him, my version of "Searching for Yellowstone" is a search for self, for new self-understandings. And these understandings emerged out of an engagement with that symbolic space known as Yellowstone National Park. The congressional act of 1872 which established Yellowstone National Park reads, in part:

> "This land is reserved
> and withdrawn from settlement, occupancy or sale....
> Dedicated and set apart
> as a public park or pleasuring-ground
> for the benefit and enjoyment of the people."
>
> (HAINES 1996A, 167)

I went there in 1988 as a tourist, and twenty years and fifty visits later I became convinced that a new cultural politics is being played out in the park and its surrounding communities.[3] Indeed, the park is more than a pleasuring-ground. It is a magnet for national discourses and performances about Native Americans, history, gender, nation, and nature. In borrowing my title from Schullery, I am suggesting that this search extends beyond self—it speaks to the soul of a nation, and to the kind of nation we want America to be.

CONSTRUCTING THE TEXT AS "MYSTORY"

Guided by Gregory Ulmer's concept of "mystory" (1989), I write from
the scenes of memory, rearranging, suppressing, even inventing scenes,
foregoing claims to exact truth or factual accuracy, searching instead
for emotional truth, for deep meaning (see Stegner 1992, iv; Blew 1999,
7). Translating experience and memory into "fictional truth...is not a
transcription at all, but a re-making" (Stegner, quoted in Benson 1996, 114).
In so doing, I'm in the "boundaries of creative nonfiction [which] will always
be as fluid as water" (Blew 1999, 7).

My texts travel among three levels of discourse: personal experience;
popular representations of Yellowstone and the Old West and New West;
and scholarly discourses on these topics. Following Walter Benjamin's
directions, these narratives rip the present and the past out of their current
contexts. History unfolds as a series of interconnected presents, memories,
a montage of moments quoted out of context, "juxtaposed fragments from
widely dispersed places and times . . ." (Ulmer 1989, 112). To represent the
past this way does not mean to "recognize it 'the way it really was.' It means
to seize hold of a memory as it flashes up at a moment of danger" (Benjamin
1969, 257), to see and rediscover the past not as a succession of events but
as a series of scenes, inventions, emotions, images, and stories (Ulmer 1989,
112).

In quoting from these histories and discourses surrounding Native
Americans, Yellowstone Park, and Lewis and Clark, I hope to expose and
criticize the racist politics buried deep inside the American democratic
imagination. Thus these interrogations represent an opportunity to take up
again Kittridge's (1996) and Limerick's (2001) challenge to rethink western
history and mythology by starting out at ground level, starting all over again.
In bringing the past into the autobiographical present, I insert myself into
the past and create the conditions for rewriting and hence reexperiencing
it. I want to invent a new version of the past, a new history. I want to create
a chorus of discordant voices (and images) concerning Native Americans
and their place in Yellowstone Park, as well as in our collective imagination
(Spindel 2000, 8).

I read Yellowstone, America's first national park, metaphorically. In and
across the discourses that historically define the park are deeply entrenched
meanings concerning nature, culture, violence, gender, wilderness, parks,
whites, and Native Americans (Langford 1972/1905; Chittenden 1964/1895;
Haines 1996a, 1996b; Bartlett 1985; Schullery 1979a, 1997; Brown 1971). The
presence of Native Americans in the collective white imagination is almost

entirely a matter of racist myth, shifting meanings of the color line, the "veil of color," theatricality, and minstrelsy (Du Bois 1989, xxxi, 2–3; Crue 2002; Spindel 2000).

Driving or walking into the park occasions these reappraisals, whether one enters through the Grand Arch at Gardiner, through the east entrance at Cooke City, over Sylvan Pass outside Cody, past the Grand Tetons at the southern entrance of the park, or through West Yellowstone. The spaces of Yellowstone invite introspection, memory, forgetting, critical reflection on what is not here, lost innocence.

So these chapters are about memory and forgetting, nostalgia, a longing for the unspoiled, a desire to confront nature in its pure essence, its sheer beauty. They ask, "What do we forget when we remember?" Visits to the park and celebrations of Sacagawea and Lewis and Clark occasion only selective glimpses into the past. In these glimpses we neglect experiences that need to be examined in the light of a new day. In looking back into our own personal rearview mirrors, we also catch glimpses into our nation's past. We reenact that past, in some version, every time we visit the park. We must learn a new form of remembering. This will allow us to recover and then forget what was never in our memory in the first place. So, transformed, Yellowstone can become a utopian site for imagining and constructing new beginnings and new memories, and for forgetting by no longer honoring such ugly pasts as those connected to Lewis and Clark and Sacagawea.

GRANDFATHERS AND PARKS AND STATE FAIRS

In the summer of 1952, when I was eleven, my grandfather almost took me to Yellowstone Park. My grandfather was Waldo William Townsley, named Waldo, perhaps, after another famous Waldo, Ralph Waldo Emerson. And Townsley: Paul Schullery (1997, 160, 213) notes that John Townsley was a midcentury Yellowstone Park superintendent (see also Everhart 1998, 164–65). I do not know if John Townsley was related to Waldo William Townsley. Still, his name on the list of park superintendents somehow makes the Townsley and now the Denzin presence in Yellowstone all the more real.

Grandpa went to Yellowstone in the summer of 1932. He loved to tell me stories about Old Faithful, about the trout fishing on the Madison River, about the sun setting over the mountains, about the beautiful Yellowstone River. But we never made the trip. When I was ten years old we did get as far as Des Moines for the last day of the Iowa State Fair. It rained on our tent, but Grandpa made pancakes for breakfast and that made it special.

I have a memory of a picture of Grandpa smiling, standing beside a Lincoln roadster, wearing a white shirt, proudly holding a string of trout (Plate 20).[4] Whenever I stayed overnight with my grandparents, I fell asleep in the bedroom which had Grandpa's Yellowstone picture sitting on the dresser. I awakened each morning to the sight of grandpa and his fish.

Today I search for that spot in Yellowstone where my grandfather caught those trout. I have followed that picture into the heart of Yellowstone Park, to the Old Faithful Inn. I have walked along the banks of the Madison and the Firehole rivers, where he surely fished. My wife and I have stood, as he surely did, with other tourists and waited for Old Faithful to erupt skyward. I have hiked past Upper Geyser Basin to the campground at Fountain Paint Pot, wondering if Grandpa camped here. I drove to West Thumb, Grant Village, and Geyser Basin, looking for his footprints.

My grandfather's smile in that picture was an invitation to come to this site, to Yellowstone. Like others in his generation, he searched for meaning in his life. He was drawn to and found Yellowstone, and in this place he felt fulfilled and complete, fulfilled in a way that he never felt anywhere else. This is why he wanted to take me to Yellowstone, so I could experience this feeling for myself, so I could find myself in the fast-running waters of the river named Yellowstone, in the sacred places in the park named Yellowstone.

My grandfather was a Republican, boasting that our family had voted Republican since Lincoln. When I broke with tradition and voted for Kennedy against Nixon, Grandpa refused to talk to me for a month. There is a sense in which his Republican politics embodied the values of those Montana capitalist investors, including Nathaniel P. Langford, who sought to promote tourism in Yellowstone as a way of making money for the Northern Pacific Railroad. In 1872 this group succeeded in convincing Congress to make Yellowstone America's first national park, set aside for "the benefit and enjoyment of the people" (Kittridge 2000, 247). Soon trains were bringing rich people to the park. Grandpa might have been one of them, except he chose the rich person's transportation of the 1930s: the Lincoln roadster.

But I have followed my grandfather to this park, and today I attempt to find myself in ways that his Republican self might not like. Like him, I am a transplanted midwesterner struggling with these myths of the American West.

In America today, in the brutally cruel, cold days since 11 September 2001, we are struggling to revise our dominant mythology. Just who are we as Americans? Are we western cowboys, as President George Bush seems to imagine, hunting down and killing terrorist outlaws? Are we seeking new frontiers and new worlds to conquer and control? Can a violent form of democracy be imposed on others against their will? What story about ourselves do we want to inhabit? Who are our storytellers? Whose stories will we accept? Which laws will we allow to control our lives? What does democracy mean after 9/11/01? Like Walter Benjamin and C. Wright Mills (1959), I want a writing form that helps me make sense of the history I am living, a form that allows me to insert myself into the violent events of the day, including life in America after 9/11/01 (see Denzin and Lincoln 2003, xx; Denzin 2007a).

We must return to a new starting point. Yellowstone is a good place to begin. Working forward from this site, we may find what we are looking for. We want laws designed to preserve a model of a radically peaceful democratic society, a society which is nonviolent and nonracist. We want laws and courts based on a post–11 September mythology. We want a new mythology for America. We must reimagine our myths. Only then can we coherently remodel our laws and hope to keep our society in a realistic relationship to our utopian democratic ideals. In a modest way, the essays in this book are meant to speak to this new mythology.

READING/PERFORMING THE TEXT

Except for this introduction and Chapters 7, 9, and 10, the five plays and one autoethnographic narrative which follow are intended to be performed—that is, read aloud. The act of reading aloud in a group, or coperforming, creates a shared emotional experience that brings the narrative alive in ways that silent reading cannot. In each play the speakers are designated as Speaker 1 or Speaker 2. Among these speakers are narrators who speak in various voices, pairs or groups of individuals, and organizations. When the plays are performed, group members rotate through the speeches, taking their turns as Speaker 1 or Speaker 2. Each speaker identifies the character—for example, Thomas Jefferson, a Native American, narrator as child—before reading the speech. Performers should play across race, age, and gender lines. Additional stage directions are suggested, such as the use of "whiteface," "redface," and "blackface" masks. The plays may be performed around a seminar table, on a simple set, or on a stage before an audience with costumes, sets, and props as "ornate as one imagines" (Smith 2004, 6).

If audiovisual equipment is available, images and the text of some of the documents in the plays, such as timelines and letters, may be projected. The three photo essays and the map in Chapter 4 are examples of material that could be used. A spotlight that moves from speaker to speaker could enhance a production.

In creating these performance texts I had in mind the trilogy *U.S.A.* by John Dos Passos (1937). He used Newsreel sections to incorporate news of the day into the text, The Camera Eye passages to capture personal experience in a poetic stream of consciousness, and most important, he caught the speech of the people. I present my material as a layered text, a montage of original sources and documents, newspaper clippings, memories, events, history, personal experience, and interpretations.

The lines that are spoken are not mine: they are all taken from published texts. I have imposed a narrative order upon them. My procedure is borrowed from Anna Deavere Smith: "All words that are spoken are verbatim (or paraphrased) from historical texts" (2004, 5). For the passages from the Lewis and Clark journals, original spelling and punctuation has been maintained whether the passages were quoted or paraphrased.

A CRITICAL PERFORMANCE PEDAGOGY

As with the earlier books *Performing Ethnography* (Denzin 2003a) and *Reading Race* (Denzin 2002b), this project reflects two concerns. For nearly four decades I have been working with undergraduate and graduate students at the University of Illinois, experimenting with new ways of reading, writing, and performing culture. We learned how to write and coperform texts based on epiphanies surrounding race, gender, and the politics of identity. I owe these students a great debt: together we worked through many of the themes and issues in this book. This book is partial payment on this debt.

Second, I continue to believe that the current generation of college students in North America has the opportunity to make a difference in the race relations arena. It is possible to imagine and perform a multiracial society, a society in which differences are honored. If this generation is to make a difference, that difference will be defined, in part, in terms of opposition to the current representations and interpretations of the racial order and the color line that circulate in the media and in social science writings. This resistance, in turn, will be shaped by how we read, write, perform, and critique culture.

In challenging these myths and cultural representations, I follow Stuart Hall (1997) and Valerie Smith (1997), who argue that it is not enough to replace negative with positive representations. The positive-negative debate essentializes racial identity and denies its "dynamic relation to constructions of class, gender, sexuality [and] region" (Smith 1997, 4). It takes two parties to do racial minstrelsy. Race is performative, contextual, and historical. Stereotypes of whiteness are tangled up in racial myth, in minstrel shows that replay the Wild West, leading whites to look western, and Native Americans to look Indian (Dorst 1999).

By unraveling these myths and their meanings and origins, I point to the diversity and complexity of racial representations and racial performances in American popular culture. I seek to replace old stereotypes with new understandings. I want to show how historical discourse can in fact turn back on itself, revise its stance toward the past, and perform new, progressive representations of cultural difference.

I advance a critical performative pedagogy which turns the ethnographic into the performative, and the performative into the political. This pedagogy hopefully allows us to dream our way into a militant democratic utopian space, a space where the color line disappears, and justice for all is more than a dream.

Chapter 2

INDIANS AND COWBOYS[1]

"White domination is so complete that even
American Indian children want to be cowboys."
(WARD CHURCHILL 1992, QUOTED IN MICHAEL YELLOW BIRD 2004, 33)

In the 1950s my brother, Mark, and I spent our summers, until we were young teenagers, with our grandparents on their farm south of Iowa City, Iowa.[2] Saturday nights were special. Grandpa loved those "cowboy and Indian" movies, and so did I.[3] Every Saturday Grandma fixed an early supper. After supper, Grandpa and I, wearing going-to-town clothes, drove to Iowa City to catch the first of a double feature at the Strand Theatre starring John Wayne, Glen Ford, Henry Fonda, or Jimmy Stewart. Soft summer nights in cool darkness, nighttime dreams of cowboys, Indians, the cavalry, six-guns, stage coaches, barroom ladies, school marms—and blond-haired little boys running after a lonely rider on a horse: "Shane, Shane, Shane, come back." I still remember the names of the movies: *Stage Coach, Broken Arrow, Colt 45, She Wore a Yellow Ribbon, Winchester '73, High Noon, The Naked Spur, The Far Country, Bend of the River,* and *Shane,* the only film I ever watched with my father. Grandpa and I would leave home by six o'clock and often not get back until after eleven.

I wanted to be a cowboy when I grew up. So did Mark. On Saturday mornings, while Grandma made hot doughnuts for us in the new deep-fat fryer in her big country kitchen, we watched cowboy and Indian television shows: *The Lone Ranger, Red Rider and Little Beaver, Roy Rogers and Dale Evans, Sky King.* Mark and I had cowboy outfits—wide-brimmed hats, leather vests and chaps, spurs, little pistols and gun belts. Grandpa bought us a horse. There is a picture of Mark and me in our cowboy outfits on the back of swaybacked Sonny, the horse who was deaf in the right ear. We'd ride Sonny round and round the corral, waving at Grandpa and Grandma. In fourth grade I was Squanto in the Thanksgiving play about the pilgrims.

A blue, wind-swept Montana night, a red sun setting over the Beartooth Mountains. It's hot inside the crowded Red Lodge Civic Auditorium. "Montana Night," a special part of this year's Festival of Nations celebration, is about to begin.[4] The Montana Tune Smiths softly play their new song, "Montana Miners' Story."[5] Tall, slender, blue-eyed Miss Rodeo Montana waves and smiles at the audience.

Everyone sings the "Festival of Nations Anthem." A tall cowboy walks to the podium. The mistress of ceremonies asks the audience to "Please give a friendly Montana hello to Bill Greenough of the famous rodeo-riding Greenough family."[6] Bill removes his cowboy hat and, in a swooping gesture, waves to the crowd, which stands and cheers.

I can still hear Waylon Jennings in the back of my mind. I remember all those times I listened to Waylon and Willie Nelson sing "Whiskey River." I remember drinking myself to sleep. Country music floats through these memories. Stealing a line from Willie, I used to think of myself as an "angel flying too close to the ground." Like Waylon, my heroes were cowboys in those days, and it seems they are even tonight. Like them, I am "sadly in search of myself, one step in back of my slow movin' dreams." A midwesterner in a small Montana town, dreaming about the West, cowboys and Indians, whiskey rivers. So for years I turned off the country music, fearful that its soulful sounds would take me back to those drunken nights. Tonight, here in Red Lodge on Montana Night, I come face to face with those suppressed, painful memories. I thought I had left that past behind me.

The lights dim. The mistress of ceremonies asks the audience to "Give a big Red Lodge welcome to Crow Indian Chief Haywood Big Day and his family, who are visitors tonight from the Crow reservation near Pryor." In full tribal regalia, Chief Big Day walks to the center of the stage. I flash back to those cowboy and Indian television shows of my childhood. The chief looks like a television Indian. Maybe he is another version of "Kaw-Liga," the drugstore wooden Indian in the Hank Williams song; the sad Indian who never smiled at the little Indian maiden next door.

But Haywood Big Day is no wooden drugstore Indian. He stands in a circle of white light in the middle of the darkened auditorium.[7] He extends his arms skyward, as if praying. Turning slowly, he bends four times from the waist, first to the north, then to the east, the south, and finally to the west. A "real" live Indian in Red Lodge. Sherman Alexie says, "Indians make the best cowboys" (1993, 18).[8]

As if on cue, Bill Greenough, this evening's version of Roy Rogers and the Lone Ranger, walks to the center of the gym floor. Chief Big Day turns, smiles, and speaks to Bill and the audience:

> "Hello. My family used to come to Red Lodge during your
> ceremonies. We would come to the rodeo. We rode down
> Broadway with you and your family. Then they stopped asking us. It
> is good to be back. My family joins me tonight."

The chief, now acting like the Lone Ranger's Tonto, beckons to his family. In full ceremonial regalia, his wife and daughter solemnly walk across the floor and stand behind him. Wearing Los Angeles Lakers basketball jerseys, his four young grandsons follow their mother to the center of the gym. Their blue and gold L.A. Lakers–like jerseys have Shaquille O'Neal's face on the front and his number, 34, on the back. Seven Crow Indians stand in a row in the center of the Red Lodge Civic Auditorium. In the fifty years since the Festival of Nations began, Indians have never shared the stage. Cowboys and Indians together again.

Bill extends his hand to Chief Haywood Big Day:

> "Welcome to the Festival of Nations You are First Nation! You were
> here before us! Thank you for coming back. I remember when we
> rode together in the rodeo."

Then, as if remembering a line from *Red Rider* or *The Lone Ranger*, Bill says to tonight's Tonto, "Please entertain us."

The chief demurs: "There will be no square dancing tonight! We are First Nation. We will do a war dance." Seven Indians, four dressed in L.A. Lakers jerseys, do a war dance, heads bowed, arms moving up and down, across the gym floor.

For a brief moment, all who are present bear witness to a colorful montage. Everything is mixed up at the same time: race, ethnicity, the NBA, Shaquille O'Neal and the Los Angeles Lakers, rap and hip-hop, Miss Rodeo Montana, Crow Indians on reservations, war dances, cowboys, country music, dead miners. The crowd of over eight hundred stands as one, applauding Chief Big Day and his family, chanting "First Nation, First Nation." I can hear Paul Revere and the Raiders: "They took the whole Cherokee Nation and put us on the reservation."[9]

A postmodern racial performance right here in Red Lodge. All that's missing is Lyle Lovett singing "If I Had a Boat" (1987), and at that moment, these lines from Lyle's song run through my mind:

> "The mystery masked man was smart
> He got himself a Tonto
> 'Cause Tonto did the dirty work for free
> But Tonto he was smarter
> And one day said Kemo sabe
> Kiss my ass I bought a boat
> I'm going out to sea"

I wonder if Haywood Big Day will tell Bill to "shove off."

I wonder how the chief got here tonight. Four years earlier a controversy raged in Red Lodge about the Redskin mascot and its use by the men's and women's high school athletic teams (see Beaumont 1997). The Lady Redskins stopped using the name, and the boys' teams started calling themselves the Red Lodge Pride. Semiotic warfare right here in this little mountain Montana village. Last week I asked one of the anti-Redskin advocates about Chief Big Day's performance. She told me the performance was hypocritical: "It was an insult. The people of Red Lodge drove the Crow Indians away."

We take a cab to the Billings airport. Our young cab driver says he is a Crow Indian from the rez. He tells us family stories as we make our way through the snow-packed city streets. "My father was an alcoholic. A drunken Indian like in the movies. I never see him." In early May of 1981 I spent a morning on Hennepin Avenue in Minneapolis drinking with Chippewa Indians. Four drunken days later I entered a treatment center in a Minneapolis suburb. Indians, drunk and sober, have been a part of my recovery ever since. And so it is tonight in the Red Lodge Civic Auditorium.

I think now back to those childhood days with Grandpa and Grandma. I did not know then that my father was an alcoholic. I just knew he drank a great deal. During our long summers on that Iowa farm I dreamed my way out of a painful family situation, away from those fights Mother and Dad had all the time. I dreamed my way into cowboy heaven, into a small, snug, safe space that opened up on Saturday nights when Grandpa and I drove to Iowa City. I would sit in the passenger seat, my arm out the window, the soft, warm summer breeze blowing through my hair, my face level with the green fields of corn that flashed by. We'd drive through those tunnels of green. We'd drive, like Dorothy in *The Wizard of Oz*, straight into another world, where I imagined life was better.

In front of the big and little silver screens, with Dale and Roy, John and Jimmy, Red Rider and Little Beaver, I became a boy-man, a warrior of sorts, a brave man, a cowboy, a rancher, a man of property who fought Indians. On Friday nights we listened to *Gunsmoke* on the big Philco radio next to Grandpa's desk in his corner of the kitchen. I loved Matt and Kitty and Festus, and I loved knowing that there could be justice on those Kansas plains. You just might have to kill drunks, rowdies, crooks, and Indians to get it.

Now on this blue August night, which is turning cold, I dream myself past those childhood reveries. Here in Red Lodge I come face to face with real Indians and cowboys. I wonder how I could have been so naive, how *we* could have been so naive. Indians were people, too, not performers put here to entertain us. But those movies I watched as a child with my grandfather created a discourse that exists to this day, for we only know Native Americans in their relationship to our whiteness (see Deloria 1998). We were never shown how to take them on their own terms, or on any terms for that matter.

And that is why the lines to Lyle's song are so important to me today:

"If I had a boat
I'd go out on the ocean
And if I had a pony
I'd ride him on my boat
And we could all together
Go out on the ocean
Me upon my pony on my boat"

I'd ask Tonto and his wife if they wanted to come with me. They could choose to come or stay. They both could ride upon my pony on my boat. They could have the boat and the pony.

These thoughts ran through my mind that night when I walked away from the Civic Auditorium in Red Lodge, Montana.

In March of 2001, as I was writing an earlier version of "Indians and Cowboys," debates raged on the University of Illinois campus about Chief Illiniwek (see Ebert 2001a, b; and Chapter 9 in this book).[10] Those debates wage to the present day. This official mascot and symbol of the university was created in 1926. The dancing Chief has been a presence at university athletic events ever since (see Spindel 2000; King and Springwood 2001; Crue 2002). In February 2000 the North Central Association of Colleges and Universities stated in its accreditation report: "There are inconsistencies between exemplary diversity policies and practices, and the university's policies regarding the Chief."

I had gone to Red Lodge for a vacation, for an escape to the mountains, and to leave racial politics and Chief Illiniwek behind. But as I sat in the Red Lodge Civic Auditorium on Montana Night in August 2000 and watched the performance of Chief Haywood Big Day, I was thrown back inside the very situation I thought I had left. Here a live version of Chief Illiniwek unfolded before me!

I attempted to write the two stories as one, a crisscrossing performance tale of negative images of Native Americans in two community contexts, Red Lodge and Urbana, Illinois. But the story got out of hand. There was too much material. I decided to narrow the focus to just the memories and feelings I had that night in the Civic Auditorium in Red Lodge. I had made notes the next day on the memories and the images I experienced that night, including memories of going to cowboy movies with my grandfather. But the story would not write itself until I returned to the music of Hank Williams, Willie Nelson, and Waylon Jennings. That music brought all the memories together: summers on my grandparents' farm, my father's drinking, my own drinking, listening to Willie sing and getting drunk, media images of Native Americans, painting my skin red and brown and playing Squanto in my grade school Thanksgiving play.

Seeing Tonto as the embodiment of all Indians, I awakened from a fitful sleep. As if in a dream, with Waylon singing in the background, the story poured out of me.

The discourses that circulate through the story came, it seems now, from my unconscious. As a young man I was not consciously aware of how those cowboy movies provided symbolic escape from the world of family alcoholism. I had never made the connection between First Nations persons, drunk and sober, and these slices of family history. Tonto emerged from my childhood memories as a stand-in for all Native Americans. That night Chief Heywood Big Day stood in for Tonto. But here was a Tonto with a family—a wife, a daughter, grandchildren—a Tonto with a history. This was a Tonto from Lyle Lovett's song, a Tonto who would not play second fiddle to the Lone Ranger.

The cowboy movies of my childhood divided the world into dualisms: cowboys and Indians, men and women, children and adults, country and city, West and non-West. In writing my story I fell into these tropes. They write themselves over and over again in my story. Indeed, gender inscriptions carry out the work of the cowboy/Indian split, and reproduce in gender the white/nonwhite racialization that I wish to deconstruct (see Nagel 2001).

I attempt to undo these splits and dualisms in the moment when the chief's grandsons appear in Los Angeles Lakers basketball jerseys. In that postmodern space everything slides together. All dichotomies dissolve into a single, blurring performance: the spectacle of seven Native Americans doing a war dance for a predominantly white audience.

In giving Tonto a life in the figure of Chief Heywood Big Day, I rescue myself from my past. Tonto and I now circulate through the lines of the Lovett song. I'm no longer a boy-man. Reworking a line from Bob Dylan, for just that moment I become the chief, I become Tonto, and stand inside his shoes, and see what a drag it is to see the Lone Ranger. I should call my story "Indians and Cowboys" or "Tonto and the Lone Ranger."

What if, as Mary Weems writes in "Brotha Wearing a Mask and a White Earring":

"If the Lone Ranger
  had been a brotha
  him and Tonto woulda
  hooked up
  kicked butt
  and took the long way
  Home."

(WEEMS 2002, 123)

What if?

Chapter 3

∵

INDIANS IN THE PARK

"Perhaps the most intriguing perpetual legacy of Native Americans in Yellowstone...was the belief that Indians were afraid of the park area."

(SCHULLERY 1997, 106)[1]

Contemporary Indians often respond with a chuckle when they are told of the theory that their ancestors cowered before those places (the geysers).

(NABOKOV AND LOENDORF 2004, 283)

"Buster...was wearing a blue cloth headband with a turkey feather stuck over his ear...'We late, man,' Buster said....Buster said Indians didn't eat chicken....We didn't have a troop, only the *Boy Scouts Handbook*....We were more interested in being *Indian* scouts than simply *Boy* Scouts."

(ELLISON 1996, 63–65; ITALICS IN ORIGINAL)

PROLOGUE

SPEAKER 1

Narrator as Dramatist, as Historian

This is a coperformance text, with multiple speaking parts—a four-act play of sorts (Denzin 2003a, 184). It can be performed on a simple set, around a seminar table, or from a stage in front of an audience. Images can be projected onto a full-size screen if audiovisual equipment is available. A spotlight can move from speaker to speaker.

"Indians in the Park," enacts a critical cultural-political issue concerning Native Americans and the representations of their historical presence in Yellowstone Park and elsewhere.[2] More than thirty-five individuals speak, some more than once. (See Chapter 1 for suggestions for performing this and the other plays in the book.)

SPEAKER 2

Narrator as Child

As a child I lived inside a white imaginary world.
I played dress-up games called cowboys and Indians,
and I was usually the Indian.

ACT 1

Scene 1: Sacagawea and Other Myths

SPEAKER 1 *(in whiteface)*

Sidney Horton: Keeping the Legacy Alive

Two hundred years ago the Corps of Discovery, led by Captains Meriwether Lewis and William Clark, struck out from the Falls of the Ohio, near Louisville, Kentucky, to explore the newly acquired territory of the Louisiana Purchase. Their 8,000-mile trek took them through perilous, forbidding country by canoe, horseback, and foot. Lewis, the party's scientist, and Clark, its surveyor, mapped geological features and fixed the longitudes and latitudes of the rivers and plains. Lewis described or preserved specimens of some 178 plants and 122 animals—the majority previously unknown to science....

> None of this, of course,
> would have been possible
> without the aid of the Native Americans
> [nearly fifty tribes in all]
> they met along the way.
> Their Shoshone guide,
> Sacagawea, a fifteen-year-old girl,
> proved indispensable.

(HORTON 2003, 90)

SPEAKER 2

Skeptic

This is revisionist white history!

SPEAKER 1

Thomas P. Slaughter

Sacagawea is elusive,
fictive, mythic, and real.
She is the Indian princess
required by myths of discovery and conquest.

(SLAUGHTER 2003, 86)

Scene 2: Park Performances

SPEAKER 1

Narrator

Staged performances based on lore and myth from Hollywood westerns and Wild West shows represent and connect Indians with war bonnets, horses, western landscapes, parks, wilderness, tourism, nature, and danger. These representations simultaneously place Native Americans within and outside white culture, hence the title "Indians in the Park." Parks are safe places, sites carved out of the wilderness and other spaces where whites go to view and experience nature and the natural world. Indians are not part of this cultural landscape. The "natural world" they inhabit is outside the park. It is a wild, violent, and uncivilized world.

(SEE JANETSKI 2002, 119; SPINDEL 2000, 8)

Scene 3: Indians and Other Wild Beasts

SPEAKER 1 *(in blackface)*

Nathaniel Pitt Langford

The story of Indian murders and cruelties would fill volumes.... The region of the Yellowstone...was inhabited by wild beasts and roving bands of hostile Indians.

(LANGFORD 1972/1905, XXIV, XXVI)

SPEAKER 2 *(offstage)*

A Native American

This is pure rubbish,
white-man rubbish.
Come on, roving bands—
what do they think my people
were doing anyway?

SPEAKER 1 (*IN REDFACE*)

Richard A. Bartlett

In 1877, 1878, and for brief periods in the following decades, Indians frightened park visitors.... Until the mid-1890s, small parties, mostly of Bannocks and Shoshones, continued to hunt in the south and southwest sections of the park....

In 1895 a false rumor spread
that ten Princeton men
had been captured by hostiles,
but the Indians by this time
were cowed and restricted to reservations.
Yellowstone was off-limits.

(BARTLETT 1985, 21, 28)

Scene 4: A Tourist's Genealogy and Historical Background for Yellowstone National Park

SPEAKER 1

(The timeline may be projected onto a screen as well as spoken.)

Narrator: Yellowstone National Park Timeline

1700s   Native American tribes in the greater Yellowstone region include the Flathead, Nez Perce, Kalispel, Coeur d'Alene, Shoshone-Bannock, Sheepeater, Blackfoot, and Crow. They hunted, fished, camped, and 'hard, reflective stone that had multiple uses.

1797   A map of unknown authorship names a river *R. des Roches Juanes*, translated in 1798 as "Yellow-Stone"; also called the Elk River by Crow Indians.

1805   "River Yellow Rock" appears on a map prepared by Lewis and Clark.

1807   John Colter detours into what would be called the Upper Yellowstone region.

1810–60   The region is explored and mapped by mountain men, trappers, hunters, and the military, who virtually destroy the beaver, buffalo, and Native American populations.

1860   A military party led by mountain man Jim Bridger explores the region but is forced back by winter storms.

1861–63   The Civil War slows explorations.

1863–69   The transcontinental railroad is completed, bringing tourists and tourism to the West.

1869   Private citizens from Montana Territory journey to the Yellowstone region.

1870   Jay Cooke sells $100 million of Northern Pacific Railway bonds to encourage tourism in the region, with the possibility of a railroad connecting Cooke City with Gardiner, Montana.

1870   The Washburn Expedition explores and maps the region. A historic campfire conversation inspires the idea of a national park.

1871   A bill is introduced in Congress to establish a preserve at the headwaters of the Yellowstone River. President Ulysses S. Grant signs the bill the following spring, creating the world's first national park.

1871   Photographer William Henry Jackson and artist Thomas Moran join the Hayden Survey, which is mapping the region. Moran is financed by Jay Cooke and the Northern Pacific Railroad.

1872   Moran's painting of the Yellowstone Grand Canyon is purchased by Congress for $10,000 and is hung in the Capitol to encourage and legitimize the creation of Yellowstone National Park. Moran is later hired by John Wesley Powell to paint the Grand Canyon of the Colorado River.

1872   The park opens for tourists and is managed by the Army Corps of Engineers until 1918.

1873   Tourist hotels begin to appear in the park, along with the first tourist guide.

1875   F. Jay Haynes contracts with Jay Cooke and the Northern Pacific Railroad to make stereopticon pictures of important natural sites. In 1881 Haynes sets up the first photographic studio in Yellowstone Park. In 1890, under the auspices of the park and the Northern Pacific Railroad, he publishes the first *Haynes Guide to Yellowstone*, which would be published annually until 1968.

1877–95   Native Americans periodically frighten park visitors.

1877   The Nez Perce War in Yellowstone involves tourist groups, including the Cowan party.

1878   The Bannock war ends on 4 September near Index Peak. Colonel

Miles surprises a Bannock camp, killing eleven and capturing thirty-one Indians, thus ending the Bannock and Indian problem in the park.

1877–1915   Poachers hunt illegally in the park and highwaymen stage holdups and robberies.

1883   Road construction begins, eventually creating a grand loop of two smaller loops, linking Mammoth Hot Springs, the Grand Canyon, Old Faithful and other geysers, and Yellowstone Lake. Construction is completed by 1905.

1883   The Northern Pacific Railroad extends the rail line from Livingston, Montana, to Cinnabar (now Gardiner).

1903   The Roosevelt Arch, at the northern entrance to the park, in Gardiner, is dedicated by Theodore Roosevelt. The inscription on the arch reads: "For the benefit and enjoyment of the people, Yellowstone Park, created by Act of Congress, 1 March 1872."

1915   Automobiles are allowed in the park.

1918   The National Park Service takes over management of the park.

(BARTLETT 1985, 14, 28, 155; HAINES 1996A, 4, 214, 229–30;

JANETSKI 2002, 39; NORTON 1873; PYNE 1998, 88)

Scene 5: Unfounded Fears

SPEAKER 1

Paul Schullery

Indian attacks were of great concern to the early explorers of the Yellowstone.... Such fears were largely unfounded. Yet an occasional encounter with unfriendly Indians did occur in the park, with unfortunate results for tourists. The Nez Perce tribe had a record of cordial coexistence with white men until whites cast greedy eyes on their ancestral homeland in eastern Oregon. When pressured to move to a reservation, part of the tribe refused and began a long fight. Their travels were interrupted by several battles with the United States Cavalry, who finally defeated and captured them in Montana. It was on this journey, in the summer of 1877, that the Nez Perce passed through Yellowstone. They encountered a few tourist groups, and small raiding parties left the main group...and attacked other visitors.

(SCHULLERY 1979B, 1)

ACT 2

Scene 1: Blind Man's Bluff

SPEAKER 1

Aubrey L. Haines

Yellowstone National Park thus became the vast and rugged arena for a two-week struggle resembling a military version of that childhood game known as blind man's bluff....Entirely by chance, several parties of pleasure-bent tourists were involved, effectively drawing the attention of the press and public from the fact that the army had again muffed a chance to catch the Nez Perce.

(HAINES 1996A, 219)

SPEAKER 2

Narrator

According to Haines, at least four groups were involved in this game

A group of six hundred Nez Perce led by Chief Joseph and Yellow Wolf

General Oliver O. Howard's force of six hundred men

Three tourist groups: the Radersburg party of nine from Helena and Three Forks, Montana; another Helena group of ten men, including a black cook; and a small party of English tourists led by 'Texas Jack" (John Omohondro)

A miscellany of miners and settlers

(HAINES 1996A, 219–23)

Scene 2: Mrs. Cowan's Story

SPEAKER 1

Mrs. George Cowan, Summer 1887, Yellowstone Park

In the summer of 1877...my brother Frank...told us of his intention to visit the Park....We soon made preparations for the trip...with an easy double-seated carriage, baggage wagon, and four saddle horses,...a [black] cook named Myers,...provisions, tents, guns, and...musical instruments. With J. A. Oldham as violinist, my brother's guitar, and two or three fair Speakers, we anticipated no end of pleasure....Thursday the twenty-third of August...we received the very unpleasant impression that we might meet

SPEAKER 2

Sven Liljeblad

The Sheepeaters were…big game hunters and the most skilled hunters on foot of all Idaho Indians.

(LILJEBLAD 1959, 33; ALSO QUOTED IN JANETSKI 2002, 52)

SPEAKER 1

Aubrey L. Haines

The Sheepeater Indians, who were the only residents of the Yellowstone Plateau in the historic period (A.D. 1700), were never recognized by the government as having a valid claim to the area. Instead, an unratified treaty of 24 September 1868 was used as justification for placing all the Shoshonean groups on small reservations.

(HAINES 1996A, 29)

Scene 4: No sign of Indians

SPEAKER 1

Joel C. Janetski/William T. Sherman

With the banning of all Indians from the park, the region soon looked deserted. When General Sherman inspected the area in 1877, just before the Nez Perce War, he wrote, "We saw no signs of Indians."

(JANETSKI 2002, 67; QUOTING SHERMAN)

SPEAKER 2

Paul Schullery

Yellowstone on the eve if its formal discovery and establishiment as a national park was already a culturally complex and ecologically subtle place.

(SCHULLERY 1997, 50)

Scene 5: Native Yellowstone

SPEAKER 1

(The course descriptions may be projected onto a screen as well as spoken.)
Yellowstone Association Institute

Course Description: Native Yellowstone

Yellowstone National Park has a rich Native American past and present that is only beginning to be appreciated. The Bannock, Shoshone, Crow, Nez Perce, and Kiowa are just some of the at least twenty-six tribes that used the park as a source of game, traditional medicine, and spiritual sustenance.... Today the park's affiliated tribes are returning to Yellowstone and fueling nothing less than a revolution in our understanding of the park's native heritage. Join us as we explore the past, present, and future of Native Americans in Yellowstone National Park.

(YELLOWSTONE ASSOCIATION INSTITUTE 2003, 13)

SPEAKER 2

Yellowstone Association Institute

Course Description : The Nez Perce in Yellowstone

The Nez Perce were Yellowstone's most reluctant tourists. Their only desire was to stay on their ancestral lands, but conflicts with white settlers flared into a war with the U.S. Army.... Fleeing to Canada, the Nez Perce crossed through Yellowstone National Park and left an indelible mark on its history. We'll visit the site where the Nez Perce bumped into tourists and the army.... We'll talk about not just the 1877 war but Nez Perce history in general, from pit-house days until the present.

(YELLOWSTONE ASSOCIATION INSTITUTE 2003, 12)

SPEAKER 1

Yellowstone Association Institute

Course Description: Flight of the Nez Perce

Learn about the Nez Perce Indians and their dramatic 1877 foray through Yellowstone by heading into the backcountry to follow portions of their actual route. Historian Lee Whittlesey (an expert on the Yellowstone route of Nez Perce) and cultural anthropologist

Rosemary Sucec (who, on behalf of the park, has consulted
with various Nez Perce tribal members about their views of the
Yellowstone landscape and how they related to it both during
and before 1877) will accompany you on a trip from the Lamar
Valley…to the Clark's Fork.

(YELLOWSTONE ASSOCIATION INSTITUTE 2003, 36)

SPEAKER 2

Contemporary Tourist

The sign at the top of the lookout over Clark's Fork Valley, on Chief Joseph
Highway, reads: "Dead Indian Pass." The sign names the white settlers in
Crandall and Sun Light Basin who survived the Indian wars before and after
1877.

SPEAKER 1

Yellowstone Association Institute

Course Description: Horse-packing the Nez Perce Trail

In the summer of 1877, in one of the most tragic episodes in the
history of the American West, the United States Army chased
several hundred members of the Nez Perce tribe on a meandering
path from Idaho through western Montana and north toward
Canada. Along the way, the Nez Perce fled through present-day
Yellowstone National Park and left an indelible mark on the park's
history. Join us as we learn about the flight of the Nez Perce.… We
shall discuss Nez Perce culture, the antecedents to the Nez Perce
War, the evidence we use to reconstruct the route today, and the
activities of the tribe during their time in the park.

(YELLOWSTONE ASSOCIATION INSTITUTE 2003, 38)

Scene 6: Indians in the Park

SPEAKER 1

Narrator as Recent Tourist

In the gift shop at Old Faithful Inn, alongside shelves of books celebrating Lewis and Clark, they are selling books—new, old, and reissued—about Sacagawea:[4] cookbooks, trail guides, biographies, books about her son (Jean Baptiste Charbonneau), stories about her life, refrigerator magnets with her picture, wall plates, trivets, postcards. She is everywhere, a rediscovered commodity. She has new market value. It is no accident that she comes back into the park under the sign of Lewis and Clark. In this year of the bicentennial, the chronicles of Lewis and Clark are still being read as blueprints for the future (*New York Times* 2003). No surprise, then, that this future would include revisionist histories of Indians in the park.

Coda

SPEAKER 1

Narrator as Audience Member

On 3 May 2003 I gave the keynote address at the Fourth International Conference on Qualitative Research in the University of Calgary Conference Center in Banff, Alberta, Canada. After my address, a Native American drumming and dance group performed for the audience. It was a moving experience and everyone applauded when the dancers and drummers were done. The dancers wore colorful costumes and performed complex dances. The loud, rhythmic beat of the drummers was powerful and very moving. I felt entertained, moved, and inadequate, not knowing how to respond to this live version of Native Americans performing indigenous dances for a largely white North American audience. The Native American drummer, who was also master of ceremonies, informed the audience about the awards and prizes each dancer had received at regional dance and performing contests. I left wondering if this was another version of a Wild West show, like those staged by Sitting Bull and Buffalo Bill Cody. And if so, who was tourist and who was performer? I felt like I was a little boy again, back on the reservation in Tama, Iowa.

Narrator as Historian

And so, 200 years later, still riding on the shoulders of the Corps of Discovery, we have come full circle. Indians in the park have passed through at least four historical stages. In stage 1 they were in the parks and the natural world, but they left no history, and we learned nothing from or about them. In stage 2 they reappeared in nature and the park as primitive, violent, bestial others who scalped and murdered white people. In stage 3 they were killed and forcefully removed from the park and placed on reservations to be assimilated into white culture, from which they would occasionally be brought out as entertainers. In stage 4 they were rediscovered, given complex histories, and brought back into the park.

In stage 4 they are again located within our national imagination. The posters for Lewis and Clark, Sacagawea, and the Northern Pacific Railroad that are on sale in the Yellowstone tourist shops fold three myths into one: Lewis and Clark, with the aid of this Native American woman, explored the Pacific Northwest. It was their work that the Northern Pacific Railroad carried forward by pioneering access to and then developing and serving the Pacific Northwest, and the larger project called the United States of America.

The Northern Pacific Railroad, of course, created the need for the park. Yellowstone became a destination for tourists, who would ride on Jay Cooke's trains and stay in the hotels he and his capitalist friends built. The park had to be policed, and the United States government directed the army to provide this service. There was no place in the park for Indians, and those who strayed into Yellowstone were either killed or run off by Sherman's soldiers.

And so today and yesterday this pioneering spirit remains represented in the Lewis and Clark and Sacagawea posters. This spirit is embraced by both progressives and conservatives who imagine themselves in pristine nature, in a natural world of beauty and wonder, in a world not unlike that Wonderland called Yellowstone, which in 1872 had no place for Native Americans.

❦

REMEMBERING TO FORGET: LEWIS AND CLARK AND NATIVE AMERICANS IN YELLOWSTONE

PROLOGUE

"Remembering to Forget: Lewis and Clark and Native Americans in Yellowstone" is a three-act play that enacts the cultural and political biases and behavior of the Lewis and Clark expedition of 1804–1806, Lewis and Clark's relations with Native Americans in the greater Yellowstone region, and the bicentennial commemoration of that presence in 2003 and 2004.[1] Building on Chapter 3's treatment of the negative history of Native Americans in Yellowstone Park, this play suggests that much of the history makes sense when Lewis and Clark's relations with Native Americans are critically examined. The performance of the embedded cultural myths and the relations based upon them suggests a new set of understandings about the Corps of Discovery,[2] and about Yellowstone today.

ACT I

Scene I: Getting Started

SPEAKER 1 *(offstage)*

Historian as Social Critic

"If the Lewis and Clark bicentennial is to have lasting value, we need to reject...simple romance...and epic heroism....In the process we might begin to recognize how current efforts to commemorate the expedition

SPEAKER 1

(The timeline may be projected onto a screen as well as spoken.)
Narrator

Timeline: Lewis and Clark in the Greater Yellowstone Area, 1805–14[4]

1805:

7 April: Lewis and Clark send Jefferson a map showing the "River Yellow Rock."

25 April: Lewis camps at the mouth of the Yellowstone River: "This river, which had been known to the French as the *Roche jaune*, or as we have called it, the 'Yellowstone,' arises according to Indian information in the Rocky mountains" [in Yellowstone National Park].

13 August: The expedition camps 120 miles west of the current Yellowstone National Park boundary.

1806:

17 July–7 August: Clark and a small expedition explore the Yellowstone River from Livingston to the mouth of the Missouri River.

14 August: John Colter leaves the expedition and returns to the Yellowstone River area during the summer and winter of 1806 and 1807; camping along Yellowstone Lake, Tower Falls, Lamar River, and Soda Butte Creek, to the headwaters of Clark's Fork.

1814:   Biddle publishes Clark's map of the river.

2003:   Summer celebrations of the Lewis and Clark Bicentennial begin. The entire greater Yellowstone region celebrates the accomplishments of

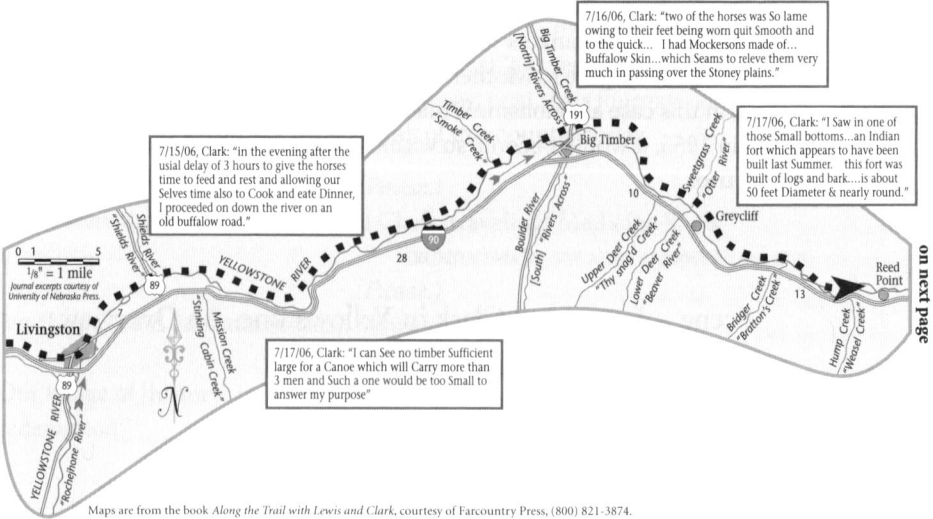

Maps are from the book *Along the Trail with Lewis and Clark*, courtesy of Farcountry Press, (800) 821-3874.

CHAPTER FOUR

the expedition.

(COUES 1965/1893, VOL. 1, 283; HAINES 1996A, 5, 34, 36–37; JACKSON 1987, 3; MOULTON 2003, 353–62; SPENCE 1999, 159)

Scene 4: Airport Sightings

SPEAKER 1

Narrator as Dramatist, as Traveler

In the summer of 2003, passengers waiting for their luggage in the Billings, Montana, airport were forced to walk around a large diorama—20 feet long by 10 feet high, a three-dimensional exhibit titled "Lewis and Clark on the Yellowstone: July 1806." In order to get out of airport, you had to confront and walk past Lewis and Clark and the legacy of their journey in the Yellowstone region.

A version of the exhibit is reproduced below

(and may also be projected onto a screen).

The trail of Lewis and Clark, with notes from Clark's journal

(FIFER AND SODERBERG 2001, 188–200).

SPEAKER 2 *(aside)*

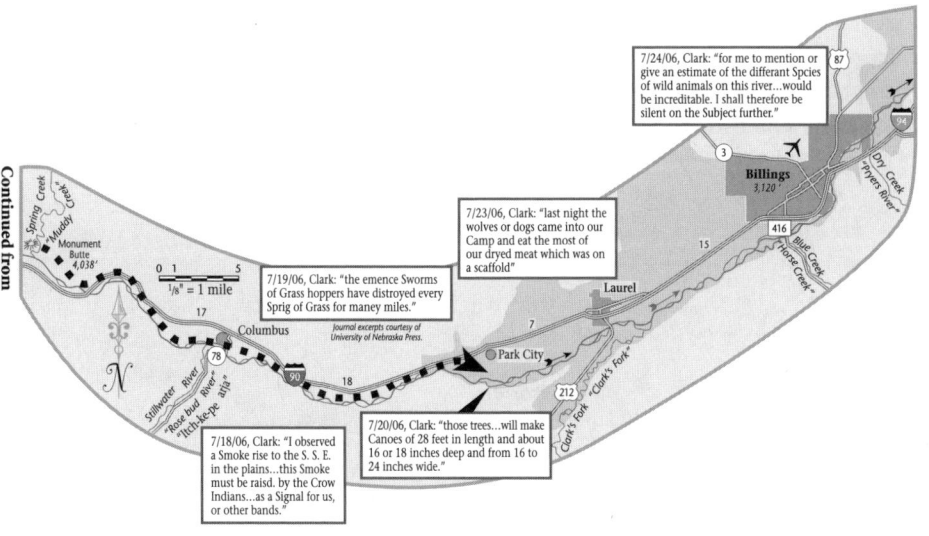

The 2003 and 2004 bicentennial commemoration of Clark's 1806 journey along the Yellowstone was marked by flag-waving parades and historical reenactments. Museums, city squares, and riverside parks in Livingston, Big Timber, Greycliff, Reed Point, Columbus, Laurel, Billings, and even Red Lodge had displays honoring the Corps of Discovery. The Hamilton General Stores in Yellowstone Park sold posters celebrating the bicentennial. In Mountain Men Rendezvous across the region, white males dressed as traders, trappers, and Native Americans reenacted the exchange rituals that were so basic to the expedition.

These performances treat Lewis and Clark and the past as if historical events could be fixed in time and then restaged in the present without problems. Indeed, the reenactments of the expedition are endowed with special powers: they stand outside time.

There is great danger in these historical masquerades. The past is frozen in time. Particular versions of whiteness and white history are performed. The sins of the past are ignored, and a peaceful bond between the imagined past and the present is forged. In this nostalgic space, the benign "pastness" of Lewis and Clark comes alive. Their historic journey of conquest is celebrated. A particular version of territorial expansion and cultural destruction is signified. The white community owns this land, this river, this park, this place, these meanings. The white community and its city fathers have the right to recreate on this land and in these cultural spaces their version of the past, their version of how these two men helped win the West for Thomas Jefferson and white America.

Under such a utopian scenario, redemption for the handful of sins committed by the explorers is sought and easily given. Indeed, redemption gives way to celebration, to a displacement from conquest to ecoenvironmentalism, to nature, and to the joy of floating the Yellowstone or the Missouri rivers under the banner of Lewis and Clark.

(SEE GROSSMAN 2003, 2–5; WILLIAMS 1997)

Scene 5: A Time for Nostalgia:

SPEAKER 1

Historian

"A few years ago I was helping my friend Stephen Ambrose lead a group of people along some of the most scenic stretches of the Lewis and Clark Trail. On a warm summer evening, after a pleasant day of paddling canoes on the

Missouri River, we camped amid the eerie and majestic White Cliffs of north-central Montana, close to the exact spot where, on 31 May 1805, Meriwether Lewis wrote one of his most lyrical journal passages about the wondrous landscape he and his men were encountering with fresh eyes. 'As we passed on,' Lewis concluded, 'it seemed as if those seens of visionary inchantment would never have an end.'

"Nearly two centuries later, we found the enchantment equally palpable as we sat around the campfire and gazed at the silent cliffs reflected in the river, tinged pink by the setting sun."

(DUNCAN 2002, V)

SPEAKER 2

Author

I question this nostalgic New West model of the cultural marketplace. It structures these performances as nostalgic consumption events. In these celebratory spaces no mention is made of how Lewis and Clark and the corps exploited, threatened, stole from, belittled, killed, and sexually exploited Native Americans.

(SEE SLAUGHTER 2003, 160–85)

SPEAKER 1

Skeptic

And the celebrations continue. Listen to this ad for the Sacagawea Hotel, Three Forks, Montana, from *Montana Magazine*, March/April 2003:

> "Lewis and Clark Never Stayed Here—Undaunted Hospitality: The Sacajawea Hotel"

And this ad for Wheat Montana Farms:

> "I commanded a most perfect view of the neighbouring country[;]...a distant range of lofty mountains rose, their snow-clad tops above the irregular and broken mountains which is adjacent to this beautiful spot" (Meriwether Lewis, atop the limestone cliffs on the edge of our farm of the Three Forks of the Missouri River, in 1805.
>
> The perch where Lewis penned his description happens to be only a few hundred yards from where we now farm acres of the "beautiful plains" he describes,...the land we now call Wheat Montana Farms.

(*WHEAT MONTANA JOURNAL* 11 [2003], 1)

Scene 6: Savages:

SPEAKER 1

Meriwether Lewis, 20 July 1806

"We believe that the surest guarantee of savage fidelity to a nation is a thorough conviction on their minds that their government possesses the power of punishing promptly every act of aggression committed on their part against the person or property of their citizens."

(LETTER TO HUGH HENRY, IN JACKSON 1962, 310)

SPEAKER 2

Expert on Frontier Race Relations

When…Lewis and Clark looked at an Indian, they saw a noble savage ready to be transformed into a civilized citizen. When they looked at a Negro, they saw something less than human.

(AMBROSE 1996, 55)

SPEAKER 1

Thomas Jefferson

"The Indian [is] as ardent as the white man, free, brave, preferring death to surrender. moral and responsible…loving to his children, caring and loyal to family…and equal to whites in vivacity and activity of mind…The Negro is physically ugly, is offensive in body odor, and oversexed."

(IN WALLACE 1999, 77–78)

SPEAKER 2

Anthony F. C. Wallace on the Theory of Savagism

The picture of the Indians presented in [Jefferson's] Notes on the State of Virginia (1785)…articulated an American theory of "savagism"—that the savage [is] one whom circumstances, for good or bad, have held in an early state of society.…Thus the Indians could be regarded as…culturally inferior, childlike, in their savage state…The theory of a scale of progress or Great Chain of Being was fully current in the literature of the Enlightenment by the time Jefferson was writing in the 1780s.

(WALLACE 1999, 95)

ACT 2

Scene 1: Getting Situated in the Present

SPEAKER 1

Narrator

Let me read from this piece of mail I received from the University of Iowa Alumni Association 30 September 2003 (see Plate 13).

(Holds up imaginary brochure to audience.)

In the Wake of Lewis and Clark: A Voyage along the Columbia and Snake Rivers
Iowa Voyagers
May 18–24, 2004
Aboard the Sea Bird

(aside)

There's a photo of the Sea Bird in harbor.

Dear Iowa Voyagers:
In the summer of 1803 Thomas Jefferson appeared before Congress to request money to fund an exploratory odyssey across the vast unmapped section of the American continent.... Jefferson's dream fueled the Lewis and Clark expedition.... There's something in the story of the Lewis and Clark expedition for everyone—fans of adventure, history, science, nature.... And now, two hundred years after they completed their exploration, Lewis and Clark have never been more popular. Their original "Corps of Volunteers for Northwest Discovery" officially began in May of 1804 and lasted two years. Ours will begin on 18 May 2004 and last seven days. Come with us and add this chapter to your life history. (Accommodation prices range from $3,750 to $2,390.)

(Pause.)

I don't think I want these experiences in my life history!

Scene 2: Getting Situated in the Past: The Object of the Trip

SPEAKER 1

Alexander MacKenzie, 1801

"By opening the intercourse between the Atlantic and Pacific Oceans, and forming regular establishments through the interior...the entire command of the fur trade of North America might be obtained[.]...To this may be added the fishing of both seas and the markets of the four quarters of the globe."

(IN DEVOTO 1997/1953, XXXIX)

SPEAKER 2

Historian as Interpreter

Thomas Jefferson read MacKenzie's book in the summer of 1802. MacKenzie's geography...interested Jefferson less than the challenge MacKenzie posed: to discover the continental passage, colonize the Pacific Coast and tap its fur resources, and establish commerce with the Orient....By the spring of 1803, Congress having assented, he commissioned his private secretary (Meriwether Lewis) to organize such an expedition.

(UTLEY 1997, 3)

SPEAKER 1

Thomas Jefferson: The President as Trip Organizer, 20 June 1803

"The object of your mission is to explore the Missouri river, & such principle stream of it, as, by it's course & communication with the waters of the Pacific Ocean, may offer the most direct & practicable water communication across this continent, for the purposes of commerce[.]...In all your intercourse with the natives treat them in the most friendly & conciliatory manner which their conduct will admit; allay their jealousies as to the object of your journey, satisfy them of it's innocence [and]...furnish them with authority to call on our officers, on their entering the U.S."

(INSTRUCTIONS TO LEWIS, IN DEVOTO 1997/1953, 482, 484)

SPEAKER 2

Thomas Jefferson: The President as Theorist of Indian Affairs

"The ultimate purpose of engaging Indian leaders is to obtain lands from them[.]...If ever we are constrained to lift the hatchet against any tribe, we will never lay it down til that tribe is exterminated[.]...[W]e shall destroy all of them."

(JEFFERSON 1803,1807; QUOTED IN SPENCE 2003, 59–60)

Scene 3: Conquest and Domination

SPEAKER 1: A NATIVE AMERICAN RESPONDS

William Least Heat-Moon

"The adventure and romance of the great expedition have blinded many Americans to its central aims, which were more political and economic than scientific. A key duty of Captain Lewis was to inform people who had dwelt on the land for twelve thousand years…that they were now 'children' under the hand of the great and distant White Father. That is an act of conquest, not science."

(HEAT-MOON 1999, 264–65)

Chorus 1: In Their Own Words: Frontier Race Relations II

SPEAKER 1

Thomas Jefferson, 4 July 1776

"The King of Great Britain…has…endeavoured to bring on the inhabitants of our frontiers, the merciless Indian savages, whose known rule of warfare is an undistinguished destruction of all ages, sexes and conditions."

(DECLARATION OF INDEPENDENCE)

SPEAKER 2

Narrator

Let's get this straight. Jefferson is claiming that the King of England has caused the Indian "savages" to harm white settlers.

SPEAKER 1

Meriwether Lewis

"Children, we have been sent by the great Chief of the Seventeen great nations of America to inform you…that it was decided that the Missouri River now belonged to the United States, so that all those who lived in that country, whether white or red, are bound to obey the commands of their great Chief the President who is not your only great father…he is the only friend to whom you can now look for protection, or from whom you can ask favours, or receive good councils, and he will take care to serve you, & not deceive you."

(AMBROSE 1996, 156–57; ALSO BIDDLE 1962/1814, 23–24)

Scene 4: Manners, Morals, and Sex in the West

SPEAKER 1

Meriwether Lewis on the Sioux as Pirates, 23 September 1804

"These [Teton Sioux] are the vilest miscreants of the savage race."

(IN ÇOUES 1965/1893, 128; ALSO MOULTON 2003, XX; ALSO RONDA 1984, 27,
WHO ATTRIBUTES THIS STATEMENT TO CLARK RATHER THAN LEWIS)

SPEAKER 2

Meriwether Lewis on Shoshone Dinner Manners, 16 August 1805

"I sent Drewyer and Shields…to kill some meat as neither the Indians or ourselves had any thing to eat[.]…When they reached the place where Drewyer had thrown out the intestines, [the Shoshones] all dismounted…and ran tumbling over each other like famished dogs; each tore away whatever part he could and instantly began to eat it; some had the liver, some the kidneys[.]…It was indeed impossible to see these wretches ravenously feeding on the filth of animals, and the blood streaming from their mouths, without deploring how nearly the conditions of savages approaches that of the brute creation."

(IN BIDDLE 1962/1814, VOL. 1, 229; ALSO COUES 1965/1893,
503; MOULTON 2003, 183)

SPEAKER 1

William Clark: Sex and the Medicine Dance, 5 January 1805

"We Sent a man to this Medisan Dance last night, they gave him four girls all this to cause the buffalow to Come near So that They may kill him."

(IN MOULTON 2003, 77)

SPEAKER 2

Patrick Gass and Others, 5 April 1805

"[W]e ought to give some account of the fair sex of the Missouri; and entertain [readers] with narratives of feats of love[.]…It may be observed generally that chastity is not very highly esteemed[.]…The fact is…the women are generally considered an article of traffic…for an old tobacco box[.] [O]ne of our men was granted the honour of passing a night with the daughter of the head chief of the Mandan nation.

(IN MOULTON 2003, 90)

SPEAKER 1

James P. Ronda and a Native American Disclaimer: On Sex with Strangers

Native American interest in sex with traders [and strangers] was based on three distinct cultural sanctions: (1) A desire to obtain European goods.

Giving sexual relations meant receiving these objects in payment for favors—ironware, paint, blue beads, cloth [blankets] were part of the exchange. (2) Sex with strangers was also an integral part of northern plains hospitality. (3) Sexual conduct was perceived as a means of transferring spiritual power from one person to another. Sex became a conduit for power.

(RONDA 1984, 62)

SPEAKER 2

Meriwether Lewis on Native Women's Dress, 21 January 1806
"The usual dress of females…covers the body from the armpits to the waist, it conceals the breasts, but on other occasions they are suffered to remain loose and exposed, and present, in old women especially, a most disgusting appearance."

(IN BIDDLE 1962/1814, VOL. 2, 369–70)

SPEAKER 1

Meriwether Lewis on Chinook Female Sexuality, 21 January 1806
"Among these people, as indeed among all Indians the prostitution of unmarried women is far from being criminal or improper, that the females themselves solicit the favours of the other sex, with the entire approbation of friends…In most cases…the female is farmed out for hire…[with] regular prices…The little intercourse which the men have had with these women is…sufficient to apprise us of the prevalence of…venereal disease. The women were very found of carressing our men…The young women sport openly with our men."

(CLARK, QUOTED IN RONDA 1984, 64, 209;
IN BIDDLE 1962/1814, VOL. 2, 369–70)

Scene 5: Additional Commentary on Glitter and History

SPEAKER 1

Larry McMurtry
This journey of the Corps of Discovery is a buddy story of gigantic proportion:…white men conquering wilderness and the western frontier—prototypes of other famous buddy teams—the Lone Ranger and Tonto, Butch Cassidy and the Sundance Kid.

(MCMURTRY 2001, XII, 140–41)

SPEAKER 2

Chorus of Wise Men: Dee Brown, Robert Utley, Stephen Ambrose, Alston Chase
It opened up the frontier for economic expansion and the colonization of
the American West. It shaped the conditions for the Indian wars of 1860–
1890, the short-lived, transnational, intermountain fur-trade economy, the
transcontinental railroad, the erasure of complex Native American cultures,
the near destruction of the beaver, bear, and buffalo, and it helped create
the notion that white men could play God in the West, and perhaps even in
Yellowstone.

(AMBROSE 2000, 19; BROWN 1971, 11–13, 300–301, 335;

CHASE 1986, 107, 145; UTLEY 1997, 3, 6)

Scene 6: Packing for the Trip: Indian Givers —Collecting Gifts for the Trip

SPEAKER 1

(Project onto screen a montage of pictures of Jefferson peace medals,
medallions, U.S. flags, guns, ammunition, whiskey bottles,
blue glass beads, cheap rings with glass stones, mirrors, scissors,
sewing needles, brooches, brass kettles, fishhooks, hawks bells,
ruffled shirts, red-handled knifes, fifteen 3-point Hudson's Bay blankets, fif-
teen match coats, face paint, packets of tobacco, cloth fabric, combs,
armbands, ear trinkets, thimbles, awls, two corn grinders.)

(AMBROSE 1996, 88; JACKSON 1962, 63–74, 93–99; RONDA 1984, 8–9)

Narrator
By the time Jefferson created the corps,…gifts were a recognized part of the
protocol of Indian diplomacy.…Lewis knew the gift-giving tradition:…blue
glass beads headed his list;…second on his list were common brass buttons.

(RONDA 1984, 8)

Scene 7: Stealing Horses and Killing Indians along the Yellowstone in 1806

SPEAKER 1

Narrator as Historian

On 26 July 1806 Lewis and his men meet a group of Blackfeet in Two Medicine River valley. Early on the morning of the 27th, the Blackfeet attempt to steal the guns of Drewyer, Fields, and Lewis.

(FIFER AND SODERBERG 2001, 176)

SPEAKER 2

Meriwether Lewis: The Two Medicine Incident

In retaliation, R. Fields, as he seized his gun, stabbed the Indian to the heart with his knife. The fellow ran about fifteen steps and fell dead.... I reached to seize my gun and found her gone.... Turning around, I saw the Indian making off with my gun.... They then endeavored to drive off our horses. I called to them [the Blackfeet] that I would shoot them if they did not give me my horse.... One of them (Side Hill Calf) jumped from behind a rock.... I shot him through the belly.... We gathered up their horses and ours, took the Indians' guns, put four shields and two bows and quivers of arrows on the fire,... retook out flag, and left the medal about the neck of the dead man that they would be informed who we were.

(MOULTON 2003, 344–45; SEE ALSO RONDA 1984, 243–440;

UTLEY 1997, 8–10)

SPEAKER 1

Narrator

The Two Medicine incident left two Native Americans dead, killed by Lewis and Fields.

Scene 8: Wrapping Up Affairs: Clark as the Godfather

SPEAKER 1

Narrator

In his final report to Jefferson in 1807, Clark said of Charbonneau (Sacagawea's husband), "[He] was a man of no peculiar merit [but] useful as an interpreter[.]... His wife was particularly useful among the Shoshones. Indeed, she has borne with a patience truly admirable the fatigues of so long a route encumbered with the charge of an infant[.] ... We therefore paid

Charbonneau wages amounting to $500.33, including the price of a horse and a lodge [tent] purchased of him." No wages were paid to Sacagawea.

(CLARK AND EDMONDS 1979, 82)

SPEAKER 2

William Clark to Charbonneau

"As to your little Son (my boy Pomp), you well know my fondness for him and my anxiety to take and raise him as my own child[.] . . . [I]f you will bring your son Baptiest to me I will educate him and treat him as my own child."

(TINLING 2001, 19–20)

SPEAKER 1

Jean Baptiste Charbonneau

On the return trip in 1806 Mother [Sacagawea] and I were put ashore with Papa Toussaint Charbonneau at the Mandan villages. . . . Three years later, when I was six, my family accepted Captain Clark's offer to educate me and Lisette, my sister. So in 1809, dressed in white boys' clothes, I was sent to St. Louis to live. I was baptized in the Catholic Church by a Trappist Monk. My father, Toussaint, signed the record with an X. My mother's name was not given. She was described only as "____, savage of the Snake Nation." . . . Because I was a half-Indian I lived in a boarding house, not with Clark's family. Clark's wife did not accept me because I was half-Indian. I did not have a place in white society. When I was 18 I went to Europe for six years with Prince Paul of Württemberg, who had been an early tourist of the American West.

(MCMURTRY 2001, 155–56; FIFER AND

SODERBERG 2001, 202; TINLING 2001, 23, 103)

SPEAKER 2

Meriwether Lewis on Sacagawea

If she has enough to eat and a few trinkets I believe she would be perfectly content anywhere.

(RONDA 1984, 259)

ACT 3

Scene 1: Of Memories, Blankets, and Myths

SPEAKER 1

Narrator Re-Remembers the Past: 1957

(Here's another short story within a longer story.) I want to go back to the spring and summer of 1957. That spring my father sold me a $5,000 life insurance policy from the Farm Bureau Life Insurance Company. I was sixteen years old, and a life insurance policy at that age seemed a stretch. But Dad was desperate.[5] He said this sale would put him over his quota for the month and qualify him for a fishing trip to Ontario, Canada. It did and that summer he came home to our little house in Indianola, Iowa, with a four-pelt Hudson's Bay wool blanket. Today that blanket is upstairs in the guest bedroom. Nate and Heidi used it the last time they visited.

SPEAKER 2

Narrator Remembers Another Version of the Past: 1994

The Hudson's Bay blanket that my father bought for me and my wife at a farm auction in Kalona, Iowa, in the winter of 1994 was expensive. He and his best friend bid against one another, driving the price up over $300. The price was fitting, for the blanket is marked with four black pelt or point lines, which defined the blanket's worth in that nineteenth-century economy in which pelts were traded for blankets. A four-pelt blanket is indeed pricey. Today that four-pelt blanket is in the guest room in our cabin outside Red Lodge.

SPEAKER 1

Narrator Remembers the Past: 2002

For Nate and Heidi's twenty-eighth birthdays we went shopping at the Red Lodge Mountain Man Rendezvous. We found a trader from Fort Worth who was selling Hudson's Bay blankets. We bought two four-pelt blankets and shipped them to Seattle. The trader explained that the short black lines on the blanket referred to the number of fur pelts the blanket was traded for.

Scene 2: The Blanket Story from Hudson's Bay Company

SPEAKER 1

Hudson's Bay Historian Peter C. Newman

The Hudson's Bay blanket, the most durable legacy of the company's involvement in the fur trade, was developed so that Indians could trade "the very fur off their backs" and still have something warm to wear on their way home. Introduced at the end of the eighteenth century, the blanket's trademark coloured marks were added later on, and the modern blanket still bears a set of small black stripes along its edge representing the number of made beaver pelts that size of blanket was worth. Hudson's Bay blankets were often cut into coats and leggings, their snowy colour allowing a hunter to blend in with the winter landscape.

(NEWMAN 1989, 61–62)

SPEAKER 2

Hudson's Bay Salesclerk #26

What Burberry's plaid is to London, the Hudson's Bay blanket is to Canada in all its Far North glory.

(FULSANG 2003, L5)

SPEAKER 1

(The workshop ad may be projected as well as spoken.)

Narrator

Make Your Own Blanket Coat: A One-Day Workshop

For those inspired by the Hudson's Bay iconic blanket, one-day workshops are available. For about $200 you can sign up to get a sewing kit, instructions by a specialist, a history lesson, and you can make your own point blanket coat. While you make your blanket coat, you can listen to aboriginal stories and music and have a traditional plowman's lunch.

(FULSANG 2003, L5)

Scene 3: Historically Authentic Trade Blankets

SPEAKER 1

Narrator: Summary of Information from the Web

Okay, Hudson's Bay Company sold the blankets, but somebody else made them and put the HBC label on them. It is generally understood that the practice of hand-weaving points into blankets for HBC started in 1780 with Thomas Empson, who was at that time the major supplier of blankets to HBC.

SPEAKER 2

Bernard DeVoto: The Size and Cost of Blankets

Points were lines woven into blankets to denote their size, from one to four. A four-point Mackinaw measured 72 by 90 inches. The Hudson's Bay Company four-point blanket today is the full/double blanket, 144 inches long. At one period the blanket cost one beaver pelt per point.

(DEVOTO 1997/1953, 290)

Scene 4: Germ Warfare, Diseased Blankets, and Smallpox Epidemics

SPEAKER 1

Skeptic

These blankets were not innocent commodities. The concept of the "diseased, smallpox blanket" circulated during the French and Indian wars between 1755 and 1760. Stories of disease-infected blankets deliberately given to Native Americans surfaced after the first European contact and continue to circulate. In 1763 General Amherst, British commander-in-chief for America, sent a letter to Colonel Henry Bouquet, wondering if it could be contrived to send the smallpox to the Indians by inoculating blankets with the disease—suggesting that every possible method be used to "extirpate this Execreable Race."

(MAYOR 1995)

SPEAKER 2

Medical Historian

Nothing instilled fear in American soldiers and civilians so much as the prospect that the British might use smallpox as a weapon of war. . . . British officers had already demonstrated their willingness to use biological warfare in 1763. When Indians organized under the Ottawa leader Pontiac...on the Pennsylvania frontier,..."[O]ut of our regard to them," wrote a trader on the scene, "we gave them two Blankets and a Handkerchief out of the Small Pox Hospital. I hope it will have the desired effect." This act had the sanction of...Sir Jeffery Amherst.

(FENN 2001, 88)

SPEAKER 1

Thomas Jefferson: The President as Trip Organizer, to Lewis and Clark, 20 June 1803

"Carry with you some matter of kinepox, inform those of them [Indians] with whom you may be of it's efficacy as a preservative from the small-pox; and instruct and incourage them in the use of it."

(INSTRUCTIONS TO LEWIS, IN DEVOTO 1997/1953, 485)

SPEAKER 2

William Clark: 14 August 1804: Omahas Ravaged by Smallpox

"The ravages of the Small Pox (which swept off 400 men & women & children in perpopotion) has reduced this nation not exceeding 300 men and left them to the insults of their weaker neighbours."

(IN DEVOTO 1997/1953, 19)

SPEAKER 1

Narrator

We are going to fast-forward to 1837.

SPEAKER 2

Donald Jackson: William Clark as Superintendent of Indian Affairs and the Smallpox Epidemic of 1837

In 1807 William Clark was named Superintendent of Indian Affairs. In 1832 the U.S. government decided to fight a severe outbreak of smallpox that was raging through white and red populations. Funds were allocated by Congress, which stipulated that it was the duty of Indian agents, under the secretary of war, to put a smallpox vaccination program into effect. Two doctors were hired to treat the Indians on the Missouri, including the...Arikaras and Mandans. Their work went well but they were unable to complete their assignment before winter....A debacle followed: over half of the...Arikaras and Mandans were left untreated and died.

In the spring of 1837 smallpox broke out on the Upper Missouri....The epidemic took lives in most of the tribes along the Missouri....By February 1838 Clark was reporting to his superiors that the Mandan nation had been reduced to a handful of persons. Clark did not intervene. It is not clear if he felt any responsibility for the genocidal neglect of the tribes.

(JACKSON 1987, 41–42)

SPEAKER 1

Contemporary Journalist Ron Franscell

The idea of a "smallpox holocaust" haunts Indians to this day. [XT]Sunday, October 13, 2002—Washburn, N.D. When the state of North Dakota returned some museum bones to Indian tribes for reburial... Mandan-Hidatsa elders blanched at actually touching their forebears' remains. They feared that even breathing the bone dust might infect them with smallpox.... It is a widely held belief that the U.S. government deliberately infected Indians during westward expansion.... The Mouache Utes of Colorado's San Luis Valley believed disease-ridden blankets deliberately distributed by government officials caused an 1854 epidemic.

SPEAKER 2

Contemporary Metis Adult

It is common knowledge that the Bay blankets were infested with smallpox. I learned this as a child. Nobody doubts it.

SPEAKERS 1 AND 2

Conversation at a Local Thai Café, 28 October 2003
(A small dialogue within the larger dialogue)

Server: What are you reading?

Author: A book on the smallpox epidemic of 1775–82.

Server: Oh, I know about that. My brother had a book about it that I read. Did you see the *Southpark* [the TV show] episode about SARS and diseased blankets? The Native Americans give the Americans a SARS-infected blanket and spread the disease to them! Cool.

Author: No, I didn't see it—so it was a play on the diseased smallpox blanket story?

Server: Yah, it was called "Crossing Borders."

SPEAKER 1

Historian DeVoto: The Infected Stolen Blanket Story

However it started, in the summer of 1837 smallpox nearly destroyed the Mandans. In 1843, Francis A. Chardon (who commanded for the American Fur Company),... told John James Audubon that in 1837 Mandan Indians stole a blanket from a dying crew member, and that 'though a reward for

it was offered at once, it could not be got back."…The story of the stolen
blanket has a quality of legend, and it reappears at Fort McKenzie, and
in fact nearly everywhere else. (There is nothing improbable in it; the
smallpox virus is long-lived and infection from a blanket is thoroughly
possible.)…Soon between ten and twenty Mandans were dying every day.

(DEVOTO 1997/1953, 280, 283)

Scene 5: Indian Traders

SPEAKER 1

Meriwether Lewis, 26 July 1806

"They [the Blackfeet] informed me that they trade on the Suskasawan river
[which] is only 6 days easy march…from these traders [Hudson's Bay, North
West]. [T]hey obtain amunition, speritous liquor & blankets in exchange for
wolves and some beaver skins."

(MOULTON 2003, 343)

SPEAKER 2

Historian: Lewis and Clark and Blankets

Lewis and Clark took blankets for purposes of trade, packing, and gift giving.
Fifteen three-point blankets are listed on Lewis's summary of purchases of
18 May 1803.

(JACKSON 1962, 98)

Imagined Dialogue: Hugh McCracken of North West Trading Company Trade, Meriwether Lewis, and Stephen Ambrose

SPEAKER 1

McCracken

I'm with the North West Company. We are competing with Hudson's
Bay Company for control of the Mandan market. We are supplying
manufactured goods to the Mandans, including blankets, clothing, and guns.
In return, we get their furs and hides.

SPEAKER 2

Lewis

We want this market. We are opening the Missouri River from St. Louis to
the Mandan villages for the St. Louis and American trading companies. You
no longer have any authority in this region—we own it all.

Ambrose

Here is what Lewis and Clark had in mind. In 1808 they became partners in the St. Louis Missouri Fur Company. (Lewis was a silent partner.) As the newly appointed governor of the Territory of Louisiana, Clark was superintendent of Indian affairs. Lewis granted a trading monopoly to the new company, giving it the right to establish a fort at the mouth of the Yellowstone River. Lewis then authorized funds for a private militia to accompany a trading flotilla up the Missouri River to the Yellowstone. The militia would protect the interests of the new company.... The Indians would be made dependent on the St. Louis Missouri Fur Company, allowing the fur trade to prosper, bringing great profit to Lewis and Clark and the St. Louis investors in their company.

(AMBROSE 1996, 185, 452,454; SEE ALSO LEWIS [1808], IN
COUES 1965/1893, VOL. 3, 1215–43)

SPEAKER 2

Historical Skeptic

As Stephen Ambrose writes, this plan kept Indians—these wretched peoples—in a state of economic dependency, allowed an American fur-trade empire to flourish, and was consistent with Jefferson's policy toward Indians—that is, if they don't cooperate, kill them.

(AMBROSE 1996, 431–32)

(Pause)

You've got to be kidding! So Lewis and Clark used their great western adventure to personal advantage.

SPEAKER 1

Another Skeptic

Yes, and they traded blankets, whiskey, and guns for furs, and had dreams of getting rich!

Diseased Family Blanket Short Story Continued

SPEAKER 1

Narrator

Now I see the link. The British made and traded the blankets for furs. The Americans—Lewis and Clark—did not have the HBC blankets but they had blankets, beads, guns, Jefferson peace medallions, whiskey, and trinkets to trade. These blankets were complex cultural objects. They were known to be and would continue to be seen as carriers of the smallpox disease.

When my father brought that HBC blanket home to Indianola, he brought a part of this history right into our house—a history of disease, exploitation, and destruction. He kept the history alive when he bought us the blanket for the cabin. In turn, we carried that history into the new cabin.

When we bought Nate and Heidi their new HBC blankets, we passed the history right along to the next generation. As you can see, my family has a long, somewhat indirect and troubled history with Canada, Hudson's Bay blankets, the fur trade, nineteenth-century British and French traders, and Native Americans.

Uncomfortably, this history takes me right back into the myths about Yellowstone Park, Lewis and Clark, the Corps of Discovery, Sacagawea, and the bicentennial commemoration activities in 2003–2004.

CODA: LEWIS AND CLARK'S FOOTPRINTS

SPEAKER 1

Narrator

Today, two years after the bicentennial celebrations, Lewis and Clark's footprints are still present in our national imagination. The bicentennial celebration is central to America's understanding of itself in this new century. Celebrating Lewis and Clark means celebrating colonial and postcolonial mythologies about nature, science, the natural world, the wilderness, the frontier, race, gender, and race relations in the nineteenth century. The Lewis and Clark story is about forgetting, about memory, about remembering only certain memories. Searching for Yellowstone is about searching for new memories.

The two projects intersect, because if in 2008 America honors white men with undaunted courage, then it honors men who kept slavery and racism alive. Clark, like Jefferson, never really freed his slaves. In honoring this journey, Americans honor two men who were guided through the Rocky Mountains by a Native American woman they sometimes called Sacagawea but more frequently called "our squaw," "our Indian woman," "the Frenchman's [Charbonneau] wife," "the Frenchman's squaw." And once she is called "Janey," the nickname given her by Clark.

Remember too that both Lewis and Clark were committed to implementing Jefferson's goal of obtaining land and furs from Native Americans, and this included killing Indians, waging war with Britain if necessary, and enacting a form of democracy that was ethnically exclusive.[7]

If Native Americans could not assimilate to the American way of life, they were doomed to extinction.

(AMBROSE 1996, 452–53; MCMURTRY 2001, 157; SLAUGHTER 2003, 102; WALLACE 1999, 18; WALLACE 1997, 30)

A Counternarrative

Narrator

It is possible to imagine another version, or telling, of the Lewis and Clark myth. Like Robert Williams, who turns Jefferson back on himself, it is possible to use the Lewis and Clark narratives as an occasion for reimagining indigenous human rights. Williams argues that Jefferson's theory of democracy should be taken up by indigenous peoples, who can claim, as whites did, the natural, inalienable rights of self-recognition, self-governance, survival, autonomy, life, liberty, the pursuit of happiness, and sovereign authority over their own lands.

Similarly, the Lewis and Clark celebrations of 2003–2004 can be turned into political performances—transgressive events. In this form of historical theater, Lewis and Clark would be pushed aside, ignored. In their place, performers would enact a disruptive utopian theater, reclaiming and celebrating the inalienable rights of Native Americans to own and control their own history. These performance texts would be occasions for indigenous peoples to write their way into the journals, to offer their stories and narratives about the effects of Lewis and Clark on their ancestors and on themselves.

Like William Least Heat-Moon, also known as William Lewis Trogdon, these tellings would recover buried history, moments, representations, ancient pictographs that write across "all of us—red, white, mixed." This theater would advance the project of indigenous decolonization. These performance events would represent Lewis and Clark as colonizers whose "undaunted courage" will no longer be recognized or honored or celebrated.

(HEAT-MOON 1999, 216–17; HOXIE 2006; WILLIAMS 1997, 62–67)

In producing this performance text I have attempted to disrupt history. I have performed an alternative version of the Lewis and Clark project. In doing this I was taken back to childhood memories, to my father and mother in Indianola, Iowa, to stories about illness, alcoholism, disease, Hudson's Bay blankets, gift giving between generations in my family—in short, to my family's place in the Lewis and Clark mythology.

YELLOWSTONE PARK AND LEWIS AND CLARK, CIRCA 2006

Many of the 2004–2006 Lewis and Clark Bicentennial celebrations occurred in and around Yellowstone National Park. The bicentennial became an occasion for celebrating Yellowstone as America's first national park. Montage 2 reproduces iconic images of the park, including several from the 1953 *Haynes Guide* to the park (Plate 6). Haynes's photograph *Old Faithful* was on the cover of every edition of the guide.

In the late 1870s F. Jay Haynes (1853–1921) was hired by Jay Cooke's Northern Pacific Railroad to become their official photographer. Haynes's job was to produce photographs that could be used as advertisements for the NPR. Soon thereafter, Haynes proclaimed himself the official photographer of Yellowstone National Park, and thus was borne the annual *Haynes Guide*, which was published continuously from 1890 till 1967. Tourists were encouraged to buy the guide when they entered the park.

Thomas Moran's 1872 *Grand Canyon of the Yellowstone* (Plate 8) is the most famous painting of the park. The painting includes a Native American, whose back is turned away from the canyon (Plate 9). This painting was celebrated in the 2005 in *Drawn to Yellowstone* exhibit at the Buffalo Bill Historical Center. The *Haynes Guide*, of course, included photographs and discussions of Moran's *Grand Canyon of the Yellowstone*.

Four advertisements are included in this montage: an NPR travel brochure showing Old Faithful (Plate 10); an ad for the 2005 *Drawn to Yellowstone* art exhibit (Plate 12), and two photos from the brochure for the 2006 Lindblad expedition, "In the Wake of Lewis and Clark." Notice that the second of these images (Plate 14) reproduces the standard historical image of Sacagawea.

Crazy's Mule's Map 1 (Plate 15) is the only known nineteenth-century Native American representation of the greater Yellowstone region. This map is discussed in detail in Chapter 7. This montage also includes a highway map of the park from the Haynes Guide (Plate 16). Of course every image in the *Haynes Guide* functioned as an ad to bring tourists to Yellowstone.

Plate 5. Postcard, Old Faithful.

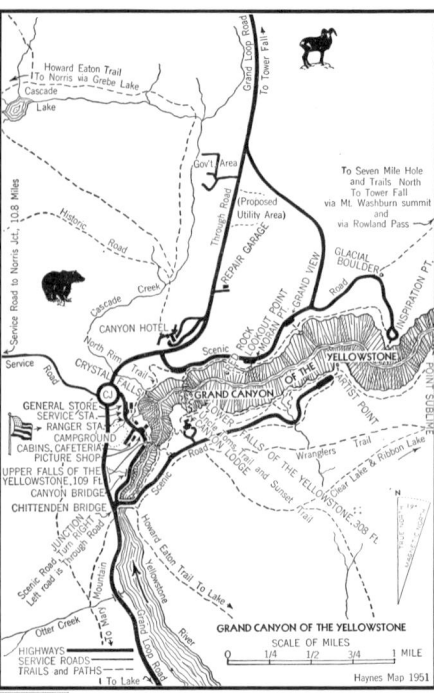

Plate 7. Map of the Grand Canyon area from the 1953 *Haynes Guide to Yellowstone National Park.*

Plate 6. Cover, 1953 *Haynes Guide to Yellowstone National Park.*

Plate 8. Thomas Moran, *Grand Canyon of the Yellowstone*, 1872.

Plate 9. Detail, Thomas Moran, *Grand Canyon of the Yellowstone*.

Plate 10. Cover of Northern Pacific Railroad travel brochure showing Old Faithful, 1933.

Plate 11. Front cover, *Along the Trail with Lewis and Clark.*

Plate 12. Guide to *Drawn to Yellowstone* exhibit, Buffalo Bill Historical Center, 2005.

Plate 13. Cover of brochure for Lindblad expedition, "In the Wake of Lewis and Clark, 2006."

Plate 14. Back cover of Lindblad expedition brochure showing (left to right): Clark, York (Clark's slave), Lewis, Sacagawea, and Charbonneau. The sixth figure is an unidentified member of the expedition, probably Patrick Gass or John Ordway.

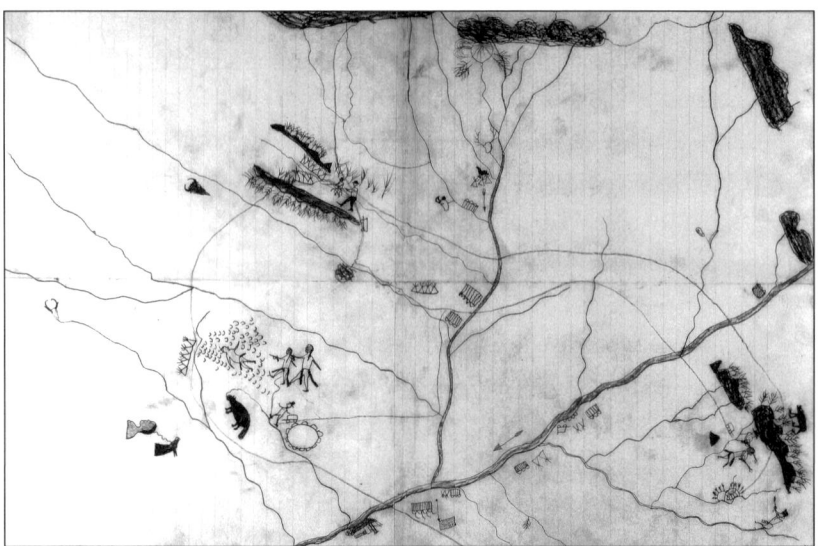

Plate 15. Crazy Mule's map

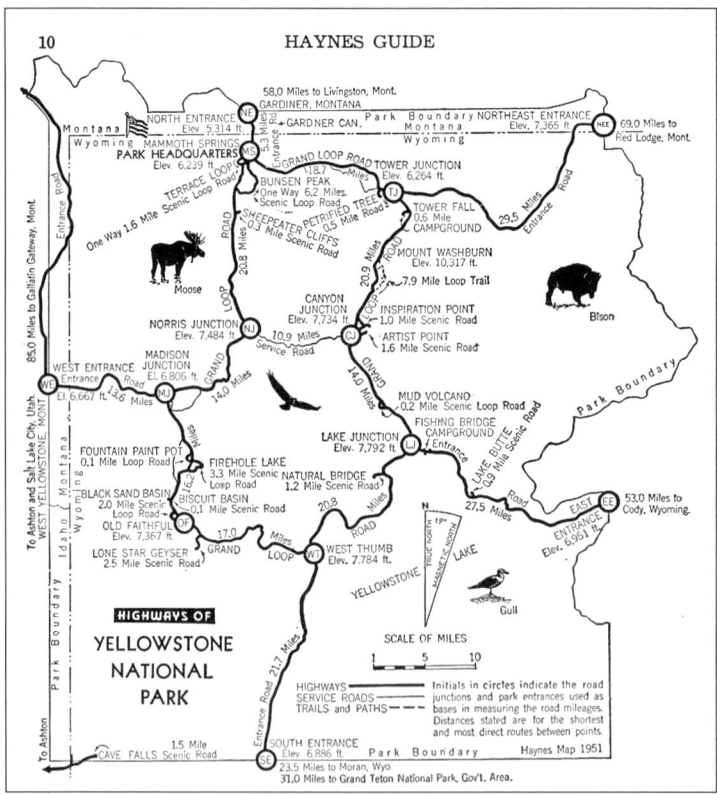

Plate 16. Map of Yellowstone National Park highway system

꩜

SACAGAWEA'S NICKNAME,[1]
OR THE SACAGAWEA PROBLEM

The tropical emotion that has created a legendary Sacajawea awaits
study.... Few others have had so much sentimental fantasy expended on
them. A good many men who have written about her...have
obviously fallen in love with her. Almost every woman who has written
about her has become Sacajawea in her inner reverie.

(DEVOTO 1958, 618; SEE ALSO WALDO 1978, XII)

Anyway, what it all comes down to is this: the story of Sacagawea
...can be told a lot of different ways.

(ALLEN 1984, 24)

Many millions of Native American women have lived and died...
and yet, until quite recently, only two—Pocahontas and Sacagawea
—have left even faint tracings of their personalities on history.

(MCMURTRY 2001, 155)

PROLOGUE

SPEAKER 1

Narrator as Dramatist

"Sacagawea's Nickname, or the Sacagawea Problem," is a four-act play which
offers a revisionist history of Sacagawea and the representation of Native
American women in two cultural and symbolic landscapes: the Lewis
and Clark journals and *The Big Sky* by A. B. Guthrie Jr., Montana's most
famous novel (1947).[2] In the summers of 2003, 2004, and 2005, Sacagawea's
footprints, like those of the two explorers, were all over the greater
Yellowstone region.[3]

The Lewis and Clark Bicentennial corresponds with the fifty-year anniversary of *The Big Sky*. Guthrie's book is the source of Montana's "big sky" origin myth. The Lewis and Clark journals and *The Big Sky* are, at one level, interchangeable texts,[4] for Guthrie "drew from the journals…and in some cases…incidents appear to be lifted almost verbatim." *The Big Sky* is the foundational novel for modern western literature. Its West is the West of white males, Turner's (1920) frontier, a West that is "innocence, anticivilization, savage and beautiful and doomed." Guthrie's West is an imaginary site for "a dream that most Americans, however briefly, or vainly, have dreamed and that some have briefly captured."[5]

In the summers of 2003, 2004, and 2005, you could not pass a bookstore without seeing Sacagawea's face or name on the cover of a new publication or a revision of a so-called classic, such as Anna Lee Waldo's expanded (1978) epic novel Sacajawea.[6] This play reinterprets Sacagawea's place in the Guthrie and Lewis and Clark mythology.

The presence of the Native American woman in the collective white imagination is almost entirely a matter of racist myth and Euro-American patriarchal stereotypes—stereotypes which confine her to one of two categories, squaw or princess. It is necessary to critically interpret the legend and the myth of Sacagawea. If we fail to come to terms with the Sacagawea problem, a problem symbolized by her American nickname, Janey, we fail to confront our own past, and the place of the Lewis and Clark legend and its sexual politics in that past.

(BLEW 1988, 633, 634; ALSO BOOK 2003; CLARK AND
EDMONDS 1979; FARR AND BEVIS 2001; FRADIN AND
FRADIN 2002; GARCEAU 2001, 120, 151; GILMAN 2003;
HUNSAKER 2003, 2001; METCALF 2002; ROWLAND 1989;
SLAUGHTER 2003; STEGNER 1965, VIII; TINLING 2001)

ACT 1

Scene 1: Getting Started

SPEAKER 1: *(offstage aside)*

Narrator

If the woman named Sacagawea had not appeared in front of Lewis and Clark in November of 1804, she would have to have been invented. The Corps of Discovery needed a gendered presence that would define proper, civilized, white, American male [and female] conduct—conduct that was not

Indian-like, and not French or British or half-breed. She served this function and served it well. She is central to the Lewis and Clark narrative. In this telling, writers have created the proper place for the fully assimilated Native American woman and her family.

SPEAKER 2

Donna Kessler and James Ronda
There are multiple versions of Sacagawea as she appears in legend and myth, versions which have undergone successive revisions since her original presence in the journals. Three questions have preoccupied Sacagawea scholars:

The spelling of her name

Whether or not she was an indispensable guide for the expedition

The date and place of her death

(KESSLER 1996, 98, 104, 109) (RONDA 1984, 256–58)

SPEAKER 1

Narrator
From the moment she joins the corps, 4 November 1804, until 17 August 1806, when she is set back ashore at the Mandan villages in North Dakota, Sacagawea is a hovering presence in the journals.[7] There are more than 125 references to her.[8] Of course there are multiple spellings of her name—Sacajawea, Sacagawea, Sakakawea, Sah ca gah we ah—plus other names: Janey, the squaw, "Bird Woman," "Boat Launcher," interpretress, wife of Shabano [Charbonneau], the Indian woman, remarkable little woman.

(SLAUGHTER 2003, 102) (RONDA 1984, 256–57)

SPEAKER 2

James Ronda
The two recurrent spellings of her name—Sacajawea and Sacagawea—indicate membership in two different tribal communities. Sacajawea is Shoshone and means "boat launcher." Sacagawea is Hidatsa and translates as "bird woman."

(RONDA 1984, 257)

SPEAKER 1

Narrator as Interpreter
In the diaries and in the second published version of the journals, she is a savage, a guide, and a heroine. In turn-of-the-century novels, popular history, drama, and suffragist literature, she is transformed from a savage into a

princess, a guide, a heroine—to a model of modern feminism's independent American woman. By the 1950s, novelists suggested that she and William Clark were involved in a romantic relationship, thereby "bringing interracial comity to Anglo-American conquest."

(KESSLER 1996, 67, 104; SLAUGHTER 2003, 87)

SPEAKER 2

Narrator Summarizing History

On the occasion of the bicentennial, she appears as a captive mother and interpreter; a source of family for Clark; our "national Indian, our founding princess." Images of her appear on coins, stamps, paintings, and crockery, and in comic books.

(HALL 2003; MCMURTRY 2001, 161; SLAUGHTER 2003, 112)

Scene 2: An Obituary

SPEAKER 1 *(offstage)*

Narrator as Historian

For Sacagawea
    Sacagawea was a Wind River Shoshone
    also known as "Bird Woman,"
    born in 1788 or 1789 in Salmon, Idaho.
    The two accounts of her death
    discredit each other.
    In one, she died 20 December 1812
    at the age of twenty-five,
    of a putrid fever,
    at Fort Manuel, South Dakota.
    In the second account
    she was joined by her son
    on the Wind River Reservation,
    where she died on 9 April 1884,
    at Fort Washakie, Wyoming.
(Pause.)
We would honor her best
by celebrating her accomplishments
as a slave who
transcended and escaped her condition.

(HUNSAKER 2001, 72; MOULTON 2003, 380;

SLAUGHTER 2003, 88, 91, 113)

Scene 3: *The Big Sky*

SPEAKER 1

Narrator as Literary Critic, as Literary Historian

Modeled after the Lewis and Clark narrative,[9] A. B. Guthrie Jr.'s 1947 novel *The Big Sky* is the story of Kentuckian Boone Caudill, who, when the story begins, is seventeen years old and leaving home with hopes of becoming a mountain man. Boone meets, falls in love with, and fathers a blind son with a Native American woman named Teal Eye. Teal Eye is a fictional woman, much like Sacagawea, Lewis and Clark's Bird Woman. She is Guthrie's Indian princess, his Pocahontas. But she is more than Pocahontas.

By falling in love with Teal Eye and taking her into his tepee, Boone has become a "white Indian" and has symbolically "married the wilderness," turning his back on ordinary white society. Teal Eye represents the freedom from constraint that he desires. But as he embraces the Native American and mountain man way of life, he experiences a "fatal moral lapse from civilization." He is self-reliant, courageous, and larger than life. But he is also ruthless, resentful, conspiratorial, and violent in his savagery. This savagery, "which has become his strength, is revealed as his fatal weakness." Untamable, he is called to the western territory beyond the edge of civilization, and he cannot go back. In a jealous rage, he shoots his best friend, Jim Deakins. This murder shuts him off from all connections to the wilderness and to civilization. Doomed, he has nowhere to go. And it all started when he fell in love with Teal Eye, the Indian princess.[10]

> The simplistic gender system
> princess/squaw, virgin/whore
> operating in the journals and in *The Big Sky*
> reveals an unbridgeable gap
> between…fictional squaws
> and the actual lives of mid-nineteenth-century
> native…women.…
> There is an adamance to…[these] caricatures
> of women, native and white,
> that suggests strong feelings
> about gender and power in American society.…
> Economic productivity and active sexuality
> are desirable traits in the women
> who inhabit the pages of the journals and *The Big Sky*,
> but only if these women
> do not challenge white male authority.

When Boone takes Teal Eye as a wife, he marries more than the wilderness. He marries into an imaginary gender system that, in the words of Dee Garceau, bears "little resemblance to either actual women of the historic Plains or Mississippi Valley…or to the seamless metaphors of kinship and intermarriage that knit together First Nations women and Spanish, French, and English colonizers, Hispanic and Anglo emigrants, and European immigrants."

This flat conception of feminine identity is also evident in the journals when Clark (22 November 1804) calls Sacagawea "the squar [squaw] of the interpreter." It is also present when he says (12 October 1804) that the Sioux have a curious custom "to give handsome Squars to those whome they wish to show some acknowledgements."

(CHRISTIAN 2004, 86; GARCEAU 2001, 121, 122, 150;
MOULTON 2003, 57, 70; STEGNER 1965, X, XII)

Scene 4: Miscegenation

SPEAKER 1

A. B. Guthrie Jr.

Sex in *The Big Sky:*
Boone's squaw lifted her gown and…lay back,…lay waiting, thinking about the scarlet cloth her man had bargained for.…She wasn't bad—straight and young and so light-colored a man might take her for white in the dusk.

(GUTHRIE 1947, 125–26)

SPEAKER 2

Narrator: Reading Sexual Politics: Childbirth and Mixed Breeds

The racial politics and miscegenation message are clear. The races cannot successfully mix.

SPEAKER 1

Shirley Christian

Hold on here. Lewis and Clark and Guthrie were operating with only one possible model of racial and sexual politics. There was another model, the one the French followed. Based on strictures of the Roman Catholic Church, children born from sexual relations between First Nations women and French trappers and businessmen were christened and treated as French, not as outcasts or half-breeds.

(CHRISTIAN 2004, 86)

SPEAKER 2

Lewis and Whitehouse

The ease with which the women of the aborigines of North America bring fourth their children is rather a gift of nature. . . . Indian women who are pregnant by white men experience more difficulty in childbirth then when pregnant by an Indian.

(LEWIS AND CLARK JOURNALS,

IN MOULTON 2003, 198, 228)

SPEAKER 1

Narrator: Back to Sexual Politics and the Sacagawea Problem

White men such as Boone, who fall in love with Indian women, have no place in white or Native American society. Native American women like Teal Eye or perhaps Sacagawea, who fall in love with white men, will be trivialized, abandoned, or killed. This is the message buried deep inside the Sacagawea problem.

But there is another side to Janey's problem. The gender and sexuality system that operates in the journals allows Lewis and Clark (and their coauthors) to write as if they were the first to witness or write about First Nations women and their place in a political and sexual economy. By ignoring what had gone before them, they, like Guthrie, were able to freely deploy the Euro-American tropes of whore and virgin.

SPEAKER 2

Narrator : Back to Our Main Story Line

In continuing to mythologize this woman—by minting coins, naming her Janey, printing stamps, and erecting new statues in her honor— contemporary culture keeps a mythic, feminized West alive. In this version of the Old West, women such as Sacagawea and Teal Eye helped white men do the civilizing work of American capitalism. But the Native American woman has no space of her own in this territory. And in folding her presence into myth and statues, the contradictions that surround her sexuality and her status in the white community are erased. Thus in myth she is stripped of her sexuality and turned into an "earth mother."

ACT 2

Scene 1: Squanto in Coralville, Iowa, Grade School, 1950

SPEAKER 1

Author as Squanto

As a child I lived inside a white imaginary world. With my classmates
in primary school I played dress-up games. Sometimes I was an Indian,
sometimes I was a cowboy, a pilgrim, or a rancher. Sacagawea and Lewis
and Clark were not topics of the day, but other Native Americans were. In
one of our school plays my classmate Mary Anderson played Pocahontas,
the Indian princess, to Billy Bruckner's John Smith, the white man
that Pocahontas supposedly saved in 1607. In fourth grade our teacher,
Mrs. Valentine, painted my face brown with food coloring, gave me a
headband with a feather in the back, and said I was to play Squanto in
our Thanksgiving play, which was about the pilgrims at Plymouth. And so
I played Squanto in our class play, looking into the audience to see if my
grandparents and parents had come to see my performance.

SPEAKER 2

Narrator as Adult: Mrs. Valentine Never Met Howard Zinn

Mrs. Valentine told us that there really was an event called Thanksgiving
that took place between the pilgrims and the Indians. She did not tell us
that Thanksgiving as a national holiday was created in 1863, or that it was
established as a commercial holiday in 1934 with the first Macy's parade in
New York City. Nor did she tell us that the second Thanksgiving celebration
excluded the "heathen natives" who had been defeated in battle. Nor did
she tell us that Squanto's real name was "Tisquantum," that he had been
captured by an English merchant in 1605, taken to England, taught English,
sold as a slave in Spain, and returned to America as a guide and interpreter
for English sea captains and businessmen. Nor did she tell us that Squanto
died of smallpox. I was informed that as Squanto I had befriended the poor
pilgrims, taught them how to survive in the wilderness, and showed them
how to plant crops. Mrs. Valentine probably did not know any other history.

Scene 2: Another Version of History

SPEAKER 1

Chorus of Radical Historians: Howard Zinn,
Dee Brown, James Virgil Vogel, Alan Taylor[11]

Contrary to the first Thanksgiving myth of mutual trust, the Plymouth colonists regarded the Indians as "savage" people who were cruel, barbarous, and most treacherous. Periodic warfare broke out, culminating in the hanging of three Wampanoags in 1675. In a war that lasted more than a year, the Indian community was destroyed.

Indian women and children were sold into slavery in the West Indies. So much for peace and gratitude in Plymouth Colony. In 1676 the colonists held a second thanksgiving celebrating the defeat of the Wampanoags.

(BROWN 1971, 4; TAYLOR 2001, 194; VOGEL 1972, 32;

WILSON 1998, 79; ZINN 2003, 16)

Scene 3: Escaping Squanto

SPEAKER 1

Author as Adult Confronts Squanto

When I joined the faculty of the University of Illinois in 1966, Squanto was the official logo of the Department of Agronomy and its newsletter. Squanto appeared as a cartoon caricature on orange and white hats. He had a long hooked nose and feathers in his headband, and he held a tall soil augur. He was retired in 1989.

(PROCHASKA 2001, 163, 174)

Scene 4: A Short History of Thanksgiving in North America

SPEAKER 1

(The timeline may be projected onto a screen as well as spoken.)

Narrator

A Thanksgiving Timeline

1621: English pilgrims in Plymouth Colony feast with Tisquantum (Squanto) and other members of the Wampanoag tribe.

June 1676: Another day of thanksgiving is proclaimed, but it does not include Indians for the celebration is in recognition of the recent victory over the "heathen natives."

1777: During the American Revolution (1775–83), the Continental Congress proclaims a national day of thanksgiving following the victory at the Battle of Saratoga.

1789: George Washington proclaims another day of thanksgiving in honor of ratification of the U.S. Constitution.

1817: New York State adopts Thanksgiving Day as an annual custom.

1863: Abraham Lincoln proclaims the last Thursday of November as Thanksgiving Day.

1879: The Canadian Parliament sets 6 November for its Thanksgiving celebrations.

1934: The first Macy's parade celebrates the day after Thanksgiving as the first day of the Christmas shopping season.

1939: President Franklin D. Roosevelt moves Thanksgiving from the last Thursday in November to one week earlier. Critics called this "Franksgiving."

1941: President Roosevelt establishes the fourth Thursday of November as the national Thanksgiving holiday.

1957: The Canadian Parliament moves Thanksgiving to the second Monday of October.

Scene 5: Sacagawea and Thanksgiving

SPEAKER 1 (*offstage*)

Narrator

An imaginary ad for the Sacagawea Hotel, Three Forks, Montana:

"Lewis and Clark never had Thanksgiving dinner here, but you can."

(*MONTANA MAGAZINE*, OCTOBER/NOVEMBER 2004)

ACT 3

Scene 1: Meeting Sacagawea and Her Little Family

SPEAKER 1

Narrator

When and how does Sacagawea first appear in the journals?

SPEAKER 2

William Clark

She arrived in our little world on 4 November 1804, at Fort, Mandan, North Dakota: a french man by the Name Chabonah (Toussaint Charbonneau), who speaks the Big Belley language visit us. we engau him to go on with us and take one of his wives (Sacagawea) to interpret the Snake language.

(MOULTON 2003, 67)

SPEAKER 1

Meriwether Lewis, 11 February 1805

About five o'clock this evening one of the wives (Sacagawea) of Charbono was delivered of a fine boy (Jean Baptiste Charbonneau).

(MOULTON 2003, 83)

SPEAKER 2

Audience Member

How did they put this expedition together? They were on boats, right? What were the sleeping arrangements?

SPEAKER 1

Clark, 7 April 1805

Our vessels consisted of six small canoes, and two large perogues. This little fleet altho not quite as rispectable as those of Columbus or Capt. Cook were still viewed by us with much pleasure[.] ... [W]e were about to penetrate a country ... on which the foot of civilized man had never trodden.

(MOULTON 2003, 92–93)

SPEAKER 2

Narrator

This was a lie and Clark knew it. He had the maps from the Mackay and Evans Expedition of 1795–97, nine years before Lewis and Clark left St. Louis.

(WOOD 2003, 6)

SPEAKER 1

Historical Critic

Clark's favorable comparison of his fleet with Columbus and Cook is chilling because we know that they were colonizers who brought violence, illness, and slavery to indigenous peoples.

SPEAKER 2

Stephen Ambrose

Lewis's bed was a buffalo-skin and a blanket inside a buffalo skin tepee, apparently put up (and taken down) and packed the next morning by Sacagawea, and perhaps with some help from York.... Joining Lewis in his lodge were Clark, Charbonneau, Drouillard, Sacagawea, and her baby. Putting her in the tent, surrounded by the two captains, the hunter, the interpreter (her husband), and her son removed temptation from the men. This sleeping arrangement persisted until Sacagawea and Charbonneau returned to the Mandan villages.

(AMBROSE 1996, 211–12)

SPEAKER 1

Larry McMurtry and James P. Ronda

Legend has it that Sacagawea was a guide and an interpreter for the corps, but this is early-twentieth-century fabrication: she was neither. She did not guide the expedition to the Pacific Ocean. She was not part of the advance party that met and negotiated with the Snake Indians. Her guiding consisted primarily of identifying Beaverhead Rock in southwestern Montana,...a landmark the captains could probably have figured out for themselves.

(MCMURTRY 2001, 156; RONDA, 1984, 256–57)

SPEAKER 2

Narrator as Interpreter

But she never speaks, she is only spoken for, described, written about, an enigma. Her silent presence serves to reinforce the narrow Euro-American representations of Native American women in the journals.

(SEE GARCEAU 2001, 123; ALSO ALBERS 1983, 3;

KESSLER 1996, 22–23).

SPEAKER 1

Clark, 9 August 1806

"She gave me a gift.
The Squar brought me
a large and well flavoured Goose Berry
of a rich Crimson colour,

and [a] deep purple berry
of the large Cherry of the Current Speces."

(MOULTON, 2003, 361)

SPEAKER 2

Popular Culture Historian

Sacagawea is the journal's Pocahontas.
She is the good Indian mother, earth mother,
the gatherer of herbs and berries,
the proper mythical Indian woman
subservient to her white husband.

Scene 2: Who Is Pocahontas?

SPEAKER 1

Narrator

Timeline: Pocahontas and Powhatan

1595:   Pocahontas is born, the daughter of Chief Powhatan of Jamestown, Virginia.

December 1607:   Pocahontas rescues John Smith by throwing her body across his as he is about to be clubbed by Indians.

1609:   John Smith returns to England.

1610:   Pocahontas marries an Indian named Kocoum.

1611:   She is captured and held for ransom.

1613:   She is moved to a new settlement, is educated in Christianity, and she meets a tobacco planter named John Rolfe.

1614:   Rolfe attacks Powhatan's village, and Pocahontas is reunited with her brothers. She is baptized, christened Rebecca, and she marries Rolfe.

1616–17:   She is taken to England, presented to the Royal Court. She meets John Smith and sets sail for America in 1617. She dies of smallpox on 21 March 1617, leaving a son, Thomas, to whom some famous Virginia families trace their ancestry.

(VOGEL, 1972, P. 332)

SPEAKER 2

Historian

As you can see, it's not a straightforward story. She was an Indian princess. The Walt Disney Studio made a movie about her life.[12] She was born about eighty-five years before Sacagawea, but there are parallels between their lives. Both married older white men, bore sons, and traveled far from their people in boats. Pocahontas is famous for saving the life of Captain John Smith. Both women were aligned with white racial ideology and became symbols of the properly assimilated Native American woman. Consistent with the Pocahontas legend, Sacagawea chose a white man as her husband, a French Canadian.[13]

SPEAKER 1

Audience Member

So she's also a little like Squanto: she has an important place in American myth; she helped the starving colonists get food; she defined the proper "Indian" for whites.

SPEAKER 2

Narrator

They gave her a white name, Rebecca, just like Clark gave Sacagawea a white name, Janey. This represents a profound shift in identity. It states that the Native American woman will be known only by the name given her by a white male.

Scene 3: Sex and a Little Tenderness on the Trail with Lewis and Clark

SPEAKER 1

Narrator

But back to Sacagawea. Her silent presence is contrasted with the sexually aggressive Native American women who engage in sexual exchanges with the men in the corps. The presence of these two images in the journals—the proper princess and the sexually aggressive squaw—reinforces the white, masculine nationalism of Lewis and Clark. Indeed, the sexual conduct of the squaw can be read as justifying white conquest, sexual exploitation, rape, smugness, aggression, deceit, ridicule, capture, violence, murder, genocide.

SPEAKER 2

Cynic

Can you be more specific?

SPEAKER 1

Narrator

Just listen to Clark.

William Clark: Just a Little Tenderness, 11 June 1805

The Indian woman verry sick. I blead her which appeared to be of great Service to her[.]...(June 12) I moved her to the back part of the Covered part of the Perogue which is cool, her own situation being verry hot one in the bottom of the Perogue exposed to the sun[.]...(June 17) [She] is much better today...there is every rational hope of her recovery.

(IN MOULTON 2003, 128, 137)

SPEAKER 1

Meriwether Lewis on Tawny Damsels
and Shoshone Female Sexuality, 19 August 1805

The chastity of their women is not held in high estimation[.]...I have requested the men to...have no connection with their women... [but] I know it is impossible to effect, particularly on the part of our young men whom some months of abstinence have made very polite to these tawney damsels.

(IN MOULTON 2003, 190)

SPEAKER 2

Narrator as Interpreter

Clearly Lewis and Clark place Sacagawea, who was Shoshone, outside their discussion of Shoshone sexuality. She may be tawny but she is not a damsel, and she is not farmed out for favors by her husband. She is a woman who requires a little tenderness and protection from the sun when she is ill.

SPEAKER 1

William Clark: Christmas presents, 25 December 1805

I recved a present of...two dozen white weazils tails of the Indian woman.

(IN MOULTON 2003, 251).

SPEAKER 2

Bernard DeVoto: Clark's Christmas with Sacagawea

And the warm heart of Sacajawea, whose ailments he had treated,...[s]he had but inadequate words to give him on Christmas...but...knowing that he had been kind to her and that this was a day of kindness, she gave him what she had. History will remember William Clark as one of the greatest captains, and, remembering him, it will not forget the twenty-four white weasel tails that Janey gave him on Christmas day.

(DEVOTO 1936, 28, REPRINTED IN RONDA 1998)

SPEAKER 1

Narrator as Interpreter

Indeed! And what did Clark give her?

Scene 4: Guys Talk about Sex in *The Big Sky*

SPEAKER 1

Mountain Men (and Guthrie as Omniscient Narrator)

"They're sweet pumpkins, them Ree squaws,
best outside a Taos woman[.] ...
Light-colored and tall and long-legged
and purty as a young filly,
and nigh everyone of 'em willin',
for beads and vermillion[.] ...
A man got calluses,
handling the price to the bucks the squaws belong to[.] ...
And nigh every squaw with the clap
and every man catchin' it."

(Pause.)

"A squaw in a blue dress ... kept watching ... putting one forefinger on
top of the other ... making a sign[.] ... She pointed between her legs
and looked up while she made the sign again, her little eyes asking a
question[.] ... Underneath the old skin dress that was pulled in at the middle
Boone could see the fat of her breasts jiggle."

(Pause.)

In the open grass behind the clay huts the boatmen and the squaws made
moving heaps, the men writhing over the squaws, rising and pushing and
writhing and sometimes groaning like a stud horse as the stuff of them
pumped out. Once in a while you heard a giggle from a squaw.

(GUTHRIE 1947, 87, 102, 103, 125)

SPEAKER 2

Narrator as Interpreter

Guthrie's fictional sexual accounts
could have been written by Lewis or Clark:
sex for hire,
soft ethnographic pornography,
fishhooks and beads,
tawny virgin damsels,

venereal disease,
wild women,
the Wild West "purty" like a virgin,
boatmen writhing over squaws,
moving heaps of flesh,
stud horses pumping out sperm,
giggling squaws,
young men too long without a woman,
the women sport openly with them!

ACT 4

Scene 1: Sexual Voyeurs, Dress Codes, and Tawny Damsels

SPEAKER 1

Narrator as Interpreter

It seems that Lewis and Clark were preoccupied with what they defined as the indecent appearance of Native American women. They write in vivid and graphic detail about garments, leather breechcloths, robes, exposed breasts, openly visible groin areas, hips, and necklines.

SPEAKER 2

Lewis the Observer, 29 March 1806

Their women...wear a kind of leather breech clout about the width of a common pocket handkerchief....[T]he two corners are...confined over the hips and the other end is brought between the legs...and tucked at the groin[.]...[T]he leather truss or breech clout constitutes the whole of their apparel. This is a much more indecent article than the tissue of bark, and bearly covers the mons vens to which it is drawn so closely that the whole shape is plainly perceived.

(IN MOULTON, 2003, 290–91)

SPEAKER 1

Clark the Observer, 10, 17, and 19 October 1805

[Of Snake women] The women are more particular than any other nations which I have passed in Secreting the parts.

[Of Nez Perce women] The women are more inclined to Copulency then any we have yet seen[.]...The women have only a tiny piece of leather about the waste, the breasts are huge and hang down verry low lilly Shaped.

(IN MOULTON 2003, 217; 221, 224)

Cynic

Secret parts, exposed groins, breasts shaped like lilies! What were these ethnographers, these great explorers doing? This was not a project focused on female dress, sexual codes, and the female body. Nowhere in the journals (by my reading) do they report in such graphic detail on male dress and the norms organizing male sexuality. This is sexual voyeurism, plain and simple. The bodies of Native American women have been turned into objects of the male sexual gaze. This gendered sexual gaze introduces into and exposes the erotic, political sides of everyday life under patriarchy. The active, aggressive gaze of Lewis and Clark is harsh and masochistic. It affirms their power over Native American women. At the same time, it suggests that sexual gazing was commonplace in the expedition, and sexuality was never far below the surface.

> In blurring the investigative
> with the sexual gaze,
> Lewis and Clark's story
> crosses over into the pornographic,
> a sexual tale of domination
> disguised as scientific discovery.

Scene 2: Medical Voyeurs, Venereal Diseases, and Prostitutes

SPEAKER 1

Cynic

Lewis and Clark understood that sexual relations would be part of the expedition's experience. They included in their supplies…remedies believed effective against venereal diseases. Symptoms of the disease were first recorded in mid-January 1805. Lewis and Clark looked for native cures and gave close attention to whether or not the women [and men] in a particular tribe appeared to have one or more forms of a sexually transmitted disease.

(SEE BEARS 2005; LOWRY 2005; RONDA 1984, 106–107)

SPEAKER 2

Lewis: Sexual Illness Narrative I, 27 January 1806

Goodrich has recovered from the Louis veneri which he contracted from an amorous contact with a Chinnook damsel. I cured him as I did Gibson last winter by the use of murcury. I cannot learn that the Indians have any simples which are sovereign specifics in the cure of this disease; and indeed I doubt very much whether any of them have any means of effecting a perfect cure…[but] many support this disorder with but little inconvenience[.]…[T]his disorder doe exist among the Indians on the Columbia…in my whole rout down this river I did not see more than two or three with the gonnaera and about double that number with the pox.

(IN MOULTON 2003, 269–70)

SPEAKER 1

Lewis: Sexual Illness Narrative II, 19 August 1805

There seems a strong proof that these disorders bothe gonaroehah and Louis venerae are native disorders of America…[but] perhaps they might have been contracted from other indian tribes who by a round of communication might have obtained them from Europeans.

(IN MOULTON 2003, 269, 191–92)

SPEAKER 2

Gass: Carnal Desire and Prostitution Narratives, 21 March 1806

The women are much inclined to venery[.]…To the honour of the Flatheads, who live on the west side of the Rocky Mountains[,]…we must mention them as an exception; as they do not exhibit those loose feelings of carnal desire.

(IN MOULTON 2003, 286–87)

SPEAKER 1

Lewis: Clatsop and Chinnook Prostitutes, 6 January 1806

We were visited this afternoon by Delashshelwilt, a Chinnook Chief[,] his wife and six women of his nation[.]…[T]his was the same party that had communicated the venerial to many of our party in November last[.]…The Clatsop's do not hold the virtue of their women in high estimation, and will even prostitute their wives or daughters for a fishinghook or a stran of beads.

(IN MOULTON 2003, 283, 258–59)

SPEAKER 2

Ronda on Sex with the Men in Expedition

Of course, as previously noted, Native Americans had a complex theory of political economy, gender, and sexuality. They exchanged sexual favors for European goods. They believed that sexual conduct was a way of transferring spiritual power from the European male to the Native American woman. She in turn transmitted this power to her husband. This was not a secret theory. The corps chose to ignore it, in favor of a moralistic evaluation of Native American women which defined them as whores and prostitutes.

if you will bring your son to me
I will educate him and treat him as my own child.
And his father and mother agreed to do so:
Provided he has been weened, and sufficiently old to leave his mother.

(IN MOULTON 2003, 366; TINLING 2001, 19–20)

SPEAKER 2 *(offstage)*

First Narrator

And thus ends Sacagawea's presence in the journals. Historians disagree on
her contributions. Moulton, for example, argues that "despite her limited
but useful contributions to the expedition, geographic landmarks have been
named for her; markers, monuments, and memorials have been placed
in her honor; and numerous literary and artistic works have given her a
prominence that competes even with that of the captains."

(MOULTON 2003, 380)

SPEAKER 1

Second Narrator

Indeed! And twenty-four white weasel tails. Now what did Clark give her?

SPEAKER 2

Clark

We paid Charbonneau wages of $500.33. His wife deserved a greater reward
then we had in our power to give her. We paid her no wages.

(IN CLARK AND EDMONDS 1979, 82;

ALSO TINLING 2001, 19–20)

CODA: THE SACAGAWEA PROBLEM

In giving her the nickname Janey, or, rather, in recording her name as Janey, Clark, like Guthrie with the woman he names Teal Eye (aka Bird Woman), engages in a form of cultural politics that trivializes while it westernizes Native American women. Ironically, Sacagawea is named Janey in that moment when the expedition members are asked to vote on where they should construct their winter camp. In recording Janey's vote ("a place where there is plenty of Potas"), along with York's, instant suffrage is granted to a Native American woman and a black servant (Moulton 2003, 243).[14] The name Janey functions in this context as a proxy for this one time when the black man and the Indian woman are given the power to vote.

These names—Janey, Teal Eye—are conferred by white male narrators. The act of naming strips the women of their subjectivity even as it relocates them within a fraudulent participatory democracy in which males control the right to vote. The act of naming erases their sense of personal agency. It places them in a linguistic, sexual, and cultural borderland somewhere between princess and sexual slave. Paraphrasing Kessler (1996), in this hinterland, which includes the frontier West, native female compliance functions as a metaphor for a feminized territory awaiting male exploration and domination (Kessler 1996, 180).

Herein lies Sacagawea's problem. She can only be recognized from within this white male mythology and its signifying apparatuses. This mythology celebrates conquest and submission. It requires a Native Indian princess who is willing to be complicit with America's sacred male narratives about the frontier, democracy, and the inevitable march of civilization across the virginal, violent West. Sadly, there are few, if any, Native American signifers which would allow her to be recognized differently. This is the other side of her problem. She is known only from within this racist mythology, where she performs her obligatory service to the dominant culture.[15] She is earth mother embedded in a timeless western landscape (Green 1975, 714; also Kessler 1996, 178).[16]

The David Lemon Bronze: *Welcoming Pomp*

Welcoming Pomp by David Lemon, bronze 31.

Consider David Lemon's recently cast bronze statue titled *Welcoming Pomp: Charbonneau and Sacagawea with Baby Pomp*. A full-page photo in the winter 2004 issue of *Big Sky Journal* advertises the statue as the first in a series of limited-edition bronze sculptures commemorating the two hundredth anniversary of the voyage of Lewis and Clark. The 31-inch-tall, hand-patinaed statue is exclusively marketed by Stellar Art Publishing and is exhibited at the James-Harold Galleries in Lake Tahoe, California; the May Danela Galleries in Scottsdale, Arizona; the Downey Gallery in Sante Fe, New Mexico; and the West Lives On Gallery in Jackson Hole, Wyoming.

In this work, the figures of Sacagawea and Charbonneau are standing on a circular, three-level marble and granite base. The sculpture is simultaneously maternal and paternalistic. Sacagawea holds baby Pomp in her arms. She gazes at him. His tiny face is barely visible from inside the blanket that wraps around his body. She is clothed in a flowing buckskin dress. A multicolored shawl with beaded piping covers her shoulders. Her long black hair partially hides the turquoise necklace and matching earrings she is wearing.

Charbonneau, the protector of this little family, is dressed in dark buckskin. A pipe is in his mouth. He stands close to Pomp and Sacagawea. They share the same circular space. His left leg appears to touch her shin, and his foot is next to her right foot. He gazes into the distance, his eye on potential danger. His extended left arm touches Pomp's head. His right arm balances on his shoulder what appears to be a gun enclosed in a leather-fringed case. A brown stocking cap with three white feathers is perched on the side of his head. A powder horn hangs from his waist.

The statue defines Sacagawea in terms of her identities as Native American mother and wife: she is protected by her husband; in turn, she protects and cares for her child.

The photograph of the statue makes an additional statement. It situates the sculpture—and Sacagawea—outside civilization, in an unbounded winter space that could be the frontier: a large bearskin nestles against the base of the sculpture, which is placed in front of a bare tree; patches of snow dot the landscape. (This is the winter issue of *Big Sky Journal*!)

Of course the statue could be placed anywhere—on a coffee table in a living room or on a stand in an art gallery. As this tableau moves from place to place, it reproduces the legend of Sacagawea and her innocent, gendered, complicit place in the story of Lewis and Clark and the voyage of discovery. In valorizing her, in buying David Lemon's statue, we reassert and do not contest the truth of their narrative. In this way their tale takes on new life in its third century of telling.

Sacagawea in the Buffalo Bill Historical Center

Now another statue. Located on either side of a glassed-in breezeway, two gardens, the Greever and the Braun[17], separate the Plains Indian Museum from the four other museums in the Buffalo Bill Historical Center (BBHC) in Cody, Wyoming.[18] Harry Jackson's 10-foot polychromed bronze monument of Sacagawea (Plate 1) is displayed in the Greever Garden.[19] Three statues—*Crazy Horse*, *The Unknown*, and *Male Warrior with Loincloth*—are located in the Braun Garden. Thus Sacagawea is hemmed in by images of Indian male violence. In her peaceful plenitude, she acts as a stark contrast to these violent males. Completed in 1980 and dedicated on 4 July 1980, titled *Sacagawea*, the monument places her "firmly at the crossroads of the American Frontier" (Goddard 1980, 14; also quoted in Kessler 1996, 179), and at the crossroads of the museum as well. She is connected to the earth and the sky. She stands on a granite base, which is located in a small field of flowers. Wooden benches for visitors, a stone courtyard, a rock garden, and mountain spruce and cottonwood trees fill out the courtyard, which nestles alongside the Plains Indian Museum.

Sacagawea is more than a mere presence in this landscape: she commands the landscape. All visitors are drawn to her. She is wrapped in a full-length, off-white blanket with horizontal earth-brown stripes. She faces eastward. A compliant, gentle, at-peace-with-herself earth mother, she gazes into the morning sun as it shines on the statue of William Cody, which stands outside the east entrance to the museum (Kessler 1996, 180).

It is as if she were created by the wind, a wind that "sweeps her long hair and…enshrouding blanket into diagonal ridges and contours that suggest geological formation.…She is herself part landscape,…she is the native woman who guided Lewis and Clark into unknown wilderness" (Kessler 1996, 179).

She is Sacagawea, a Native American woman in the center of a Wild West museum; a museum designed to celebrate, at one level, the very way of life she represents and honors by her presence. Is she here out of guilt?

Sacagawea is surrounded on all sides by the five museums that make up the Buffalo Bill Historical Center. She is re-remembered on this site. Her presence across from the other statue garden locates Native American women in a historical place that celebrates the American frontier. The Cody Firearms Museum is a monument to the conquest of the West. It celebrates whiteness, and in so doing, as Dickinson, Ott, and Aoki observe (2005, 85), it makes violent conflict between Anglo-Americans and Native Americans a central part of its story.

Jackson's statue of Sacagawea locates Native American women alongside and inside that violence. She bears witness to it. By helping to guide Lewis and Clark, she facilitated the conflict between whites and Native Americans that would come later. Of equal importance, then, and perhaps unintentionally, her statue at this site locates the Lewis and Clark narrative inside the story of the West and how it was won. Indeed, the museum does not repudiate the violence that was central to winning the West. Instead, the violence is celebrated. The posters of Wild Bill Cody and his Wild West Show "reenact the dream of excitement, adventure and conquest that was what the Wild West meant to most people in this country" (Tompkins 1992, 192; also quoted in Kessler 1996, 179).

Sacagawea's presence in the courtyard of the Buffalo Bill Historical Center signals more than acquiescence to this myth. It is a ringing endorsement of it! Why is she there? The answer is obvious. She is a central part of the Pocahontas complex, the Native American princess who helped white males conquer the frontier. The native princess complex is basic to Americans' sacred narratives concerning the West and manifest destiny (Kessler 1996, 178). In honoring her presence, the BBHC reinscribes the old stereotypes that continue to harm Native American women (Kessler 1996, 184). And herein lies another version of her problem. In refusing to forget her, in creating statues of her, white America reminds all Native American women that they have only one of two sexualized places within our national imagination: squaw/whore or Pocahontas/princess.

If Sacagawea is to be set free, she must be remythologized, taken out of and away from the Lewis and Clark and Wild West narratives.[20] The following ad from *Yellowstone Journal*[21] (12 June 2005: 65) is not how to do this.

> Visit the Grave of Sacajawea
>
> The famous Indian woman guide of the Lewis and Clark Expedition, Sacajawea, is said to be buried on Wyoming's Wind River Reservation.
>
> After helping guide the "Corps of Discovery" to the West Coast and back, Sacajawea spent several years wandering the Northern Rockies before she settled with the Eastern Shoshone in Wyoming. Here she was called Wad-ze-whipe—Lost Woman, and lived to be 100.
>
> Sacajawea is reported to have taken part in negotiations that created the reservation, acting as an interpreter because of her language skills.
>
> Her grave and memorial are located in the Sacajawea Cemetery, situated just north of the Robert's Episcopal Mission on Trout Creek Road near Fort Washakie.

Lost Woman!

And then there is the previously cited imaginary ad from *Montana Magazine* (March/April 2003) for the Sacajawea Hotel in Three Forks, Montana—"Undaunted Hospitality: Lewis and Clark Never Stayed Here." Untangling Sacagawea from the legends of Lewis and Clark and *The Big Sky* seems impossible.[22]

To return to the beginning—Janey, Pocahontas, Lewis and Clark on the edge of America (Volmann 2005, 121):

> The East, where the
> United States began:
> John Smith, Pocahontas—
> where we became Americans.
> The West, the Pacific shore:
> "Ocean in View! O! the joy!"
> The Pacific Ocean,
> the beginning of the end,
> the end of the beginning.
> And Janey casts her vote:
> What kind
> of beginning
> for her?

Chapter 6

DRAWN TO YELLOWSTONE I[1]

Jay Cooke's Railroad and Thomas Moran's
Grand Canyon of the Yellowstone

"The establishment of Yellowstone National Park was a great incident
in the scenic history of America.... For the first time, a scenic
wonderland was dedicated as a 'public park...
for the benefit and enjoyment of all the people.'"

(MILLS 1915, 329)

The force of Thomas Moran's 1872 painting
Grand Canyon of the Yellowstone as the paradigmatic image
of Yellowstone National Park has not diminished.

(KINSEY 1992, 78)

PROLOGUE

SPEAKER 1

Narrator as Dramatist

I offer a critical reading of the most famous painting of Yellowstone Park:
Thomas Moran's *Grand Canyon of the Yellowstone* (Plate 8). This painting
from 1872 functions as the paradigmatic image of the park and the
commodification of a specific site within the park—the canyon and falls of
the Yellowstone River.[2] In the summer of 2005, because of the exhibition
Drawn to Yellowstone in the Buffalo Bill Historical Center, reproductions of

Moran's painting and those of his contemporaries and successors were all over the greater Yellowstone region.

I present a four-act performance text that follows the production of Moran's painting from its earliest sketches and woodcuts in 1870 to its public display and sale to the U.S. Congress for $10,000 in 1872. It is generally presumed that Moran painted himself into his masterpiece.[3] Hence, the painter cannot be separated from his painting, and the painting cannot be understood outside its historical moment.

Moran's painting contains a representation of a Native American male. In full regalia, his back turned to the canyon, he stands next to Ferdinand Hayden, who is looking into the canyon. Hayden gestures to the Indian to look back over his shoulder at the scene below (Plate 9).[4] In this placement, the painting functions as a metaphor for progress. Hayden embodies the presence of science and the government in this wild, beautiful, natural setting. He represents the American taming of the wilderness, opening it up for the pleasure of the tourist.

The Indian turns his back on this form of progress, yet even as he is removed from the larger western landscape, he is presented as "a dependent pupil of the 'white discoverer.'" His presence in the painting foreshadows the ways in which the park would become a site for the containment of Native Americans.

(DENZIN 2005B; KINSEY 1992, 44; 1997, 302;

HASSRICK 2002, 42)

SPEAKER 2

Narrator as Child

Today the scenes of this painting
take me back to my grandfather's dresser,
where the faded photograph
of Moran's most famous painting
stood alongside the picture of Grandpa
holding those trout
caught in Yellowstone Lake in 1932.

SPEAKER 1

Narrator as Dramatist

In quoting the story of Moran's painting back to itself, I hope to expose those contradictions and ruptures that brought science, art, capitalism, railroads, and tourism together in the production of his painting. Remember the timeline. With the completion of the transcontinental railroad in 1869, tourism emerged as a new form of cultural consumption. The soon-to-be-established national parks, Yosemite and Yellowstone, would become destinations and points of consumption for the European and American middle and upper classes. In order to get people to travel to these sites, corporate capitalists needed advertisements, photographs, paintings, and stories.

I want to interrupt and interrogate the smooth narrative that says Moran's painting supplied the necessary imagery for the establishment of Yellowstone as a national park. I want to expose the fault line that allows capitalism, tourism, and art to work together.

I also want to interrogate the memories and the fault lines that surround those two pictures on my grandfather's dresser. In my first trip to the park, in the summer of 1988, with my wife and stepson, we were drawn almost unconsciously to Artist Point and the Lower Falls of the Yellowstone. There we stood, alongside a busload of tourists from Japan, cameras in hand, taking pictures of one another. What drew us to this spot? We were drawn to it unconsciously, like my grandfather, by Moran's painting. And what drew Moran to this site?

(SHAFFER 2001, 3)

Tourism sits on top of this divide. Capitalists who build hotels and railroads pay artists to paint pictures of exotic settings. These paintings are turned into advertisements and are used to entice tourists, who read tourist guides to ride the capitalists' trains to their hotels. Soon the economic and cultural geographies of tourism take over. Pristine wilderness and wilderness experiences are quickly commodified. Indigenous peoples (Indians in the park) are relocated. Park managers play God with the natural environment, including its wildlife. Roads, bridges, hotels, restaurants, gift shops, and viewing stations soon mar the natural landscape. If tourism is a devil's bargain, then paintings like Moran's are part of the devil's toolkit.

(CHASE 1986; ROTHMAN 1998, 10)

I read *Grand Canyon of the Yellowstone* through the intertwined lives of two men, Thomas Moran (1837–1926)[5] and Jay Cooke (1821–1905). Cooke was one of nineteenth-century America's wealthiest men, one of the founding fathers of American tourism, an empire builder, the Civil War's patriot-banker, a robber baron who wrapped himself in the American flag. Cooke "had hired hands everywhere," and Moran was one of them.

(JOSEPHSON 1962, 57; SAUNDERS 2003, XIII;

SHAFFER 2001, 43–44; ALSO SILLIMAN 2003, 2–3)

SPEAKER 2
Narrator: A Disclaimer and a Diorama

Hold on just one minute! History records that this story involves at least one other man, Ferdinand Vanderveer Hayden (1829–87). Hayden was head of the American Geological Survey in 1870. At Cooke's urgings, Hayden hired Moran. In the Horace Albright[6] Visitor's Center in Mammoth Hot Springs (until recently park headquarters), visitors walk past a floor-to-ceiling diorama that intermingles art and science (geology). Lifelike replicas of Ferdinand Hayden—with telescope—and Thomas Moran—with paintbrush and easel—are presented against a mountain landscape.

ACT 1

Scene 1: Getting Started

SPEAKER 1
Narrator: Tom and Jay's Great Adventure

Let's start over. Many events had to happen before Moran painted his picture. The painter, Moran, and the robber baron, Cooke, intersect in that space that connects the painter's masterpiece with the robber baron's railroad. The railroad paid for the painting. The painter rode on the baron's railroad to Yellowstone. The painter's painting was then turned into advertisements that the robber baron used to lure tourists to the park. Paraphrasing standard history, the story called "Tom and Jay's Great Adventure" goes something like this.

(BARTLETT 1985; HAINES 1972, 1996A;

LANGFORD 1972/1905; WILKINS 1998, 81)

SPEAKER 2
Narrator as Historian

By 1870, as Cooke was promoting the Northern Pacific Railroad (NPR), he became interested in the region known as the Yellowstone. He needed to raise $100 million by selling railway bonds. Cooke needed a good public relations man and a person with deep knowledge of the Montana Territory. His first choice was Nathaniel Pitt Langford. He hired Langford to give twenty lectures about the Yellowstone region on behalf of NPR. A very important feature of the general scheme of publicity for the Northern Pacific Railroad was the employment of public relations men such as Langford. NPR agents in each district set up times and places for these lectures. Everybody knows that because of Cooke's influence, Langford got the job as the first superintendent of Yellowstone National Park (1872–77).

(HAINES 1972, VIIII–IX; ALSO LUBETKIN 2006, 76;

OBERHOLTZER 1907, 236)

SPEAKER 1 *(in blackface)*

Jay Cooke: Instructions to Langford, 1871

Give your lectures. But I want more. Get me a scientific expedition. Bring back pictures and stories for the national magazines. I'll see to it that my friend Charlie Scribner (1821–71) and his editor Richard Watson Gilder (1844–1909)[7] publish them. But be sure to include geologists and scientists because the American public likes this science, you know—Darwin and all that geology stuff. And they love pictures, so hire a good photographer—see if you can get William Henry Jackson (1843–1942).[8] I like his stuff. His pictures look good in railroad ads. They'll need a military escort no doubt.

(D. SMITH, 1999, 3)

Scene 2: Military Escorts and the Washburn-Doane Expedition

SPEAKER 1

N. P. Langford, 1870–71

After I met with Mr. Cooke, I returned to Montana and enlisted the aid of Henry Dana Washburn (1832–71)[9] to help me put together a civilian and military expedition into the Yellowstone region. This would be called the Washburn-Doane exploration of the Yellowstone region. Lieutenant Gustavus C. Doane (1840–1901), of the Second. United States Cavalry, arranged the military's support of the expedition, which included nineteen persons as well as two packers and two black cooks, named Nute and Johnny. Mr. Cooke persuaded me that this needed to be a scientific expedition if we were going to influence public opinion.

(HAINES 1996A, 108)

SPEAKER 2 *(in whiteface)*

Nute and Johnny

Science, my foot! This whole thing was a big lark! They wanted to shoot off their guns, go fishin', and make us do all the cookin' and clean up after them!

(SEE W. H. JACKSON, IN BLAIR 2005, 68)

Scene 3: First Drawings: Amateur Artists in Yellowstone

SPEAKER 1 *(in whiteface)*

Art Historians Peter Hassrick and Joni Kinsey

The Moore and Trumbull [amateur artists with the expedition] sketches are amateurish…but significant for their influence on Moran's interest in Yellowstone.

SPEAKER 2 *(in redface)*

Trumbull on Railroads and the Falls of Yellowstone

When…by means of the Northern Pacific Railroad, the falls of the Yellowstone and the geyser basin are rendered easy of access, probably no portion of America will be more popular as a watering-place or summer resort than that which we had the pleasure of viewing, in all the glory and grandeur of its primeval solitude.

(TRUMBULL 1871, 496, QUOTED IN HASSRICK 2002, 29)

Scene 4: *Scribner's Monthly* and the Moore-Trumbull Drawings

SPEAKER 1

Langford

When I got back from the Washburn-Doane Expedition I followed Mr. Cooke's instructions. I wrote a two-part article and called it "The Wonders of Yellowstone." I sent this article to Richard Watson Gilder, the editor of *Scribner's Monthly*. It came out in the May and June 1871 issues of the magazine. In the second of the two articles I told my readers that within three years they would be able to see the Great Falls and Canyon of the Yellowstone by means of the Northern Pacific Railroad. I thought Mr. Cooke would like this plug. Gilder rejected the Trumbull and Moore drawings.

(FROM KINSEY 1992, 70; LANGFORD 1871, JUNE, 128)

SPEAKER 2

Richard Watson Gilder

These drawings are terrible. I can never publish them. I'm going to ask Tom Moran to redo them. He does illustrations for us. He's a good friend.

SPEAKER 1 *(in blackface, excitedly)*

Thomas Moran to Gilder

Let me see what I can do. Gosh, I sure need the money, and this place called Yellowstone seems to be a pure wonderland of beauty. No wonder they call it a wonderland. I'll start with ink-wash drawings and then turn them into wood engravings.

SPEAKER 2

Aubrey Haines: An Origin Story

The original newspaper announcement of the park's creation (in the *Helena Herald* of 28 February 1872) referred to it as a "wonderland." The word *wonderland* was taken from the book *Alice's Adventures Under Ground*, written by Charles Lutwidge Dodgson (aka Lewis Carroll) in July 1862 and published in 1866. According to the myth, the little girl for whom this story was written visited Yellowstone Park as an adult and "seemed almost as thrilled as if she had really gotten into that peculiar place through the rabbit hole."

(HAINES 1996A, 172, 354)

SPEAKER 1

John Muir

Nature is on show in the Yellowstone Park, in the blessed old Yellowstone Wonderland.

(MUIR 1979, 42, 63; ORIGINALLY PUBLISHED
IN *ATLANTIC MONTHLY*, JANUARY 1898)

SPEAKER 2 *(in blackface, excitedly)*

Langford on His *Scribner's* Article

The engravings were perfect! Finally people could see...the wonder of Yellowstone. I can say with some confidence that Tom Moran's engravings of the Upper Falls and Castle Geyser helped mobilize public interest in the national park movement.

(STEGNER 1954, 177)

SPEAKER 1

Narrator as Critic

Don't forget, the national park movement would never have gotten off the ground without Cooke's railroad.

SPEAKER 2:

Contemporary Critic Michael Kimmelman

A haphazard, show-offy virtuoso, Moran at his best turns out to have drawn delicate scenes of the most refined atmospherics, capturing western light and air, making sensible geometry of an infinitely complicated space.

(KIMMELMAN 2006, B32)

Narrator as Cynic

Remember, this is not about just art and aesthetics; it is also about science in the service of capitalism, money, tourism, and railroads. Hayden needed paintings that would help sell his survey to the government and Cooke needed a painting that would help sell his railroad.

ACT 2

Scene 1: Moran's First and Second Big Shots at Glory

SPEAKER 1

Narrator as Historian

Several factors had to be in place for Moran to make his wood engravings of the Upper Falls of the Yellowstone:

A transportation, communication, mass production, and mass distribution infrastructure that helped Americans enact the myth of the United States as a unified nation

The desire by capitalists like Cooke to extend railroad lines into and through the American West

The sponsorship by Jay Cooke, Congress, and the military of the 1870 Langford-Washburn-Doane Expedition

A growing post–Civil War interest in the national park movement and in tourism

The romantic appeal of the American West and its unexplored, "wild," natural wonders

National interest in science, scientific exploration, and landscape art

Langford's and Cooke's favorable relationships with *Scribner's Monthly* editors

The presence of two amateur painters on the expedition

Moran's recognized talent as a painter trained in the aesthetic theories of Ruskin and Turner

Moran's friendship with Gilder as well as his prior work for *Scribner's*

When these factors were in place, Moran got his first and then his second shot at glory.

(SHAFFER 2001, 326)

SPEAKER 2 *(in redface)*

Thomas Moran

The *Scribner's* commission was a once-in-a-lifetime opportunity. I need to keep my excitement to myself. Now I've got to go West and see this place for myself, they call it the New Wonderland. I'm hoping I can do with Yellowstone what Bierstadt did with Yosemite, and Church did with Niagara. But I'm flat-out broke, and we got a new baby on the way!

(HASSRICK 2002, 32)

SPEAKER 1 *(in blackface, loudly)*

Jay Cooke to Charles Scribner

Charlie, I want those Moran engravings for some Yellowstone ads for my railroad.

SPEAKER 2 *(softly)*

Charlie Scribner to Jay Cooke

Jay, we have to be careful of those engravings. They could get out and be copied! I'll have the office send them over to you, but in order to guard against unlawful copying, it would be better if you just got Tom Moran to do his work directly for you.

(KINSEY 1992, 71)

SPEAKER 1 *(in blackface)*

Cooke to Scribner

I don't care what you think. I want those Yellowstone engravings! Now!

SPEAKER 2 *(muttering to himself)*

A. B. Nettleton

It never ends. It never ends. Now Mr. Cooke wonders if I couldn't work with the Hayden Geological Survey to see if they would provide pictures and photographs of the Yellowstone region.

Scene 2: Cooke Gets Hayden, Hayden Gets Moran, Tom Gets His Second Shot at Glory

SPEAKER 1 *(in blackface)*

Jay Cooke to A. B. Nettleton

A. B., calm down! I've got support in the Congress for the Northern Pacific Railroad. Now we need them to fund Hayden's next survey. See to it that they go into the Yellowstone region. They will need a good artist, so try to get Tom Moran. Write Hayden today. Use company letterhead.

SPEAKER 2

A. B. Nettleton to Hayden, 7 June 1871

Jay Cooke & Co., Bankers, Financial Agents
Northern Pacific Railroad
Dear Dr. Hayden:
Let me introduce you to my friend, Thos. Moran, an artist of Philadelphia of rare genius, [who] has completed arrangements for spending a month or two in the Yellowstone country, taking sketches for painting.…
I have encouraged him to believe that you will be glad to have him.

(NETTLETON TO HAYDEN, IN KINSEY 1992, 69–70)

SPEAKER 1

Hayden to Nettleton on Moran

Fantastic. It will be an honor to have this wonderful painter in our expedition!

SPEAKER 2 *(in redface)*

Thomas Moran on Money and Patrons

I had to go to Mr. Cooke and ask for another $500! Mr. Cooke wanted paintings from me as payment. I promised him a group of Yellowstone watercolors. Frankly, those watercolors were little gems, some of my best work.[10]

(ANDERSON 1997, 48; ALSO HASSRICK 2002, 43)

Scene 3: The Hayden Expedition Gets Started, 15 May 1871

SPEAKER 1

(The timeline may be projected as well as spoken.)

Narrator

Let's get an overview of the events that led up to creation of Moran's *Grand Canyon of the Yellowstone*.

Timeline for Making a Painting

August 1870: Doane-Washburn Expedition.

3 March 1871: The Sundry Civil Act funds Hayden's Yellowstone survey.

May 1871: Hayden assembles people and equipment for the expedition in Utah.

May/June 1871: Langford's *Scribner's* articles with Moran's wood engravings are published; Langford prepares to join Hayden, intending to write another set of articles, which Moran will illustrate. Moran looks for funding to pay for the trip with Hayden.

7 June 1871: Cooke through Nettleton writes to Hayden about Moran joining the expedition.

11 June 1871: The Hayden expedition sets off for Virginia City, Montana, on the way to the Yellowstone wilderness.

7–11 June 1871: Moran rides the Union Pacific Railway to Green River, Wyoming, then to Ogden, Utah. He then catches a stagecoach to Virginia City to meet Hayden.

11 July 1871: The Hayden expedition arrives in the Yellowstone region for a five-week stay, stopping first at Mammoth Hot Springs.[11]

15 July–10 August 1871: Jackson and Moran travel to the Grand Canyon areas—both Upper and Lower Falls—of the Yellowstone River, photographing, painting, and sketching.

26 August 1871: The Hayden party leaves the Yellowstone region; geologists and engineers conclude their fieldwork.

30 August–1 September 1871: Hayden departs for Washington, D.C. Moran returns home to his studio in Newark, New Jersey, and begins work on his grand painting.

SPEAKER 2

Narrator

Now let's look at the members of the Hayden Expedition—or how many different ways can politics, class, status, and science be mixed together?

Imagine that they are lined up in front of one of those large nineteenth-century cameras for the official group portrait.

James Stevenson, managing director

F. V. Hayden, geologist

H. Elliott, artist

C. Thomas, statistician, entomologist

A. Schoenborn, chief topographer

A. Smith, assistant topographer

W. Jackson, photographer

G. Dixon, assistant photographer

J. Beaman, meteorologist

G. Allen, botanist

R. Adams, assistant botanist, member of Congress from 1893 to 1906

A. Peale, mineralogist, medical doctor, scion of the Peale family

C. Turnbull, physician

E. Carrington, zoologist

W. Logan, son of Representative John Logan of Illinois

F. Huse

C. Dawes, son of Representative H. Dawes of Massachusetts

T. Moran, artist

C. Negley and J. Duncan, general assistants

Twenty men as cooks, laborers, packers, hunters, guides

(HAINES 1996A, 142)

SPEAKER 1

Historian

This list of personnel was standard fare for a scientific expedition in those days. Organizers recruited friends, neighbors, relatives, patrons, politicians, and relatives and friends of politicians.

(HAINES 1996A, 141–42; SEE STEGNER 1954, 21–22)

Scene 4: Moran in the Wilderness

SPEAKER 2

Wilkins on Moran, a Pale Rider

Moran rode trains and stagecoaches to meet up with Hayden and his group. This thin, 5-foot, 9½-inch-tall eastern artist with a long, yellowish beard soon adapted to the western style of dress, incorporating red flannel shirts, rough trousers, heavy boots, and a sombrero into his regular wardrobe.... On horseback he carried his portfolio under his arm, with a rifle slung from the saddle horn.

(WILKINS 1998, 8–85)

SPEAKER 1

William Henry Jackson and Thomas Moran

When we first came to the Yellowstone we took our time, trying to make a view of the valley, to take in the landscape, the colors, the mountains, the meandering river. As we moved up the canyon, Tom fished and Will looked up viewpoints for his camera. We were both aware that this was really important work.... We were in a place that had never been painted or photographed before. The falls were spectacular, 150 and 350 feet high!

(HASSRICK 2002, 34)

SPEAKER 2 *(from memory)*

Moran

I was finally here at the Grand Canyon of the Yellowstone. I decided I needed to study the site from every possible angle. I even tied a rope around my shoulders and waist and lowered myself down over the edges of rocky cliffs.

The gorge was over a thousand feet deep and it seemed twice as wide, and the river extended for over 20 miles into the distance. The spray of the water formed a huge arch, producing a rainbow that I tried to capture with my watercolors. I was beside myself with anxiety. Those beautiful hues and tints I felt were beyond the reach of human art.

(FROM WILKINS 1998, 91–92)

SPEAKER 1

Narrator

About the time Moran was hanging from a rope sketching the Grand Canyon of the Yellowstone (15–28 July 1871), Jay Cooke experienced a great personal loss: his wife, Elizabeth, suddenly became ill and died on 21 July. One week later Moran completed the work for his painting and left Yellowstone.

(LUBETKIN 2006, 78)

ACT 3

Scene 1: Hayden and Company Leave Yellowstone and Cooke Applies Pressure to Create a Park

SPEAKER 1 *(offstage)*

Narrator

Hayden and his survey left the Yellowstone region in late August of 1871. Upon word of Hayden's return to Washington, D.C., Jay Cooke mobilized his NPR resources to put pressure on Congress to turn Yellowstone into a national park.

SPEAKER 2

A. B. Nettleton to Hayden, 27 October 1871

Dear Doctor:

Judge Kelly has made a suggestion which strikes me as being an excellent one sir. Let Congress pass a bill reserving the Great Geyser basin as a public park forever—just as it has reserved that far inferior wonder the Yosemite valley and big trees. If you approve, would such a recommendation be appropriate in your official report?

(HAINES 1996A, 155)

SPEAKER 1

Historian

Hayden included in his report to Congress a recommendation that Yellowstone be set aside as a public park.[12]

SPEAKER 2 *(muttering to self)*

Narrator

Let's get this timeline straight.
(The timeline may be projected as well as spoken.)
Timeline for Passage of the Park Bill
1871
27 October: Nettleton sends a letter to Hayden.
9 November: Langford travels to NPR headquarters in St. Paul and is pressured to put park idea forward.
Mid-November: Hayden meets with Langford, Cornelius Hedges (attorney), Samuel Hauser (civil engineer), and communicates with William A. Claggert, newly elected to the U.S. House of Representatives from Montana.

7 December: Bozeman newspaper calls for grant of Yellowstone region to the territory of Montana.

18 December: Claggert prepares a draft bill (H.R. 764), and Senator Pomeroy (Kansas) introduces an identical bill in the Senate (S. 392). Both bills call for the creation of a park in the Yellowstone region.

18 December–15 January: Hayden, Langford, Nettleton, Hedges, Hauser, Claggert, Cooke, and others lobby Congress for the creation of a park, using news stories in Montana newspapers, Langford's articles in *Scribner's Monthly*, Jackson's photographs, Moran's sketches, and Hayden's geological specimens to make their case. Copies of the article "Wonders of Yellowstone" are distributed to all senators and representatives. Hayden writes two articles endorsing the park proposal for the *American Journal of Science*. Moran's painting had not yet been executed.

1872

30 January: The Senate passes the bill.

15 February: Hayden publishes another article in *Scribner's Monthly*, "Wonders of the West II: More about the Yellowstone," which is circulated to members of Congress.

27 February: The House passes the bill and sends it to President Ulysses S. Grant.

(The timeline is interrupted twice)

SPEAKER 1 *(offstage interruption of timeline)*

Editor, *Helena Herald*

Without a doubt the Northern Pacific Railroad will soon have a branch track penetrating this plutonian region, and few seasons will pass before excursion trains will daily sweep into this great park. Jay Cooke got his park, and he got a destination playground for the tourists who will ride on his train.

SPEAKER 2 *(continues timeline)*

Narrator

1 March: President Grant signs the bill into law.

SPEAKER 1 *(offstage interruption of timeline)*

Cynic

Talk about public relations! Cooke gets his park and Moran hasn't even finished his painting! Illusion is certainly more important than reality.

Narrator

2 May: Moran unveils his masterpiece.

June: Congress buys Moran's *Grand Canyon of the Yellowstone* for $10,000.

(HAINES 1996A, 168–69; 170–71; HAYDEN 1872)

Scene 2: The Doubting Painter

SPEAKER 1 *(offstage)*

Narrator:

Hold on a minute. When and how did Tom do his painting?

SPEAKER 2

Moran: The Doubting Painter, Letter to Hayden, March 1872

The Picture is only half done. I am convinced it will have an influence in art circles. I cast all of my claims to being an Artist into this one picture of the Grand Canyon.

(KINSEY 1992, 38)

SPEAKER 1

Moran on Doctor Hayden

· I felt I had to honor Doctor Hayden and James Stevenson (Hayden's assistant) by putting them my painting. So I hired an outstanding portrait painter and he painted miniature portraits of the two men, placing them among the figures standing in the foreground of the painting.[13]

(WILKINS 1998, 101)

SPEAKER 2 *(offstage)*

Narrator

It took Tom two months to finish the picture. He adopted the large size (7 feet by 12 feet) because the art market favored enormous canvases. Post-Civil War millionaires were buying huge paintings to hang on the walls of their palaces along Fifth Avenue in New York.

(WILKINS 1998, 99)

Scene 3: Drawing Yellowstone Canyon

SPEAKER 1 *(calm, authoritative voice)*

Anne Morand on Moran and Artist's Point

He pushes the falls deeper into space. The canyon walls are smoothed out.... He enlarged the white towers on the right side of the canyon walls.

(KINSEY 1992, 56–57; MORAND 1996, 37)

SPEAKER 2 *(in redface)*

Moran on Point of View

Every form introduced into the picture is within view from a given point, but the relations of the separate parts to one another are not always preserved[.] ... The precipitous rocks on the right were really at my back when I stood at that point, yet their representation in the painting is strictly true to pictorial nature, I wanted to draw the rocks accurately so that a geologist could determine their precise nature.

(IN STEGNER 1954, 182; ALSO KINSEY 1992, 55;

SHELDON 1879, 125; WILKINS 1998)

SPEAKER 1

Narrator: Reading Moran's Grand Painting

These are the key elements in the painting:

A massive V-shaped canyon

The Yellowstone River

The Lower Falls

A cloud of spray

Cascading yellow canyon walls

Jagged rock formations and vertical basalt columns

A Roman pine

Crevices and fallen rocks

A slain deer

Three horses

Two explorers, who may be Jackson and Moran

A bear lurking in the background

Hayden and the Native American male

SPEAKER 2

Ferdinand V. Hayden on Geology and Art

Tom asked me to stand in front of his easel and inspect it for the accuracy of the geology and the treatment of geological time.

(WILKINS 1998, 91, 100–101, 337)

Narrator

A slain deer signifies death, a lurking bear, danger. The photographer and the painter (next to the three horses), intruders in nature, are representatives of science and art. They direct the viewer's gaze to Hayden, the geologist, and to the Native American, who is distanced from the artist.

(KINSEY 1992, 43–44)

Scene 4: Exhibiting and Selling a Painting

SPEAKER 1 *(in whiteface)*

Art Historian

On 2 May 1872 Moran unveiled his great canvas in New York at Leavitt's Art Rooms in Clinton Hall for a one-night showing that was funded by *Scribner's* magazine.... Immediately after the New York showing, Moran shipped his painting to Washington, D.C., where he hoped it would be seen by members of Congress, who would authorize its purchase by the government.

(KINSEY 1992, 64–65)

SPEAKER 2 *(offstage aside)*

Narrator

Moran used all his influence to get Congress to buy his painting. I don't know how the price was set, but Congress bought the painting in June of 1872 for $10,000. In 1997 dollars that would have earned Moran $174, 300; in 2008 dollars, he would have made more than $250,000!

SPEAKER 1

Historian

The Clinton Hall exhibit set off a rage to consume images of Yellowstone.... Reproductions of Moran's work soon appeared in *Scribner's* and other national magazines. Color reproductions (chromolithography)[14] of Moran's *Grand Canyon of the Yellowstone* appeared in a series commissioned by Louis Prang. In 1872 the Northern Pacific Railroad contracted with *Harper's* to produce a promotional guidebook using reproductions of Moran's Yellowstone paintings as advertisements for the rail line. Walt Whitman even included lines about the park in the 1881 edition of *Leaves of Grass*.

(BARTLETT 1985, 214, 229; KINSEY 1992, 73)

ACT 4

Scene 1: Critics Interpret the Painting

SPEAKER 1

Peter Hassrick

Moran admired Ruskin's fascination with Turner's landscapes, especially the commitment to combine the emotional sway and meaning of a scene with a literal transcription of nature. When Hayden confirmed the veracity of Moran's geological forms, the literal interpretation was preserved, while the scale and drama of the painting proved that the artist, in creating a truly noble landscape, had invested it with the full measure of his emotional reserve.

(HASSRICK 2002, 43)

SPEAKER 2

Narrator

In creating a painting that was an assemblage of perspectives, Moran produced a literary and imaginary version of the Grand Canyon of the Yellowstone. This imaginary vision corresponded to a canyon in his mind, to his conception of grandeur, geology, beauty, the "wonderful" in Nature. But he painted a scene that no one can ever see or realize, except when they stand in front of his painting.

SPEAKER 1

Wallace Stegner

The painting opened the door for the location of the American Dream in landscapes such as the Grand Canyon. In these places the romantic and democratic self found a natural home, or at least a temporary resting place where the self as tourist could be restored.

(STEGNER 1954, 179)

SPEAKER 2 *(sternly)*

Peter Hassrick on Moran's Painting as a Great Machine

Monumental paintings such as Moran's were like rolling panoramas and were called machines because they conveyed the sense that images were moving. Moran's big machine drew people to the park, leading many to ride on Jay Cooke's big machine, called the Northern Pacific Railroad.

(HASSRICK 2002, 38)

Scene 2: Representing and Selling Yellowstone
as a Natural Wonder

SPEAKER 1

Narrator as Tour Guide

In 1883 Cooke's railroad inaugurated rail service to Yellowstone and soon
opened eleven luxury hotels, in the grand European manner, in the park.
The most famous was Old Faithful Inn, built in 1904.

(RUNTE 1998, 22)

SPEAKER 2

Narrator as Travel Agent

Bowman's 1882 *Pacific Tourist* contained a chapter on Yellowstone Park
written by Hayden and illustrated by Moran. Bowman's guide also reprinted
railroad routes, hotel listings, and mileage charts for travelers planning to
visit the park.

(HASSRICK 2002, 89)

SPEAKER 1

Joni Louise Kinsey on Tourist Guidebooks

Guidebooks of the 1880s presented the canyon as an embodiment of
the spirit of the entire national park, and in describing the scene writers
invariably referred not just to the natural setting, which many of them had
never seen, but implicitly to Moran's more accessible image.
(Kinsey 1992, 66)

CODA

Between 1883 and 1915, several iterations of Cooke's financial empire,
going by various names, including Yellowstone Improvement Company
and the Yellowstone Park Association, collaborated in the construction of
tourist hotels at Mammoth Hot Springs, Yellowstone Lake, and the Grand
Canyon of the Yellowstone (Shaffer 2001, 44–46). Thus was the park sold
to the world: through a painting, water sketches, and photographs. Moran's
acclaimed painting, along with his other Yellowstone paintings, sketches,
wood engravings, chromolithographs, and watercolors, served their
intended purpose.

Tourists read travel brochures with illustrations based on Moran's
painting, rode Cooke's trains to the park, traveled to the Grand Canyon
of the Yellowstone and to Artist's Point, the imaginary site of Moran's

painting. They then stayed in Cooke's hotels (Wilkins 1998, 91; Kinsey 1992, 78). Moran's painting became the paradigmatic image of Yellowstone National Park and as well as "one of the Northern Pacific Railroad's most important visual signatures" (Kinsey 1992, 78). Art, commerce, tourism, and consumption thus merged into a single representation, a single brand image, the Grand Canyon of Yellowstone.

Creating Yellowstone Park

Like Moran's painting, it took a great deal to create Yellowstone National Park, including: a virtual who's who of post–Civil War American members of Congress, governors, judges, generals, newspaper owners, editors of national magazines, scientists, the wealth and avarice of robber barons, and a newly emerging transnational rail system. For its success, that rail system required an effective print and advertising media. The media, in turn, required a national readership—wealthy readers who wanted to be tourists in and consumers of the newly discovered West. The media needed skilled painters and photographers, practioners who could create images and representations of these western landscapes. These artists and photographers, in turn, required aesthetic theories and training in these theories, so that they could paint their versions of the American sublime (Wilton and Barringer 2002). Turned into advertisements, these representations shaped consumer desires and helped create new consumers: the middle- and upper-class tourists who would be drawn to Yellowstone. These tourists nurtured their sense of privilege while enacting a capitalist's version of the patriotic, free, natural, and romantic democratic self. This was a self lodged in a noble landscape, in a wonderland of nature, in the Grand Canyon of the Yellowstone.

Moran (and Jackson) created the visual images of that landscape. The park, like the painting and the painter, needed to be turned into a myth, a narrative structure that enveloped the cultural logics of science, adventure, religion, selfhood, and aesthetic experience.

The park, like the painting, had to contain Native Americans. By 1 March 1872 all of the territory in the Yellowstone region, except for the Crow hunting grounds, had been ceded to the United States. By 1882 the Crow hunting grounds were purchased by the government, ending the last remaining Native American title to any land in the park. Ten years after Moran exhibited his painting, Native Americans were all gone from the park.

The location of an Indian male in Moran's painting was a historical gesture. While it may have obliquely connected Moran to the tradition, stretching from Miller to Catlin, of painting Native Americans, it did not enact the realism of that tradition. Instead, Moran's Indian represents a fictional version of how the American empire imagined and wanted Indians to be—that is, silent sidekicks to scientists, artists, and photographers like Hayden, Moran, and Jackson.

Of course the expedition required the labor of two black cooks, Nute and Johnny. These black men, like the Native American male in the painting, racialize the project. They throw into relief the suppressed Civil War narrative that is part of the history of the park and the painting. Union troops left over from the war accompanied the expedition, protecting the painter and the photographer and the scientists from marauding Indians. Slaves—turned into free men but still working as laborers for capitalism and white patriarchy—packed mules and cooked the meals. The railroads, partly built by captive Indians (Ambrose 2000, 133), newly freed slaves, Chinese, Irish, and Mormon laborers, and young Civil War veterans, carried the painter and the photographer to and from this western wilderness. On the trains and in the railroad camps, Negro mammies and black porters served the food cooked by black men (Ambrose 2000, 177). It took a complex, racialized social structure to produce the park and the painting.

We must remember that at some point in his life Moran quit doing Yellowstone paintings. Fully aware of the changes in the art market, he told a Denver reporter in June 1892, "I prefer to paint western scenes, but the Eastern people don't appreciate the grand scenery of the Rockies. They are not familiar with mountain effects and it is much easier to sell a picture of a Long Island swamp than the grandest picture of Colorado" (National Gallery of Art 1997).

So it is.

Faded Pictures and Trout Fishing in Yellowstone

A copy of Moran's famous painting leans against the wall behind me. It is not an especially good copy, the colors run together. The photograph of my grandfather holding the trout he caught in the Yellowstone Lake in 1932 (Plate 20) hangs from a hook on the bookcase to my right. Grandpa is smiling. I can see reflected in my mind's eye that faded reproduction of Moran's painting that sat on Grandpa's dresser in the large white farm house eight miles south of Iowa City, Iowa. The house was shaded by a towering evergreen. Grandmother's carefully groomed rose gardens were on every side of the house. They filled the yard with vivid color and a neat orderliness, and filled the country air with perfume.

There were no trout in our Iowa rivers, and so we were drawn, Grandpa and I, to Moran's mystic river, and to that photo with Grandpa's fish. "Someday," he said, "we'll go to Yellowstone." And so in those days trout fishing in Yellowstone became our special way of being in America (Brautigan 1967).

Chapter 7

DRAWN TO YELLOWSTONE II

Crazy Mule's Map, Geysers, Coca-Cola, and Other Fragments

We scoured the available material for Indian pictures of Yellowstone National Park, but only came up with the Cheyenne Scout's (Crazy Mule) map, which I extracted for a kind of logo for the book.

(PETER NABOKOV, E-MAIL MESSAGE, 6 JULY 2005;

SEE NABOKOV AND LOENDORF 2004, XI, 221, 229;

ALSO SUNDSTROM AND FREDLAND 1999;

FREDLUND, SUNSTROM, AND ARMSTRONG 1996)

The national parks (and Yellowstone) ultimately became rich people's playgrounds, ... presented as scenic wonders and home to various wildlife but not for indigenous human inhabitants, ... who needed permits to leave their reservations in order to visit parks like Yellowstone.

(SANDERS 2000, 198; ALSO QUOTED IN NABOKOV AND LOENDORF 2004, 306)

The government ought to establish parks where the native Indian ...
[can gallop] his wild horse ... amid the fleeting herds of elk and buffaloes.
What a beautiful and thrilling specimen for Americans to preserve
and hold up for view of her refined citizens and the World ...
A nation's Park, containing man and beast.

(CATLIN 1880, 2; ALSO IN NABOKOV AND LOENDORF 2004, 306)

"I will fight no more forever."

(CHIEF JOSEPH, 1877, QUOTED IN FREDLUND, SUNDSTROM, AND ARMSTRONG 1996, 23)

"One day we will go to Yellowstone and stay in Old Faithful Inn."

(WALDO WILLIAM TOWNSLEY TO GRANDSON, SUMMER 1951)

There were no paintings by Native Americans in the 2005 *Drawn to Yellowstone* exhibit (Plate 12) in the Buffalo Bill Historical Center (BBHC) in Cody, Wyoming.[1] With one exception,[2] there are no Native American representations of Yellowstone in the 2002 park website "Windows into Wonderland: The Influence of Art on Yellowstone." In Part 2, "Artists Interpret Yellowstone National Park," there is a reproduction of Crazy Mule's map of Yellowstone (Yellowstone National Park 2002),[3] the so-called Yellowstone-Milk Map[4] (Sundstrom and Fredlund 1999; Fredlund, Sundsrom, and Armstrong 1996, 5). The text reads, "A Cheyenne Indian scout named Crazy Mule drew this map depicting the Yellowstone region in the 1880s."

The absence of Native American representations in these shows is not surprising. There are no Native American paintings of Yellowstone in Peter Hassrick's book, *Drawn to Yellowstone* (2002).[5] The Cody exhibit, as noted in Chapter 6, reproduced Hassrick's book almost work for work. Giving pride of place to Moran's *Grand Canyon of the Yellowstone*, the 2005 exhibit snuck Native Americans in through the side door, so to speak. Deep in the center of Moran's painting stands that Indian brave with his back turned to the canyon and the Yellowstone River.[6]

By using Hassrick's book as its framework,[7] the 2005 exhibit committed itself to presenting variations on John Ruskin's aesthetic theory of painting: an artist striving for authenticity should communicate the sublime features of nature's beauty while showing the emotional effects of a wondrous scene on the soul, or the psyche. The deeper truth of nature's beauty is thus recorded. The artist is God's instrument in search of the sacred, the eternal.

At least this is how the exhibit starts out, with fine-grained representations of the canyon and the park's geysers in the classical mode— sweeping pictorial landscapes that were later turned into railroad art for Jay Cooke's trains (Kinsey 1992, 73). The closer the exhibit gets to the present, however, the more contemporary and less Ruskin-like is its aesthetic. The show ends with such works as Anne Coe's famous *Breakfast at Yellowstone* (1997): three bears—momma, poppa, baby—are eating at a picnic table; steam from a geyser rises in the background against a clear blue sky.

I offer a critical reading of selected artworks in the joint Hassrick–BBHC *Drawn to Yellowstone* exhibit. I will move back and forth in time among John Crazy Mule's 1880 map of the Yellowstone region; Frank J. Haynes's 1920

promotional photograph *Old Faithful*;[8] Frederick Mizen's 1931 ad piece for Coca-Cola, *Old Faithful Inn at Old Faithful Geyser*;[9] Anne Coe's *Breakfast in the Park* (1997); and Will Caldwell's *Bear Meets Chevy at Geyser Basin* (1997).

These five works mark four distinct representational moments and distinctive formations in the iconography of Yellowstone. Crazy Mule's map is the only known Native American representation of the park. Frank J. Haynes's 1920 photograph *Old Faithful* is the most celebrated picture of the geyser. It was used on thousands of Northern Pacific Railroad brochures and appeared on every edition of the *Haynes Guide: Yellowstone National Park* from 1920 to 1967.[10] Haynes's *Old Faithful* and Moran's *Grand Canyon of the Yellowstone* spotlight the two most famous sites in the park. Mizen's advertisement for Coca-Cola situates Old Faithful geyser at Old Faithful Inn, the most famous hotel in the park (Hassrick 2002, 189). Haynes's photograph and Mizen's ad are quintessential early-twentieth-century efforts to commodify nature and Yellowstone for "popular consumption by the masses" (Hassrick 2002, 185). Thus, as with Moran, the fine lines separating art, promotion, and advertising disappear. In contrast, the Coe and Caldwell paintings playfully challenge the notion of the park as a sacred site set apart from everyday life.

In offering this reading, I fold the 2002 Yellowstone Park online exhibition "Windows into Wonderland: The Influence of Art on Yellowstone" (Yellowstone National Park 2002) into my analysis. I want to interrupt the smooth surfaces of these exhibits, much I did as with my interpretation of Thomas Moran's *Grand Canyon of the Yellowstone*. Indeed, Moran's painting, the 2005 exhibit, and the 2002 park website are part of the same orderly historical fabric. Each reproduces the imagery necessary for the continued representation of Yellowstone as white America's and the world's premier park.

CRAZY MULE'S MAP

John Crazy Mule was a Northern Cheyenne Indian scout and auxiliary soldier stationed at Fort Keogh in Montana Territory between 1877 and 1890 (Nabokov and Loendorf 2004, 229; Fredlund, Sundstrom, and

Armstrong, 1996, 9–10; Sundstrom and Fredlund 1999, 57).[11] Under the command of General Nelson A. Miles, Crazy Mule was involved in the Nez Perce War of August 1877 (Haines 1996a, 218–37).[12] An official group photograph of twenty-three Native American scouts shows Crazy Mule, fourth man from the left, to be of medium height. He is gazing forward, into the camera's eye, a dark-colored bandanna around his neck. He is wearing a military jacket. A wide-brimmed hat is on his head. His hands are clasped. He seems to be holding a stick.[13]

John Crazy Mule produced two drawings, or maps, based on his military experience.[14] The "maps are drawn on lined ledger book paper, divided into quadrants by red lines" (Fredlund, Sundstrom, and Armstrong 1996, 5). He signed each map with "a name glyph showing a dark mule, with a wavy line extending from the head of the mule to the head of a human" (Fredlund, Sundstrom, and Armstrong 1996, 8).[15] The head and torso in the glyph are red, indicating Cheyenne identity (Fredlund, Sundstrom, and Armstrong 1996, 8). The first drawing—the Yellowstone-Milk River map—is a pictorial map of the Nez Perce military campaign. The second drawing records the removal of Little Chief from Fort Keogh to Indian territory in the summer and fall of 1878 (Fredlund, Sundstrom, and Armstrong 1996, 5).

My concern is with the first map (Plate 15). This is a pictographic narrative containing biographical references, place names, and geographic and military information. According to Sundstrom and Fredlund (1999, 50), following Native American representational convention, Crazy Mule used pictographic referents to mark specific places and geographic features: an elk head designates the Yellowstone River; a tiny steamboat, the Missouri River; a tiny shell, the Musselshell River; a bear with claws, the Bears Paw range; a tiny geyser, the location of Yellowstone Park. Settlements are indicated by various pictographs: a crow among a set of three tepees refers to the Crow village (Sundstrom and Fredlund 1999, 50); small pictures of stockades indicate forts; lines of tepees indicate Indian camps, including an Indian encampment near the Yellowstone River. Near the mouth of the Yellowstone River is a trading post, probably representing Fort Union (Fredllund, Sundstrom, and Armstrong 1996, 12). Rivers, streams, and trails are marked by dark or red lines.

The Yellowstone-Milk map records military operations which took place between April 1877 and the autumn of the same year (Sundstrom and Fredlund 1999, 53). The map "tells the story of three military events: the capture of Chief Joseph's band in the Bears Paw Mountains; the attack on Lame Deer's camp in the Wolf Mountains; and the Cheyenne scout's encounters with Lakotas in the little Missouri country" (Sundstrom and

Fredlund 1999, 57; also Fredlund, Sundstrom, and Armstrong 1996, 24; see also Whittlesey 2007).

The first pictograph, depicting the first military operation, is located in the upper right section of the map, between the Missouri and Milk rivers. It shows "a white soldier and a Cheyenne scout facing an Indian, with a striped breechcloth and hair worn in a 'horn' or knot above the forehead" (Sundstrom and Fredlund 1999, 50). All three men are firing their rifles. (The style of hair for the Indian in breechcloth is consistent with Nez Perce identity (Sundstrom and Fredlund 1999, 50). Sundstrom and Fredlund argue that this pictograph refers to the 1877 capture of Chief Joseph's band at the Bears Paw Mountains. It is likely that the Cheyenne scout is Crazy Mule.

A tiny picture of a wagon "confirms that this was the route used to transport men and material to the battle area" (Sundstrom and Fredlund 1999, 50). A line running from the Yellowstone geyser field, across the Little Bighorn, along Rosebud Creek and the Missouri River, up to the west side of Little Rocky Mountains marks the trail taken by the Nez Perce on "their run to the Canadian border of September 1877" (Sundstrom and Fredlund 1999, 50). The trails and pictographs in this section of the map clearly refer to the Nez Perce battle when Chief Joseph made his famous surrender speech, quoted at the opening of the chapter: "I will fight no more forever."

The second pictograph—and second battle—is located in the lower middle section of the map. This is the Lame Deer fight, one of the most famous battles in the post–Little Bighorn campaign (Sundstrom and Fredlund 1999, 52). It shows a Lakota Indian camp, with tepees located on both sides of a narrow canyon between timbered ridges. A white soldier and an Indian (shown with breechcloth) are attacking the camp. As was the military custom, the Indian scout, Crazy Mule (?), advances ahead of the white man (Sundstrom and Fredlund 1999, 52).

A third pictograph in the lower right segment of the map shows a fight between Lakota warriors and Cheyenne scouts. In the map the scouts are leading a white soldier to the scene of a skirmish. A dead Lakota, with a protuberant stomach, lies on the ground. Nearby, a circle with twelve loops seems to represent the military camp. A trail to this camp leads back to the Yellowstone River.

Paraphrasing Sundstrom and Fredlund (1999, 57), John Crazy Mule's map provides a window into the cultural, political, and military geography of the greater Yellowstone region circa 1878. The forts, trails, and battlefields of the military are everywhere present. Intertribal conflicts are represented. The historical Nez Perce journey into and through the Yellowstone region is carefully mapped.

As a historical document, the map includes only information relevant to the events and places recorded. There is no extraneous detail (Fredlund, Sundstrom, and Armstrong 1996, 25). The topology is event-driven, recording events in terms of their conceptual and temporal relationships to one another (Fredlund, Sundstrom, and Armstrong 1996, 25). The map is autobiographical. Crazy Mule carefully records his heroic deeds on the battlefield in pictographic form. The visual narrative is driven by a logic of conquest, a logic that moves from the personal to the tribal to the nation-state. This is, after all, a military map. But what is a map but a set of representations about places, things, and events?

Reading the Yellowstone–Milk Map

Hung on a wall, John Crazy Mule's map looks like a child's drawing or a work of surrealist art—a Chagall, Miró, or Paul Klee montage. There are traces of Marc Chagall's *I and My Village* (1935), which includes floating heads, upside-down people, lamps falling from the sky, and a person sitting on a stool milking a cow that is located inside a mule's head. Joan Miró's *Dog Barking at Moon* (1926) also comes to mind: a ladder extends into the sky, and a funny-looking dog on a hill bays at a moon that is tilted on its side. In Crazy Mule's map, alongside the Yellowstone River a flock of blue birds that might be from Paul Klee's 1919 landscape of the same name fly by.

But this playful reading of the pictographs is misleading. This is a record of military violence, guns, three separate battles, dead bodies, dead Indians. White men are shooting at Native Americans. Native Americans are shooting at Native Americans. A Native American tribe, which faces destruction, is being chased by the American military. The author of the map—the cartographer, the painter—is himself part of the story. He may or may not be present in all three battles, but his presence as a narrator touches every drawing in the map. The map is a story of cultural and political genocide—a tragedy, a holocaust, a nightmare, the death of a way of life. It was authored by a painter who had gone over to the other side.

For John Crazy Mule, the greater Yellowstone region functioned as a site of military warfare. His map, with the three military pictographs, records the last traces of Native Americans in the park. Crazy Mule did not produce drawings celebrating the Grand Canyon, the geysers, or the river. The canyon and the geysers were relevant only if they marked sites of death and destruction.

His map was cultural, not geographical. As argued in Chapter 4, unlike the federal government, Native Americans tended not to create maps that marked inviolable private property. Instead, their sense of the earth and land was sacred. The earth cannot be owned, marked, contained within the boundaries of a map. There are only special places and the sacred meanings attached to them (Nabokov 2006, xiii–xv).

Unlike Moran's, Crazy Mule's aesthetic involved a military grid, tales of violence, ancient sacred rituals of manhood and conquest, men killing men. For those white Americans who followed Moran, Yellowstone would become a sacred site of nature, beauty, and the sublime. John Crazy Mule helped make this so. As an instrument of the post–Civil War American war machine, he helped drive Native Americans out of the park so that it would be safe for white America.

FRANK J. HAYNES'S 1920 PHOTOGRAPH OF OLD FAITHFUL

It is the most famous photograph taken in the park.[16] Like Moran's *Grand Canyon of the Yellowstone*, Haynes's photograph *Old Faithful* became a symbol of the park. The geyser and the amphitheater where lectures are held are near Old Faithful Inn. The geyser and the inn are two of the most famous tourist sites in the park. Old Faithful is the most photographed geyser in the world (Haynes 1953, 93). For over fifty years Haynes's photograph of Old Faithful graced the cover of the *Haynes Guide* to the park (Plate 6), and like Moran's painting, it was reproduced in Northern Pacific Railroad brochures (Hassrick 2002, 185). Like other artists, Haynes helped commodify the park for popular consumption. The *Haynes Guide* guided people to the geyser and to Old Faithful Inn.

In the photograph the geyser looks like an erupting flow of whiteness, a huge burst of steam, a plume shooting forth from a slightly elevated hill. The tree line of a forest is in the distant background. The gushing flow of energy, like a mushroom cloud, fills the darkened frame, white on black. On the cover of the *Haynes Guide*, the geyser, all in white, is in the center. The geyser explodes vertically against a blue sky. The words *Haynes Guide* in orange print are inserted into the top of the geyser, as if the geyser were a balloon holding up the words. *Yellowstone National Park*, also in orange print, is at the bottom of the cover. Inside the guide, the black and white photo of the geyser spills out all over the page. In contrast, the color version of the geyser has the appearance of an artificial object: an art deco still life, too perfect, not quite real.

Haynes elevated geyser photography to a form of fine art (Hassrick 2002, 185). He discussed how he took the picture:

> All amateurs …think they have to have the sun at their backs.
> You'll find this is wrong: if you get the sun to one side and catch
> the shadows, you get a "Rembrandt-lighted picture" with good
> contrasts. If you try to photograph a geyser in action, you get
> nothing with the sun at your back because there is no contrast
> between the steam and the background. Better squarely face the
> sun and the light shining in against the cloud of vapor will give you
> a sharp clear negative.[17]
>
> (HAYNES, QUOTED IN HASSRICK 2002, 185)

Thus does Rembrandt in the persona of Frank J. Haynes offer technical instructions to the amateur photographer. It is not enough to take a picture of the geyser. The picture must be taken in a particular way. With these tips any amateur can create an aesthetically credible image, an image that Haynes might find at least marginally acceptable. In this way the tourist turns nature into a transportable commodity fit for framing.

The Geyser and the Inn

On the Grand Loop Road, Old Faithful—geyser and inn— are midway between Madison Junction and West Thumb. Old Faithful Inn, called the world's largest log structure, was constructed in 1903–1904.[18] It was designed by Robert C. Reamer. The lobby is a "great balconied cavern, open to the roof, with all supporting beams and braces exposed to view like the skeleton of some enormous mammal from within. In one corner is a mighty eight-hearth fireplace, 15½ feet wide with its chimney exposed to the point where it passes through the ridge 85 feet above the floor" (Haines 1996b, 120).

For the interior timber supports in the lobby, Reamer instructed his workers to search for crooked limbs of lodgepole pine (Reinhart 2004, 12).

Looking up into this complex structure of crooked tree trunks and branches, now darkened with age, creates the effect of being in a forest (Reinhart 2004, 12). One looks for birds' nests. The balcony on the second floor is furnished with cushioned davenports, settees, wicker chairs, rockers, writing tables with green lampshades, and Audubon prints. The mix of Mission and Victorian styles produces the feeling of a colonial outpost situated on the edge of civilized society.

The inn is entered through huge, 6-by-7-foot, heavy plank double doors painted a bold red. A porte cochere extending over the front doors was originally the drive-through area to the inn (Reinhart 2004, 17). A breezy veranda above the porch extension, entered from the second floor (Reinhart 2004, 17), was added in 1927. This open-air balcony, with rows of engraved, long wooden benches facing east toward the geyser, is a site for geyser gazers, wildlife photographers, and Sunday morning religious worshipers.

Besides being seen and being fashionably dressed, the "principle sport of those who stayed at the hotel was 'geyser gazing'" (Haines 1996b, 121). They had help in this from a young boy, who would have been called a bellhop in that earlier time. Owen Wister (1936, 474; also quoted in Haines 1996b, 121), who was a guest there, describes the process:

> We would be sitting tilted back, reading our mail, the tourists [would] have ceased talking and be lounging drowsily, the boy would be at the door, motionless as a set steel trap. Suddenly the trap would spring, the boy would catapult into the door, and in his piping treble scream out, "Beehive's a-goin off!" at which every tourist instantly started from his chair, and a leaping crowd gushed out of the hotel and sprinted over the formation to catch the Beehive at it. Beehive finally quiescent, they returned slowly, sank into chairs in exhausted silence; you could have heard a mosquito …and again the silence was pierced: "There goes Old Faithful!" Up and out they flew once more, watched Old Faithful and came back to their chairs and silence, more exhausted.

Today the bellhop is gone, but a bell rings each time the geyser is expected to erupt, and when the bell rings, Asian, North and South American, African, and European tourists with cameras rush to the platformed bleacher and amphitheater area to take photographs. When they do this they act like characters in Frederick Mizen's 1931 painting, *Old Faithful at Old Faithful Geyser*.

FREDERICK MIZEN'S
OLD FAITHFUL AT OLD FAITHFUL GEYSER

Frederick Mizen (1888–1964) was a commercial artist noted "for his calendar images, remembered in American art for his engaging billboards for Coca-Cola …[and his] illustrations for Packard, Oldsmobile, [and] Cadillac" (Hassrick 2002, 189). His most famous work, *Old Faithful at Old Faithful Geyser*, presents the park as a site for America's economic and cultural elite. His canvas is filled with Jazz-Age couples, like characters from F. Scott Fitzgerald's *Great Gatsby* (1925)—Nick, Jay, Daisy, Tom, Jordan. The nouveau riche from East or West Egg have been transported to Yellowstone. Here, outside Old Faithful Inn, next to the most famous geyser in the park, animals and humans drink Coca-Cola and play together (Hassrick 2002, 189).

The 4-by-4-foot oil-on-canvas painting is owned by the Coca-Cola Company. In keeping with the logic of an advertisement, the canvas, as an action drama, is filled with multiple activities, many involving the drinking of Coca-Cola. Like a Philip Russell Goodwin illustration,[19] the canvas can be read as a "predicament painting." It locates persons in a situation, or predicament, which requires action. The painting combines wildlife, the great outdoors, nature, and the adventures persons have when they have left the city but are still contained within the civilizing frame of the inn, touring autos, and the fashionable dress of 1930s high society. In keeping with the Yellowstone theme, the color yellow is prominent throughout the painting—yellow limousines, hats, sweaters, and dresses. Two Yellowstone touring limousines are parked alongside the viewing balcony that extends out over the driveway. A third limousine has stopped just inside the drive-through area to the inn and is being unloaded by a uniformed inn staff member.

In the painting are more than thirty tourists in ten groupings. They are in various poses—looking, talking, drinking, gazing, walking, being looked at. Their first predicament involves being attentive tourists in a natural setting where a geyser is erupting and four bears—two adults, two cubs, one of whom is drinking from a Coke bottle—are playing with one another.

Mizen represents Old Faithful—the inn and the geyser—as a performance space in which persons—"a tony crowd of dudes and jeunesse dorée (gilded youth)" (Hassrick 2002, 189)—enact tourist identities, making "humorous connections between human thirst and nature's innocence" (Hassrick 2002, 189). This is their second predicament, or rather Mizen's second predicament: how to naturalize the drinking of Coke in this site. The painter does this by making a playful connection between human thirst, which is satisfied by Coco-Cola, and the tourist's desire to take in nature's beauty and innocence—the geyser and the bears. You can do both things at the same time—indeed, drinking Coke enhances and authorizes the nature experience.

Four forms of consumption are presented: humans and bears are drinking Coke while producing and consuming nature and culture visually. By having the bear drink Coke, Mizen says that even an animal like the bear in its innocence finds enjoyment in this bottled beverage. Coke makes bears more human, or at least more playful, less dangerous.

Two kinds of eruption are also occurring: "the tipping bottle of mellifluous fizz stands center stage to the incidental eruption of Old Faithful" (Hassrick 2002, 189). A third possible eruption—a bear attacking humans—is ruled out of the picture. These are tame bears. Here at Yellowstone nature has been tamed for human consumption.

Their third predicament involves the bears, and this is resolved through looking. In the foreground, on a grassy area next to the driveway, a formally dressed couple looks on as the bears play. Old Faithful is erupting in the background. (Three tourists, their backs turned away from the inn, are climbing the hill to get closer to the geyser.)

The structure of the inn fills the top third of the painting. Its huge, three-story, red sloping roof, with twelve jutting dormers, flows down to the viewing porch that goes out over the driveway. Three groups of tourists stand on the porch. Two groups are taking in the lively scene down below. This scene includes the four frolicking bears and a formally dressed man, with two elegantly dressed young women drinking from a bottle of Coca-Cola, who are also looking at the bears. (Another group of three persons on the porch is looking at the exploding geyser.)

At ground level, the bears occupy the attention of still another group, which includes a boyish woman in her twenties in a yellow flapper dress and yellow hat. She is standing next to a man wearing a tan fedora, a suit, a white shirt, and a red tie. He is drinking a Coke. He is standing next to a young mother in a brown Coco Chanel jacket and light brown flapper hat. A young boy wearing a yellow racing cap, a yellow sweater, and brown knickers pulls against her hand. He is leaning forward, trying to pet the small cub who is next to the adult bear holding the Coca-Cola bottle. A fourth man, in cowboy wrangler garb, is in the center of this group. A red handkerchief is around his neck. He is wearing a cowboy vest, a cowboy hat, and cowboy boots. His right arm is extended over the young boy's head. He seems to be looking over his shoulder at the bears. He is smoking a cigarette.

A threesome—two women and a man—are behind the wrangler group.

They too are looking toward the area of the bears. In the distance behind the threesome a vaguely outlined group of tourists is mingling in the shadows of the hotel veranda.

For each tourist group attention moves back and forth among fellow tourists, the geyser, the bears, and drinking Coca-Cola. The frame of the painting naturalizes the interrelationship among these four elements. Because it is an advertisement for Coca-Cola, its themes are thirst and consumption—a thirst for new experience, a thirst for nature, a thirst to be seen in nature—thirsts that can be quenched by consuming Coca-Cola.

The viewer has traveled a great distance from Moran's *Grand Canyon of the Yellowstone*. The key elements that Moran brings to his painting, including the sense of awe and the sublime, and the artist as God's instrument, are nowhere present in Mizen's canvas. Still, the artist's job has changed only slightly: both painters are in the business of representing nature in a way that can be commodified and consumed by visiting tourists. Paraphrasing Andy Warhol, is this "commerce disguised as art, or art disguised as commerce?" (Hassrick 2002, 206).

BEARS, BREAKFAST, AND CHEVYS AT GEYSER BASIN

Stealing from Hassrick (2002, 208, 218), Anne Coe's *Breakfast at Yellowstone* (1997) and Will Caldwell's *Bear Meets Chevys at Geyser Basin* (1997) can be read as playfully manipulating and extending two artistic traditions that have been time-honored in Yellowstone art. The first is the landscape tradition connected to Moran. The second tradition, after Carl Rungius,[20] is animal or wildlife painting.[21] This tradition, which often uses the predicament motif, locates wild animals in their natural habitat, sometimes with humans, showing animals moving "with an ease, a presence that suggests an innate harmony with nature, and nature's rhythms" (Hassrick 2002, 208).[22]

Coe and Caldwell, like Mizen, turn these two traditions upside down. They go beyond Mizen by focusing entirely on bears doing humanlike things.[23] Caldwell's painting inscribes the nostalgic 1950s moment when Americans took auto vacations to the park. This moment, which extends to the present day, establishes a deep connection between that unique place known as Yellowstone, "where unforgettable landscape and intimate encounters with wildlife converge with the American psyche" (Hassrick 2002, 218).

In the foreground of *Bear Meets Chevys at Geyser Basin* are two cars, a brown station wagon and a blue sedan, each with whitewalls, fins, and ornate chrome bumpers and grills. A boardwalk, accessible from the road, extends to the geyser field. In the distance, at the end of the boardwalk, near billowing clouds of white steam, stand four barely visible humans, two adults and two children. The foursome would appear to be from one of these two vehicles. The blue sedan is parked a short distance back from the station wagon, suggesting the driver has either followed the station wagon to this spot or simply parked behind the other car (Hassrick 2002, 218).

Two bears are located between the two Chevys. The adult bear is on its hind legs, resting its paws on the rear roll-down window of the station wagon. A small cub is directly behind the adult bear, patiently waiting. The bumper grill and front portion of the second auto pushes into the space. The bears seem to have no interest in the boardwalk. This is quintessential Yellowstone. Tourists drive to clearly marked tourist sites, park, get out, and walk out into nature, while animals, as tailgaters, entertain themselves with human artifacts—cars, Coca-Cola.

The colors in the painting are soft purples, beige, white, dark green—it could be early evening or early morning. The bears, cars, boardwalk, geysers, and humans are outlined against a dark green forest, which extends into a sky filled with soft beige-white-yellow clouds. The cars and the boardwalk give the humans close-up access to the park's natural beauty. The bears, as tailgaters, "scheme of ways to exploit and enjoy humans" (Hassrick 2002, 218).

This workable and amusing arrangement disguised the underlying detrimental effect of cars and tourists on the bears' ecosystem (Chase 1986, 146). The current *Guide to the Park and Its Wildlife* reads:

VIEW LARGE ANIMALS ONLY AT A DISTANCE,
FROM YOUR CAR OR FROM ROADSIDES.
Do not stop in roadways—use roadside areas for your safety.

The parked cars and humans in Caldwell's painting violate these rules. The cars are not parked in a roadside area. The humans are out of their car, near at least one large animal.

Anne Coe removes humans from the equation, turning the tables on the concept of a picnic. In her humorous painting three black bears are having breakfast at a picnic table covered with a bright yellow-orange tablecloth. Blue napkins, white dinner plates, yellow serving and soup bowls, red cups, juice, water, coffee, and syrup pitchers complete the table-setting. A fried egg and two strips of bacon rest on one of the dinner plates, and what appears to be a slice of French toast with syrup is on another plate. This is a human breakfast for bears! The bears are resting their upper bodies on the table, noses in bowls held steady by grasping paws.

Steam from a geyser drifts across the upper left-hand corner of the painting. A blue sky nestles against the top line of a dark forest. A green meadow is in the middle distance. The picnic table is situated between two purple fence posts, as if they formed the gateway to this park setting.

Hassrick reads *Breakfast at Yellowstone* as an allegory. It pokes "fun at human arrogance, …shaking faith in the supposed 'control' humans have over nature" (2002, 218). If humans are gone from the equation, so too is Yellowstone. Unlike Caldwell's painting, which is firmly anchored in Yellowstone symbols and images (the boardwalk, geyser, bears, and cars), Coe's landscape could be anywhere. Only the small geyser marks this setting as being in the park. This is Yellowstone only because she says it is. But her bears, like Caldwell's (and Mizen's), are domesticated. Her bears are comfortable in the presence of human objects, comfortable using them and doing human things with them.

Coe's bears are humans in bear-disguise. In having them do human things, she exerts her control, however humorously, over nature. Her humanlike bears are not wild or dangerous, they are cute, not quite cuddly Thus there is a reverse arrogance in her text.

CONCLUSIONS

With the Coe and Caldwell paintings, the *Drawn to Yellowstone* exhibit comes to conclusion. Their paintings, like Haynes's *Old Faithful* and Mizen's Coca-Cola advertisement, stand in a continuous line with Moran's *Grand Canyon of the Yellowstone*. Caldwell, Coe, and Mizen, like Moran and Haynes, use Yellowstone as a site for articulating a cultural logic suited to white middle-class America and its tourist experiences. In each instance, nature is turned into a commodity to be visually and materially consumed— that is, sold, collected, and taken home as a trophy.

Only Crazy Mule's map, with its depictions of violence, death, and military expeditions, stands outside this discourse. His pictographs mark Yellowstone as a site of cultural and political genocide. In the multiple spaces of Yellowstone, Native Americans were either killed or displaced. Crazy Mule's map records these acts. Moreover, the removal of Native Americans from the territories of the park did not make it a safe place for bears, elk, buffalo, or fish. On this Alston Chase is quite clear:

> By the time white men were exploring the Yellowstone plateau, grizzlies had already been chased off the plain. Settlers had … killed the buffalo on which the bears had fed, and caught the spawning trout and salmon that once had been such an important source of food.
>
> (CHASE 1986, 145)

In the Buffalo Bill Historical Center and "Windows into Wonderland" exhibits, the painterly history of the park moves through several natural (and imposed) stages. This history is presented as if it were inevitable, as if guided by divine intervention. Why not end up with paintings of playful bears having breakfast in the park or with Will Caldwell's *Bear Meets Chevys at Geyser Basin*? It is no accident that in this exhibit the park moves from a site of reverence to a place for play, for engagement, a place where animals act like humans and stand next to Chevys. The seamlessness is deliberate, pedagogical, and ideological.

The intersection of the discourses of capitalism and the national conservation movement has transformed the park into a place where industrial and cultural tourism come together. People drive here to see and to be in nature, to be in the presence of the natural wonders in this wonderland. So in the contemporary period, Moran's Indian warrior is replaced by bears that act like humans, drink Coca-Cola, breakfast on fried eggs and bacon, and are unafraid of cars. Nature, like Yellowstone itself, has been thoroughly sanitized, civilized, and commodified. Indeed, Yellowstone itself is now a stand-in for nature.

The cultural tourists who looked at the paintings and reproductions in the *Drawn to Yellowstone* exhibit were taken on a historical journey and were encouraged to marvel at the "stunning" artistic representations of this "wonderland." This journey represented only one telling of the park. In that telling it preserved the illusion that Yellowstone remains an unchanging wonderland of natural beauty. But at what price?

##

RETIRE THE CHIEF,
KEEP THE INDIANS[1]

Americans have had an awkward tendency to define themselves by who
they are not....Playing Indian as a persistent tradition in American culture
has been one way for Americans to define who they are. They are noble
patriotic white people playing Indian.

(DELORIA 1998, 3)

PROLOGUE

SPEAKER 1

Narrator

"Retire the Chief, Keep the Indians," the three-act play in this chapter,
enacts a critical cultural politics concerning the use of Native American
representations by white communities and institutions. The events in this
play take place over the period from 2000 to 2007.

ACT 1

Scene 1: Chief Illiniwek Day Hearings

SPEAKER 1: *14 April 2000, Chief Illiniwek Day Hearings, Follenger Auditorium, Urbana, Illinois*
Narrator as University Faculty Member
It took me days to put these few words—my "speech"—together. The
auditorium is packed, filled with Chief Illiniwek partisans and opponents,
Native Americans, students of color, white male and female faculty members,

alumni in blue and orange University of Illinois jerseys with the Chief's image on the front and back. The Chief looks like this (Plate 2).

(Holds up image)
A judge (in whiteface) sits on the stage taking testimony:
fifty Speakers for and fifty Speakers against. It's called a dialogue.

My name is called. I stand and walk down the aisle, approaching the stage. Speaking directly into the microphone, I look at the judge and read my prepared remarks. My hands tremble, my microphone cracks.

> I am honored to be part of these proceedings. I am honored to be a faculty member at this great university. I cringe when I see the image of Chief Illiniwek appear on the television screen, in the pages of the daily newspaper, or on a package of meat sold by Agricultural Sales. Native Americans say this image is offensive to them. The symbol arouses great conflict. Can't we find a way out of this situation? Let us follow a higher moral principle. It is no longer appropriate for one social group to use the imagery of another racial group for political, cultural, or entertainment purposes. We must select a new school mascot.

I walk back to me seat and smile at Cyd Crue, a sociology graduate student, a campus leader of the anti–Chief Illiniwek coalition.

I leave the auditorium. Outside, Native Americans have erected a huge white tepee of white river birch lodge poles. A table with brochures stands in front of the tepee. A Native American drummer drums, and Cyd's adopted son, Wayne, a Shoshone Indian, walks by and gives me a high five.

Scene 2: Red Lodge, Montana

SPEAKER 1

Narrator

My mind drifts back to Red Lodge, Montana. When you drive into Red Lodge you can't miss the Indians. As Highway 210 curves into town, you drive by two large statues. The first is a huge metal statue of Plenty Coups, chief of the Crow Indians, mounted on a life-sized horse (Plate 3). The statue sits in front of the Red Lodge Tourist Welcome Center.

First Red Lodge Resident

That statue is so crazy! Who are they trying to fool?

SPEAKER 1: *Document in the Red Lodge Tourist Center*

Chamber of Commerce Spokesperson

Plenty Coups, Chief of the Crows

Circa 1848 to 4 March 1932

The Buffalo are gone and freedom denied him, the Indian was visited by two equally hideous strangers—famine and tuberculosis. He could cope with neither. His pride broken, he felt himself an outcast, a beggar in his own country. It was now that Plenty Coups became the real leader of his people.... Red Lodge was a place of worship, food, and protection for the Crow people when it was theirs. Please respect and love it.

SPEAKER 2

Narrator

A block past the statue of Plenty Coups, just east of the Carnegie Library, there is 40-foot wooden statue of a male Indian face.

SPEAKER 1

First Red Lodge Resident

Just when you start to think this really is a town that honors its Native American heritage, you hear something like this:

SPEAKER 2

Second Red Lodge Resident

That totem pole is an insult!

SPEAKER 1 *(in redface)*

Red Lodge Historian

Maybe the Speaker is wrong. Indeed, according to one version of local history, Red Lodge takes its name from the red clay that was used to cover the tepees of the Crow Indians. And you read in the Red Lodge Magazine that the neon sign above the Red Lodge Cafe—a sign in the shape of a tepee, with Indians waving tomahawks running in a circle—won a national award in 1965. And the weekly newspaper, Carbon County News, lists the scores of the last high school basketball games: The boys' team, the Red Lodge Redskins, won, but the Lady Redskins lost.

(LAMPI 1998, 8)

SPEAKER 2

Second Red Lodge Resident

But why do they keep using the stereotyped image of a Native American? On page 10 of the 31 May 2007 *Carbon County News,* a male Indian in full headdress speaks on behalf of the Red Lodge High School Booster Club, thanking community members for their support of the school's athletic teams.

Scene 3: Memorial Stadium, University of Illinois, Champaign, Illinois

SPEAKER 1: *Halftime, Any October Saturday Afternoon*

Narrator

The Marching Illini step out onto the bright green AstroTurf. The band calls this medley the "Three-in-One." They march down the field to "The Pride of the Illini March." … Then the band changes direction and begins to play "March of the Illini," standing so their bodies spell out ILLINI. Chief Illiniwek, who has been hiding among the band members, emerges and dances down the field to what the band calls "an Indian-flavored march melody." BOOM-boom-boom-boom-BOOM-boom-boom-boom.

"Chieeeef! Chieeeef!" yell the fans.… The Chief, a university student dressed in beaded buckskin and a trailing turkey feather headdress, performs a vigorous, rhythmic dance that ends in acrobatic leaps. Legs split wide, he vaults into the air and touches his toes, fringe flying. The crowd cheers. Then he strides to the Illinois side of the field, raises his arms wide, folds them down, one over the other, lifts his chin as high as it will possibly go, and stands facing the fans.

(SPINDEL 2000, 11–12)

SPEAKER 2 *(in blackface)*

Narrator

The situation clarifies. Red Lodge residents are just like the pro–Chief Illiniwek fans in Urbana. They believe that they are honoring Native Americans. It's what King and Springwood say: "Euro-American fans crafted themselves and their teams not simply by displaying racialized bodies but by playing, enacting, or otherwise mimicking them as well."

(KING AND SPRINGWOOD 2001, 3)

SPEAKER 1

A Native American

This is not surprising. Whites don't know how to play anything other than Indian.

Scene 4: Red Lodge, Montana

SPEAKER 1

Narrator

The lights dim. The mistress of ceremonies asks the audience to "Give a Big Red Lodge welcome to Crow Indian Chief Haywood Big Day and his family, who are visitors tonight from the Crow reservation near Pryor."

(aside)

So here is the irony. It seems that wherever I go there are Indians, real and imitated, being honored by white people, and where this happens there is controversy.

SPEAKER 2

Narrator as Lyle Lovett

Like Sherman Alexie, I imagine the Lone Ranger and Tonto fighting. In Alexie's version they fight in heaven. In my version, contained in the song "If I Had a Boat," Tonto buys a boat and tells the Lone Ranger to kiss off. Our tellings challenge the "Huck Finn" myth[2] about cowboys and Indians.[3] Tonto refuses to be the white man's trusty sidekick.

(ALEXIE 1993)

SPEAKER 1

Narrator as Sherman Alexie

In one dream, disembodied, I could see everything that was happening: whites killing Indians and Indians killing whites.... Three mounted soldiers played polo with a dead Indian woman's head.

(ALEXIE 1993, 186)

SPEAKER 2
Narrator
So here's another version of this story. It is about the Crow Indians and their place in Red Lodge, Montana, history.[4] This is also a story about where I work, a story about Native Americans on the campus of the University of Illinois, a story about Chief Illiniwek, a constructed Native American who functions as the official mascot for the Fighting Illini, the university's athletic teams. This is not a story I wanted to tell, and it seems endless.[5]

ACT 2

Scene 1: Red Lodge, Montana

SPEAKER 1
Narrator
I asked one of the anti-Redskin advocates in Red Lodge about Chief Haywood and his performance at the festival.

SPEAKER 2 *(in whiteface)*
First Red Lodge Resident
This performance is hypocritical, an insult. This is a lie. The people of Red Lodge drove the Crow Indians away. They stole their land. They destroyed a culture. This is a sham! It is an embarrassment. Indians are a taboo topic in this town. Everybody knows that. Talk on this has been silenced. This is pure public relations!

SPEAKER 1
Carbon County Historical Society
"In October of 1909, the Red Lodge city fathers asked the Crow Indian Agent if some of the tribe would attend the Carbon County Fair.... The agent replied that Red Lodge could have the Indians.... It was agreed the Indians would be allowed no whiskey."

(ZUBAN AND OWEN 2000, 6)

SPEAKER 2 *(in whiteface)*
First Reporter
Chief Plenty Coups and about two hundred squaws, bucks, and papooses traveled to Red Lodge in carriages and wagons and on horseback. The trip, via Pryor and Joliet, took two days....

SPEAKER 1

Second Reporter

The Indians rode in the relay races, performed sham battles and war dances, and were pronounced "excellent" by the Red Lodge citizens.

SPEAKER 2 *(in redface)*

First Reporter

They arrived in full regalia and were quartered at the fairgrounds, just north of town.... In later years, the Crow Indians would visit the Red Lodge Rodeo in July....

SPEAKER 1

Second Reporter

They participated in Indian relay and running games, adding a great deal of color to the celebration.

SPEAKER 2

First Reporter

It was a great mistake when the rodeo committee decided not to invite the Indians anymore, as they added so much flavor to the celebration.

Scene 2: Red Lodge Cafe

SPEAKER 1 *(in blackface)*

Local Dignitary, August 2000

We stopped inviting them because they got drunk, and they'd never show up on time.

SPEAKER 2

Carbon County Historical Society

"Now the Indian is seldom seen in Red Lodge. Even when they do visit, it is hard to recognize them as Indian. Gone are the days when one could see the men in their tall black hats and braids, accompanied by their squaws wearing their colorful blankets, head scarves, and buckskin leggings."

(ZUBAN AND OWEN 2000, 6)

SPEAKER 1

Local Dignitary, August 2000

We've found a way to get them here now. We pay them to perform and they seem to want to. So we think they will be back to the festival next year. Used to be you could never count on them.

Scene 3: Red Lodge High School

SPEAKER 1

Second Red Lodge Resident

What a lie! They just want a cowboy and Indian show for the Yellowstone tourists!

Scene 4: Historical Society

SPEAKER 1 *(in whiteface)*

Carbon County Historian

"The Indian is being assimilated into the white man's society, losing much of his color identity and culture."

(ZUBAN AND OWEN 2000, 6)

SPEAKER 2 *(in whiteface)*

Second Local Dignitary

In retrospect, it is easy to develop a strong empathy with the plight of the American Indian.... Now there are rumblings to do away with the reservation and completely absorb the Indian into the white man's society. In a few decades, any semblance of an Indian culture would completely disappear, genocide at its worst!

(ZUBAN AND OWEN 2000, 6)

SPEAKER 1

Lyle Lovett (1987)

But Tonto he was smarter
And one day said Kemo sabe
Kiss my ass I bought a boat
I'm going out to sea

Scene 4: Civic Auditorium

SPEAKER 1

Chief Haywood Big Day

Now why did you stop inviting us?

Scene 5: Red Lodge High School

SPEAKER 1 *(in whiteface)*

Third Red Lodge Resident, a Mother and School Board Member

Redskins, that name, that's what started our protest.
My daughter was a cheerleader.
They traveled to the reservation schools.
She said, "Mother, I can't sing
those chants for the Redskins.
It is an embarrassment for the school, for me.
We are not going to use this term in our chants."

So three of us on the school board
called for a vote to retire the symbol.
You should have heard the uproar.
They called us racists. They said,
"How can you do this?
We are honoring the Crow Indians
with the name Redskins."

SPEAKER 2 *(in blackface)*

Carbon County News Reporter 1

"Last spring the school board agreed to let the student body make the
decision about a name change. A student poll was taken, revealing that
the majority of students wanted to keep the Redskin name. The students
did, however, express their willingness to invite Native Americans in to
address the student body about their feelings on the issue. As yet, no such
arrangements have been made."

(BEAUMONT 1997, 1A–2B).

SPEAKER 1

Narrator

I'm imagining that they did the poll again in the spring of 2007. Same results. The students said they wanted money to buy new athletic uniforms because the Redskin images were getting pretty faded.

SPEAKER 2 *(in whiteface)*

First Parent

Asking the students to vote
is like asking your child
to make the major decisions
in your family.
What do they know?
Children cannot make this decision.
It needs to be made by the adults.

SPEAKER 1

Second School Board Member

Redskins! It's the same
as using any ethnic slur.

SPEAKER 2 *(in whiteface)*

Fourth Red Lodge Resident, a Mother and School Board Member

The Booster Club this year
is making a special effort
to not include the word
Redskin
on any of its promotional material,
including buttons and pins.
We're trying to teach
tolerance and respect.
We need to take a leadership role in this.
I'm calling for a vote by the board.

SPEAKER 1 *(in redface)*

Third School Board Member

I'm against the name change.
We've got a lot more important things
to worry about.

Scene 6: Crow Reservation

SPEAKER 1 *(in whiteface)*

Crow Indian Mother

How would you like it
if we called you Krauts?
You call us Redskins,
squaws, whores.
The reservation
is not our nation.

Scene 6: Champaign, Illinois/Red Lodge, Montana

SPEAKER 1 *(in blackface)*

University of Illinois Board of Trustee Member, 8 March 2001

"I believe it is not only appropriate but it is expected that we show respect
and honor to those who came before us.... The vast majority of the people of
Illinois think that Chief Illiniwek is that respectful honor."

SPEAKER 2

University of Illinois Board of Trustee Member Francis Carroll, June 2004

But the Chief is a racist symbol; his time has come to an end.

SPEAKER 1 *(in whiteface)*

News-Gazette Editor John Foreman, 16 November 2003

Recent ill-advised statements on social inclusiveness have diminished UI
Chancellor Cantor. She and Trustee Carroll are bringing backroom politics
into this long and complicated situation. Indeed, Carroll tried to sneak
through a resolution ousting the Chief. Chancellor Cantor's outspoken
distain of the Chief has been a source of controversy since the day she
unpacked her bags here.

SPEAKER 2

Philip Deloria

On the silver screen and musical stage... in football stadiums... Indians
evoked a nostalgic past more authentic and often more desirable than the
anxious present. By imagining such a past, projecting it onto the bodies of
Indian people, and then devising means to appropriate that (now-Indian)
past for themselves, white Americans sought reassurance that they might
enjoy modernity while somehow escaping its destructive consequences.

(DELORIA 2004, 167; SEE ALSO HUHNDORF 2001, 75;

TRACHTENBERG 2004, XXIII)

SPEAKER 1 *(in whiteface)*

Another Red Lodge Community Member

Historically, the name Red Lodge Redskins
was selected to honor the Crow Indians.
It was never intended
to be a racial slur.
The students of Red Lodge
have treated their mascot
with dignity.

According to the Indian Treaty of 1868,
Carbon County territory
was included within the Crow reservation.
It was not until 1882
that the Crow reservation
was thrown open to mining and settlement.

SPEAKER 2

Leslie Fiedler

Montana
as a white territory
became psychologically possible
only after the Native Americans—
the Nez Perce, Blackfoot, Sioux,
Assinboine, Gros Ventre, Cheyenne,
Chipewayan, Cree, and Crow—
were either killed, driven away,
or placed on reservations.
The struggle to rid the West
of the "noble savage" and the "redskin"
is integral to the myth
of the Montana frontier
as a wild wilderness.
The Indian
was Montana's Negro,
an outcast
living in an open-air ghetto.

(FIEDLER 1988, 745, 752; SEE ALSO FIEDLER 1971, A, B, C)

SPEAKER 1: *A Lesson in History*

(The timeline may be projected as well as spoken.)

Narrator

Chief Illiniwek Timeline

30 October 1926:   Chief Illiniwek is created by Ray Dvorak, assistant direc-
     tor of bands, and is performed by university student Lester Leutwiler.

1975:   First sign of protest, "A Challenge to the Chief" excerpt in *Illio* year-
     book.

1985:   Round Chief logo is licensed as a symbol of the sports teams. UI
     retires other Indian imagery for official use and licenses Chief logo
     on everything from notebooks to toilet paper.

1989:   U.S. Senator Paul Simon signs the petition to retire the Chief.

1990:   Charlene Teters protests the Chief to the board of trustees.

1990.   Board of trustees members vote 7-1-1 to make the Chief the official
     university symbol. Chancellor Weir declares the Chief is "authentic."

1997:   Jay Rosenstein's film *In Whose Honor*, a documentary on the Chief's
     history, is released.

9 March 1998:   The University of Illinois Faculty Senate passes a resolution
     calling for the board to retire the Chief immediately.

2000:   The North Central Association ten-year accreditation report states:
     "There are inconsistencies between "exemplary diversity policies and
     practices, and [the university's] policies regarding the Chief."

15 February 2000:   The board of trustees announces the reopening of the
     Chief dialogue.

30 March 2000:   The board of trustees appoints Judge Garippo to preside
     over a special intake session.

14 April 2000:   Speakers from both sides share views at the special intake
     session.

16 March 2001:   The board votes 8-1 against removal of the Chief.

13 March 2002:   Trustee Plummer presents a report on the Chief to the
     board, suggesting he be honored but retired.

(*DAILY ILLINI*)

SPEAKER 2 *(in redface)*

Student Journalist

In Earlier Days:

The Chief represented the university at a variety of educational
and humanitarian functions. After protesters objected to the Chief
representation, the university chose to limit public appearances.

The Dance:

The Chief's dance, like his authentic Plains Indian costume, is carefully passed down to each successive performer: The first students to depict the Chief were trained in traditional dance steps by Native Americans.

(CHIEF ILLINIWEK: SEVENTY-FIFTH PICTORIAL HISTORY)

SPEAKER 1

Red Lodge Community Member

"I noticed in a recent issue of your paper
that the political correctnoids
have found our town
and are attacking
the high school's Redskin mascot.
The people who are pushing
this little guilt agenda
are likely a handful of people
with no life of their own.
I have immense respect
for Native Americans....
My guess is
that a true Crow warrior
would not spend time agonizing
over a white man
who called his tribe
the Redskins.
He'd most likely laugh and think,
"How could they possibly live up to the name?"

SPEAKER 2

Graduate Proud of the Redskin Name

Well, its time to get my two-bits worth in.
Forty-six or so years ago,
I had the privilege of being
on the first Redskins football team.
The school had to come up with a new name
after the school went from Carbon County High School
to Red Lodge High School.
The change from Carbon County Coyotes
to Red Lodge Redskins
was definitely done
without ethnic slurs in mind.
Think of where Red Lodge got its name:
the color of Crow lodges.

Think of where Red Lodge is located:
on the former Crow reservation.
What could be more fitting than Redskins?

SPEAKER 1

Red Lodge Parent: Rethinking Our Mascot

Thank you for calling our attention to the swastika graffiti at Red Lodge High School.... It was probably not a "real hate crime" but perhaps just a misguided joke. Which is worse? How can we raise children who can really think such a prank is innocent, misguided humor? It did not take much to think of a reason why.

From the time our children are five years old and enrolled in our public schools, they are taught to embrace a double standard on racial slurs and culturally offensive images. Yup. Chalk it up, at least in part, to the Mighty Redskins. Now is the time for the school to move forward to a new home with a new image.

(*CARBON COUNTY NEWS*, 4 OCTOBER 2007, 4)

SPEAKER 2 *(in whiteface)*

University of Illinois Board of Trustees Member

The Chief is an important symbol of the Urbana campus, for which I have great pride.... The Chief is a tangible and dignified tradition.... I believe the value of this tradition far outweighs any objections that have been raised....

SPEAKER 1 *(in blackface)*

University of Illinois Alumnus

We live in the state of Illinois, named for the Illini tribe.... It was inescapable that the state would celebrate an Illini chief.... He is the single most positive public image of Indians in Illinois....

SPEAKER 2

University of Illinois Anthropology Department

"The Illini were primarily farmers.... The men did not wear war bonnets. It is inaccurate to dress the university's mascot in the military regalia of a Sioux warrior.... The young man portraying the Chief has not earned the right to wear Lakota Sioux military regalia."

(FARNELL 1998, 1–4)

SPEAKER 1

Native American Woman

How would you like it
if we called you Krauts?

University of Illinois Alumnus (*in whiteface*)

"In recent years Illiniwek has been under attack from a small, self-righteous coalition that wants to wipe him from the university's history."

SPEAKER 1

Paul Wood

"Nine hundred miles from here, a 13-year-old American Indian boy follows the Chief Illiniwek debate with great interest.... Wayne Crue was born on a Shoshone-Bannock reservation and spent several years in the Champaign school system before deciding that pro-Chief rhetoric was contributing to an intolerable environment—including pupils calling him a 'savage.'"

(WOOD 2001, A1)

SPEAKER 2

Michel Foucault

"The problem is not changing people's consciousness—or what's in their heads—but the political, economic, institutional regime of the production of truth."

(FOUCAULT 1980, 133)

ACT 3

Scene 1: Champaign, Illinois

SPEAKER 1

Narrator

The Chief's story did not end with the Plummer Report, although it could have. Several other events had to occur before this happened. Indeed, the Plummer Report seemed to solidify the pro-Chief and anti-Chief camps. It took until 2007, six more years of conflict, before a new ending for the Chief story could be written. It occurred as result of an NCAA policy, announced in August 2005, prohibiting the University of Illinois from hosting postseason competitions because of the Chief. A news release of 16 February 2007 announced the university's new policy.

SPEAKER 2

University Official

FOR IMMEDIATE RELEASE

Chief Illiniwek will no longer perform
—NCAA to lift sanctions on Illini athletics

Urbana—The University of Illinois today announced that Chief
Illiniwek will no longer perform at athletic events on the Urbana-
Champaign campus after this season's last men's home basketball
game in Assembly Hall on 21 February.

As a consequence, the University will immediately become eligible
to host postseason National Collegiate Athletic Association
(NCAA) championship events.

SPEAKER 1

Narrator

Random Headlines from Local Newspapers, February and March 2007:

Board Retires Chief Name, Logo (13 March)

Vandal Links Local KKK with Origin of Chief (25 March)

Board's Actions Regarding Chief Cowardly (15 March)

Leftover Chief Issues on Chancellor Herman's Hands (14 March)

Senator Calls for Probe of Chief Decision (3 March)

Thought Police Not Off Duty Yet (28 February)

Students Hold Vigil for Illiniwek (27 February)

Amid Threats, 18-Year Battle to Retire Chief Ends—For Now

(24 FEBRUARY)

SPEAKER 2

**Professor Joseph Gone, Member of the Gros Ventre Tribe
of Montana, 24 February 2007**

It's about time....
It's a relief to learn
that at the dawn of the twenty-first century

damaging racial stereotypes
of the sort Chief Illiniwek embodied
no longer have a place
in public university sporting events.

SPEAKER 1

Charlene Teters, 27 February 2007

The effort to remove the Chief
was never about the mascot.
It was and remains about racism.

SPEAKER 1

Cyd Crue: White Racism/Redface Minstrels

What's at stake in the Chief debate?

The American Indian of the past is more real than the Indian of the
present.

The Euro-American perspective determines who and what is an authentic Native American representation.

This perspective is neocolonial, masked behind a cultural altruism that
treats all criticism as an instance of political correctness.

The neocolonial perspective speaks for the greater good, the majority,
what is true and correct.

The Native American has become more symbolic than real, symbolic of
whiteness in relation to the redskin, the noble savage.

The practice of redface that structures the Chief's performances perpetuates nineteenth-century racist ideologies.

SPEAKER 2

Narrator to Self

Here at the end
I seek a way out of this story,
which seems to have no exit.
Everywhere I turn, from Champaign, to Urbana,
to Red Lodge, to Yellowstone National Park,
it seems there are representations
of Native Americans constructed by whites.
They all lead back to the same place.

Narrator as Philip Deloria

But this is not surprising.
In the late 1910s, tourism boosters
explicitly linked Indians, frontier, and automobility
in their hype for the "Black-Hills-Sioux Trail,"
a route that midwesterners took through Chicago
and across the Rosebud and Pine Ridge reservations
on their way to Yellowstone National Park.

(DELORIA 2004, 166)

CODA

SPEAKER 1

Narrator

These representations of Native Americans—of whites playing Indians—
replay two versions of white male patriarchal history. The Chief is
represented by young white men in redface entertaining other whites on
the football field or basketball court. In contrast, mountain men—that is,
nearly naked white males in Native American costume—act out wilderness,
manifest-destiny fantasies about masculinity, nature, and God.
Elizabeth Cook-Lynn says she can't read Wallace Stegner because of his
misunderstanding and dismissal of Native American indigenousness, "and
his belief in the theory that American Indians are 'vanishing.'"[6] Indeed,
Stegner's history of the West, like Red Lodge's history of the Crow Indians,
is a history written through the experiences of white Americans—first-,
second-, third-, and fourth-generation European immigrants—a history that
begins with the movement that located Native Americans on reservations,
out of sight, out of mind. Thus Stegner creates a literature and a history of
the West that has no place for nor needs Native Americans. And Stegner's
experiences "are those of a vast portion of the American public." Stegner's
West and his stories have become part of our collective unconscious. In our
unconscious fantasies, isolated from their own past and their own history,
Native Americans live as mascots, symbols from a symbolic past that never
existed.

(CALLOWAY 2003; COOK-LYNN 1996, 29, 32;

RICHARDSON 2007, 146)

The hearings and protests surrounding redskins and chiefs, in Red Lodge
and Champaign-Urbana, forcefully remind white Americans that...

SPEAKER 2

Elizabeth Cook-Lynn

... "they have to come face to face
with the loathsome idea
that their invasion of the New World
was never a movement of moral courage at all;
rather it was a pseudoreligious
and corrupt socioeconomic movement
for the possession of resources.
It may be that the Plains Indians
are not "done," as assumed by Stegner's fiction;
rather, they continue to multiply and prosper."

(COOK-LYNN, 1996, 33)

SPEAKER 1

Narrator

Cook-Lynn asks that these historical narratives and performances be
contested. These stories support a cultural nationalism and a view of nation
building that is racist and self-serving. There are several problems with these
narratives.

SPEAKER 2

Native American Chorus

These narratives allow whites to interpret day-to-day Indian/white
relationships through an imagined native response to history and historical
events.

(COOK-LYNN 1996, 36)

SPEAKER 1

Narrator as Critic

This supportive mythology writes the end of Plains Indians and their history
and excludes them from a place in this history.

SPEAKER 2

Native American Chorus

This fiction deprives Plains Indians of a valid claim to tribal lands.

SPEAKER 1

Narrator

This mythology makes the claim of nativeness of all European immigrants to this land more valid because...indigenous populations [did] not last long, and if they somehow survive their own ridiculousness, they will do so as degenerates of history, defeated and outrageous.

(COOK-LYNN 1996, 34–35)

SPEAKER 2

Narrator as Critic

The immigrant/colonist grandchild who remains tied historically and culturally to the purist's notion of the making of America as a morality play may, unfortunately, continue to exert the greatest influence on the taking of action in this country's political, social, and academic life that is inappropriate for the twenty-first century.... The results of such colonialistic imaginations are disastrous not only to Indians but, perhaps, to all the world.... I weep for Stegner.

(COOK-LYNN 1996, 34, 38, 39)

SPEAKER 1

Narrator

As do I.

SPEAKER 2 *(offstage, softly)*

Narrator

Recent items in the *News-Gazette*:

Creator Demands Chief Logo Back from Trustees (6 April 2007)

Retailers Plan to Stock Up on Chief Supplies (31 March 2007)

Chancellor Herman will be responsible for the final disposition of the Chief, a process that may take six months to a year as trademark and licensing issues are decided.

(*INSIDE ILLINOIS*, 15 MARCH 2007)

Retire the Chief but keep the Indians.

THE NEW WEST, MEMORY, AND THE AUTHOR'S FAMILY

The new, or postmodern, West reconfigures nineteenth- and twentieth-century images of Native Americans, cowboys, and the natural world. Thus, signifiers of the past ride alongside images from the present. In Plate 17 a Nez Perce mother and her son are on horseback. The mother is in native dress, and her son wears everyday clothing. The old and the new comingle, reinforcing one another. This is the postmodern West, a site of nostalgia, a yearning for the past.

Plate 17. Nez Perce woman and her son on horseback, Yellowstone. Note their clothing.

Plate 18. Gallery ad, *Midday at the Oasis*, by Dennis Ziemienski. Mark Sublette Medicine Man Gallery, Inc., Tucson and Santa Fe, medicinemangallery. com.

The ad for Dennis Ziemienski's painting *Midday at the Oasis* (Plate 18) illustrates this point: horse, man, nature, water, sun, rolling hills, trees. A pastoral setting, the world is good, no conflict here. The 2004 painting could have been taken from a nineteenth-century photograph, and maybe it was! The cover of Owen Wister's book *The Virginian* (Plate 19) is another example of an image of a romanticized western past used to sell a product.

Plate 19. Cover of *The Virginian* with illustration by Thom Ross, Buffalo Bill Historical Center, Cody, Wyoming.

The remaining images are photographs from four generations of my family, which includes the Bradley family (Johanna, Richard, and their two sons, Max and Owen); the Maehr family (Rachel, Mike, and their two daughters, Sylvia and Naomi); and the Summers family (Nate, Heidi, and their daughter, Katie). Also included are the 1932 photo of Waldo W. Townsley, my grandfather, in Yellowstone National Park, and a photo of myself looking down on the Yellowstone River.

Plate 20. Waldo William Townsley with trout, in front of Wiley tent, Yellowstone National Park, 1932.

Plate 21. Author looking at Yellowstone River, 2005.

Plate 22. Author and wife behind Old Faithful Geyser sign.

Plate 23. Max and Richard Bradley in front of Roosevelt Arch.

Plate 24. Maehr family in front of Harry Jackson's statue of Sacagawea, Buffalo Bill Historical Center.

Plate 25. Bradley family with author and wife in front of sign for trailhead to Greenough Lake, Custer National Park.

Plate 26. Summers family and
Katherine Ryan in cabin driveway.

Plate 27. Nate Summers (leaning
against tree), Heidi and Katie
Summers on Rock Creek bank,
Naomi Maehr next to water, Mike
Maehr on boulder.

Plate 28. Bradley family in front of Roosevelt Lodge,
Yellowstone National Park, summer 2006.

SEARCHING FOR YELLOWSTONE II[1]
AND ALICIA'S HORSES

"I am now ready for the Yellowstone Park, and look forward
to the trip with intense pleasure."
(GENERAL WILLIAM STRONG, *A TRIP TO THE YELLOWSTONE NATIONAL PARK*, 1876,
IN SCHULLERY 1997, III)

Indian youth and elders have articulated...the significant role their
people's Yellowstone history plays in their lives and culture. They've
described the sense of well-being that reconnecting to Yellowstone
brings.... Their ancestors found Yellowstone a sacred place, a magical
land;...[there is] a richness bestowed upon Yellowstone...by the historical
presence of the American Indian.
(CHRISTOFFERSON 2007, 6)

With mixed feelings, I ignored Elizabeth Cook-Lynn's arguments about not
reading Wallace Stegner. When I started my search for Yellowstone,[2] I was
drawn to Stegner because his autobiography and his family history helped
me find my way back to my father, my grandfather, and my mother (see
Stegner 1943, 1962, 1979, 1992).[3] Dreaming my way into a midcentury, Cold
War American landscape, I sought to understand my family's white middle-
class version of the American dream. Stegner (1954, 177) and Yellowstone
Park seemed is as good a place as any to start.

In 1932, about the same time Stegner's father (1943, 356) was taking
a shortcut through Yellowstone Park on a bootleg whiskey run to Cody,
Wyoming, my grandfather was fishing for browns and rainbow trout in the
Firehole River near Old Faithful Inn. I have a picture of Grandpa smiling,
standing in front of a Wiley tent, beside a Lincoln roadster, proudly holding
a 3-foot brown trout in one hand and two large rainbows in the other hand

(Plate 20). Today I search for that spot in Yellowstone where Grandpa caught those trout, wondering if he and Stegner's father might have been in the same place at the same time.[4]

Stegner's father was a salesman, as was Grandpa, and my father. Grandpa made his money in the depression. He invented a mechanical device somewhat like a slide rule or today's hand calculator. Used properly, it allowed persons to instantly compute sums, fractions, decibels, or ratios. The slender bronze-colored metal device was in the shape of a monkey suspended in midair. Trapped in a metal cage, the monkey is wearing a red hat. The monkey's arms and legs could be moved back and forth and up and down, across a sliding metric. If you divided 30 by 2, the monkey's hands pointed to the number 15. Grandpa talked small-town store owners into buying the franchise rights to his calculating monkey. For $10,000 a store owner could have the sales rights to an entire county. Grandpa then showed owners how they could use trading stamps, which would give customers discounts on purchases at their store, if they bought a monkey. Grandpa printed and sold these stamps. In his Lincoln roadster, Grandpa toured the Midwest, the West, and the South selling this system. He got rich and retired to the farm at the age of forty, taking hundreds of boxes of monkeys with him. One version of the family legend holds that he was chased out of Kansas City by the mob, the same mob that helped Truman gain the White House in 1945.

My father's side of the family was poor. Grandpa Denzin was a German immigrant who worked as a day laborer for the city of Milwaukee. Grandma Denzin mopped floors in hospitals. Dad sold hardware, John Deere tractors and plows, Farm Bureau life and car insurance, Ramblers, Dodges, Pontiacs, used cars, sunken treasure from pirate ships, antiques and collectibles, fake brass doorknobs. He could sell anything. Bad knees kept him out of World War II. My junior year in high school we read Arthur Miller's (1949) *Death of a Salesman*. I saw too many parallels between Dad and Willy Loman. Like one of Willy's sons, I was ashamed to have a father who was a salesman. My girlfriend at the time, whose father was a physician, said I had nothing to be ashamed of. I cried anyway, reading Willy Loman's disgrace and death as if they were my father's. My father never got rich. When I was sixteen he sold me a $5,000 life insurance policy: policy #40-98047. The premium stayed the same for fifty years, $44.80 payable 1 June and 1 November. It matured on 21 May 2006 at $13,153.50, for a net gain of $3,879.55. Every time I wrote out the check I thought of that night when he sold me the policy, telling me that this sale helped him make his quota for that month, maybe even qualify him for a ten-day company fishing trip to Canada and a Hudson's Bay wool blanket.

My father was a devout conservative, a Reagan-Bush Republican. Over his desk hung a photo of him and George H. W. Bush shaking hands. Across the top, Bush wrote, "Thanks to my good friend Ken Denzin." My father believed in the American dream, the Horatio Alger myth, a welfare-free nation, capitalism, hard work, handcrafted bookcases, dark blue serge suits, gray sweaters, home-cooked meals, community theater, and—with sobriety—kindness, generosity, and fierce loyalty to family.

When he died he left
a few clothes,
three broken Timex watches,
two oil paintings of river scenes on the Mississippi,
two pocket knives,
a woodworking shop full of hand-oiled tools—awls, files, screwdrivers,
little planes, saws, drills, bits, levels, hammers, pliers.
I gathered them up and took them home,
bought a sheet of pegboard and some hooks,
hung the pegboard on the wall in my basement shop,
and neatly arranged the awls, hammers, and screwdrivers.
It looks like a display in a museum.
My father's legacy: three wood boxes and a handful of tools.

On a Sunny Saturday morning in late October
we spread his ashes
from the upper deck of the Delta Queen
on the Mississippi River.
Bright sun shone and glinted off the water.
Seagulls squawked and soared overhead,
the day we spread his ashes
over the river that he loved.
The wind came up off the water
and blew his ashes back all over me.

He painted in his spare time,
took it up at the urging of Thelma, his third wife.

His river scenes, dated 1974,
have a quiet, calming presence.
In the first painting, a shrimp boat
is tied to a dock, and seagulls float
through a soft blue sky dotted with white clouds.
The cabin on the boat is reflected
in the slightly darker blue water of the river.
Dark green vegetation grows on the shoreline.
In the second painting a long, open-air wooden shed
nestles against the shore,
its brown colors reflected in the river.
Trees hover in the background.

In both paintings, the painter
must have been on the opposite shoreline,
looking back across the river he loved,
on these peaceful water scenes.

In the summer of 1953 I was twelve and my brother, Mark, was eight. This
was the summer my parents divorced for the first time. This was also
the summer my father joined Alcoholics Anonymous. Mark and I were
spending the summer on the farm with Grandpa and Grandma.

This was the summer
of the Joseph McCarthy hearings
on television, black and white screens.
Eisenhower was president,
Nixon was his vice president.
This was the summer
Grandpa bought the first family TV.
In the afternoons
we watched the McCarthy hearings,
and each evening
we had a special show to watch:
Ed Sullivan on Sundays,

Milton Berle and Archbishop Fulton Sheen on Mondays,
Norman Vincent Peale and Pat Boone on Tuesday.
This was the summer
my parents divorced for the first time.
This was the summer
my father's life started to fall apart.
I look today at the face of Joseph McCarthy
in George Clooney's movie *Good Night and Good Luck*—
a scared, lonely man.
Clooney's movie tells me he died from alcoholism.

I thought of that summer and Clooney's movie as I was going through Dad's
scrapbook. The pictures are all from the late 1940s and early 50s; Mark and
I were little and living with Grandpa and Grandma. Mother and Dad lived
in Coralville, just outside Iowa City. Dad was a county agent for the Farm
Bureau Insurance Company, and Mother kept house and was ill a lot.

I think this is when Dad's drinking
started to get out of hand.
He'd work late, come home drunk.
Some nights friends from work drove him home.
Mother and Dad had put knotty pine paneling
on the walls of the family rec room,
which was in the basement of our new house.
Dad built a bar,
and Mother got cocktail glasses, a blender,
    shot glasses, glass coasters—
really fancy stuff.
Dad got some bar stools
and installed indirect lighting in the ceiling.
Pretty soon the rec room looked like a bar,
even had a mirror on the wall behind the bar.
On the weekends men from the insurance agency
brought their wives over,
and the house was filled with smoke, laughter,
and Bennie Goodman and Harry James
on a little Philco phonograph.

Fats Domino was on the jukeboxes
singing "Ain't That a Shame" and "Blueberry Hill."
Mother was drinking pretty heavily.
She liked Manhattans and those maraschino cherries.
Dad drank Pabst Blue Ribbon (a "Blue")
and straight shots of Jim Beam whiskey.

Around this time the Communist scare had gotten all the way to Iowa City. World War III was on the horizon. The John Birch Society was gaining strength. *This Is Your FBI, The Lone Ranger, The Shadow,* and *Inner Sanctum* were popular radio and TV shows. We were all learning how to be imaginary consumers in this new culture: Gillettte Blue Blades, Bulova watches, Lava soap. Life Savers (Dylan 2004, 50–51).

Citizen Civil Defense groups were forming.
People were worried about Communists,
air attacks at night,
atomic bombs going off in big cities.
People started building bomb shelters.
Dad built a shelter in the backyard.
Every town had a Civil Defense team.
Dad was a team leader,
gone from midnight
to six in the morning twice a week.
He stood guard with a three other men,
scanning the skies with binoculars and telescopes,
looking for low-flying Russian planes.
He would come home drunk.

Bob Dylan wrote a song about this post–World War II paranoia: He called it "Talkin' John Birch Paranoid Blues":

The communists were coming around
They were all over
The Reds were all over,

Under my bed, in my car,
Them Reds were everywhere,
They were in my TV
Red strips in the American Flag
Betsy Ross
Eisenhower is a Russian Spy.
George Lincoln Rockwell is the only True American
Now I'm at home investigatin' myself

We became an A.A. Family in 1953. The drinking had gone too far. Every Sunday we'd drive to Iowa City for the 9:30 A.A. meeting over the Strand Theatre on Iowa Avenue. It was a big suite of rooms. Dad and the other men went into one room and closed the door. In a side room wives met for Al-Anon, and in the front room, overlooking the street, Mark and I and Billy O'Reilly sat around a table and played games and read comic books. After an hour or so passed, all of the adults came into the big center room, and Lola and Leo Smith would cook up a huge pancake breakfast. The room would fill with laughter and grow blue with smoke. After a while we would go home.

About a year later, Mom and Dad had some A.A. friends out for a cookout on the farm. There was a new couple, Shirley and George. Shirley was petite and had black hair like Mom's. She was wearing an orange dress that flowed all around her knees. Dad set up the archery set behind the lilacs in the side yard. The men gathered with the bows, and you could hear the twang of the arrows all the way back in the house. But nobody was very good.

Mom had Pete Fountain and his clarinet playing on the portable record player. Everybody came back into the house, and before you knew it, the dining room was filled with dancing couples. Men and women in 1950s dress-up clothes: men in wide-collar shirts and pleated slacks, with greased-back hair; women with Mamie Eisenhower bangs, sheer stockings, and high heels.

All of a sudden Dad was dancing with Shirley, and Mom was in the kitchen fixing snacks. I thought Dad and Shirley were dancing a little too close to just be friends.

About a month later our little world changed forever. I came home from high school and found a note from Dad that read:

> I have to leave
> you are on your own now
> you don't need me anymore.
> Tell Mark I've done all I can for him.

I was eighteen and Mark was fourteen.

> Civil Defense teams, bomb shelters,
> talking John Birch Society paranoia,
> the CIA, the Cold War,
> Communists, the axis of evil,
> another war, global terror,
> an out-of-control right-wing government.

My father's life segues into this question, "What went wrong with our generation's and our parents' generation's version of the American dream?" And as in George Clooney's movie, good luck was no longer enough.

By 1968 it had all gone sour. A dirty little war in Vietnam would doom the flickering dreams of the Civil Rights movement. Richard Nixon, Ronald Reagan, and the Bush family were waiting in the wings. By the time my father was shaking hands with George H. W. Bush, #41, it was all over. The dream was dead.

> And it is hard to see through
> our own family stories,
> into the deeper, darker histories
> of U.S. culture—
> tawdry stories of organized deception

and barefaced liars.
And we see too,
that our government is not something
removed from the stuff of our lives.[P]

That picture of George Bush shaking hands with my father is in my house!

How can we reclaim
the very soul of what it means
to be free persons in a free democratic society
when we have pictures like this
which us remind just how far we have not come?

(GOODALL 2006, 363)

Stegner says his father "was born with the itch in his bones.... He was always telling stories of men who had gone over the hill to some new place,... made their pile, got to be big men" (1943, 83). By the time I was eight we had moved ten times. The next sales job was always going to be the best, somewhere, 'if you knew where to find it,' someplace where money could be made like drawing money from a well, some Big Rock Candy Mountain where life was effortless and rich,... but not in Chicago, or Milwaukee, or Terre Haute, or the Wisconsin woods, or Dakota.... Twelve houses at least in the first four years" (Stegner 1943, 83, 374).

On the Big Rock Candy Mountain
Where the cops have wooden legs,
And the handouts grow on bushes,
And the hens lay soft-boiled eggs,
Where the bulldogs all have rubber teeth
And the cinder dicks are blind—
I'm a-gonna go
Where there ain't any snow,
Where the rain don't fall
And the wind don't blow
On the Big Rock Candy Mountain.
And the bluebird sings to the lemonade springs.

(STEGNER, 1943, P. 461; 1992A)

When Stegner's father died, the final sum totaled, "One dented silver mug,...one pair of worn shoes, one worn suit, a dozen spotted neckties, a third interest in a worthless mine" (Stegner 1943, 556).

The Big Rock Candy Mountain was always just around the corner, and my father, like Stegner's, never seemed to have the nerve or resolve to get there. Perhaps it was the fear of really getting on top of the mountain. Or was it pride or restlessness or an arrogance borne of a natural talent never fully realized? Paraphrasing Stegner (1943, 437), my father was haunted off and on throughout his life by the dream of quick money, but he was never quite unscrupulous enough to make his dream come true. He was a gambler of sorts, but not quite gambler enough. He had "a kind of dull Dutch caution" (Stegner 1943, 437). He would "gamble with one hand and hold back a stake with the other" (Stegner 1943, 437). My father was a self-centered, stubborn, stern-voiced man who was quick to anger; an egotist dependent on women who had a childhood of poverty and illness, two years of college, three wives, three divorces.

My grandfather, a stern Irish Protestant, married to an equally stern Scottish Methodist, did not have these characteristics. He realized his version of the American dream by following the Protestant ethic. He led a life of sobriety and temperance. Grandpa had no self-doubt. He always exhibited self-control. He believed in having clear-cut goals, positive attitudes.

Men like Willy Loman, my father, and Stegner's father are victims of the post–World War II version of the American dream: work hard, listen to your government, save your money, and you will succeed; do your own thinking, but restrict it to narrow terms, good versus evil. Men like my grandfather escaped this version of the dream. They learned how to get to the top of the Big Rock Candy Mountain, no dull Dutch caution in them, no self-doubt, no crippling addiction. Always self-controlled and good-humored, they never showed anger, except to family.

Grandpa left Yellowstone with a pocketful of memories and one photograph. Stegner's father drove through the park and made a bundle on the whiskey he sold to bootleggers in Cody. Surely the two men never met, but the memories of them come together in my mind—opposites, each man seeking something in this sacred site called Yellowstone.

By the time he had his picture taken, Grandpa was a man of leisure, a man of wealth. In those days such men were tourists, travelers to places of natural wonder, places like Yellowstone (see Shaffer 2001, 286–87; Pomeroy 1957, 223–24; Dorst 1999, 72; Rothman 1998, 147–48). Male tourists in those days wore suits, white shirts, and gray fedoras, and they drove Lincoln roadsters. Grandpa fit this model to a tee. Old Faithful became the place where he performed his version of this identity. He could have been in Mizen's painting. In his mind's eye, that picture represented in a timeless way what his version of the American dream had allowed him to become: a tourist from the Midwest, a man of means occupying a position of authority in nature (Dorst 1999, 72).

Stegner's father, like mine, never had time to be a tourist. There are no pictures of Dad in a park. Parks like Yellowstone were places to drive through on the way to somewhere else where money could be made. The exception was when he won a trip from the Farm Bureau Life Insurance Company: $1 million in premiums bought ten days in a Canadian fishing camp with a group of salesmen who were strangers to one another. But there are no pictures from those camps, just a story or two, and a faded Hudson's Bay blanket. "Peanuts," he said. "One day we'll go to Canada on a fishing trip, catch walleyes and pike." But we never went. On another day, Grandpa said, "One day we'll go to Yellowstone, and I'll take you to Old Faithful." And we never went.

As a child and a young man, I grew up with these two stories and this picture. Somehow they were sandwiched between and around that photograph of Grandpa and his trout. When Grandpa died and we took his belongings from the nursing home, I got the Yellowstone picture. I feel like Terry Tempest Williams (2000, 6), who also grew up with a picture hanging over her head:

> "As a child, I grew up with Hieronymus Bosch hanging over my head [the painting El jardín de las delicias]. My grandmother had thumbtacked the wings of Paradise and Hell to the bulletin board above the bed where I slept. The prints were…part of the Metropolitan Museum of Art's series of discussions designed for home education.…Whenever my siblings and I stayed overnight, we fell asleep in 'the grandchildren's room' beneath Truth and Evil."

(WILLIAMS 2000, 6)

My question is hers: What do I make of this legacy, of this picture?

Like Paul Schullery (1997, 2–3, 261–62), I search Yellowstone Park for meanings, for answers, and I find them in my reflection in the clear evening waters of the Yellowstone River itself. Rod and reel in hand, gray-haired, wearing baggy khaki shorts and faded blue shirt, Birkenstocks on my feet, I stand at water's edge. I stand not in the image of my father or my grandfather. I have become someone else, a sixty-six-year old college professor who writes books and stories about who he might have been.

The meaning of the picture is now evident: my grandfather's smile was an invitation to come to this site. Like others in his generation, he searched for meaning in his life. He was drawn to and found Yellowstone, and in this site he felt fulfilled and complete, fulfilled in a way that he never felt anywhere else. This is why he wanted to take me to Yellowstone, so I could experience this feeling for myself, so I could find myself in the fast-running waters of this river.

And finding myself is what I am doing. I use this river as a bridge between two landscapes: the plains of the Midwest and the mountains of Montana and Wyoming. And on this bridge I look in two directions at the same time. I see two reflections: my father on the one side, my grandfather on the other. And in this moment, as these two reflections come together, I see myself more clearly than ever before. There has always been too much of my father in me for me to have become someone like my grandfather: a man who would wear a suit into the park. And there has been too much of my grandfather in me for me to be like my father, a restless man of quick schemes who would race through a park to get somewhere else.

But I'm always pulled in both directions at the same time. And memories of them flow through me as I stand and look into this river. I suppose, then, this is why I read Stegner, for reading him helps me continue my search for Yellowstone, the everlasting stream (see Harrington 2002).

And Mother? When Grandpa was staying in Old Faithful lodge and fishing for trout, Mother and Grandmother were visiting Aunt Elizabeth in her summer home in the hills of Berkeley, California. Grandma did not like to travel with Grandpa—she did not like his line of work, and she did not like the women he met on the road—so they took separate vacations. So she and Mother never went to Yellowstone. I do not know who took Grandpa's picture.

There is another search, the one Schullery does not take up. This is the search that goes beyond using the beauty and power of Yellowstone to find out who I am. It is a search born out of collisions among white, Native American, and contemporary western popular culture. These are the collisions that occur when communities and nations do things like celebrate Thomas's Moran's *Grand Canyon of the Yellowstone*, produce nostalgic reenactments of Lewis and Clark's Expedition, and have Sacagawea dress-up contests. These collisions expose the violent fault lines that seamlessly fold capitalism, democracy, tourism, railroads, and Native Americans into pastoral narratives about progress and the western frontier. A postmodern western self confronts these contradictions and seeks utopian possibilities that go beyond just acknowledging atrocities of the past.

I want a new mythology for America and its place in the world. I want a democracy and a society that matches the grandeur and beauty of Yellowstone (Stegner 1080, 38). As angry as I am about what heedless persons have done in Yellowstone and in the postmodern West, I have hope. I have hope that a new generation will craft an ethic which honors the earth and all human communities, an ethic founded on love and respect (Leopold 1949, vii). I have hope that this ethic will help Native Americans regain their rightful place in Yellowstone and all of its discourses (Christofferson 2007; Nabokov and Loendorf 2004).5 That is what this search is all about.

ALICIA'S HORSES[6]

Along our stretch of Rock Creek there are six cabins, which are reached by crossing a narrow wooden bridge made of railroad ties. The bridge is about 4 miles south of Red Lodge off of Highway 212, which runs over the Beartooth Mountains into Yellowstone Park (Graetz 1997). Across the bridge a dirt road meanders past the cabins. All the cabins are small, single-story affairs with exteriors like log cabins except ours, which has wood siding painted soft forest green.[7] The James's cabin is the most elaborate. It has a loft, a floor-to-ceiling rock fireplace, and a small deck that extends out over the river.

Every cabin owner has a piece of this road, so to speak. To get to our cabin we have to drive past three other cabins. The road helps to create a sense of community. We all feel like neighbors. We wave at each other as we come and go over the bridge. In the winter, the Jameses, our neighbors to the east, keep the road free of snow, and we do the same when we come for Christmas. This little country lane eventually forms a half circle, crossing another bridge about a mile upstream.

Sun Dance Estates is upriver, past these six cabins. Indeed, the country lane runs through Sun Dance Estates and out again across a bridge onto Highway 212. Sun Dance is a large, extravagant, five-acre site.[8] It languished on the real estate market for over a year, a pricey $999,000. The two-story, lodge-style main house includes five bedrooms, a wall of picture windows overlooking the river, a swimming pool, and a great hall. At the end of the estate is a spacious four-bedroom guest house, and next to the main house is a two-story caretaker's cottage. The property curves along the river, through the forest, for almost a quarter of a mile. Several dark, deep trout pools hide along its banks, and in the evening hours I fish in these shadows for pan-sized brook and rainbow trout.

Last spring a recently divorced woman from Las Vegas named Alicia[9] bought Sun Dance. She paid cash. Somebody said she had the money in a suitcase. On the perimeter of the property she installed motion detectors, alarm bells, and floodlights. She also installed an electronic security gate. Alicia moved in with a friend named Jake, her teenaged daughter and son, a Toyota Land Rover, a silver Porsche, a gold-colored Lamborghini, two gold Rolls Royces, three motorcycles, an 18-foot speedboat, four German shepherds, and five horses. Jake, a crack marksman and self-proclaimed wild animal sportsman, brought with him sixteen stuffed lion and tiger heads, which were hung from the walls of the great room. The locals grumbled, stating that such a tasteless, garish display of wealth was to be expected of people from Las Vegas—dirty drug money, guns, and high security.

On the curve of the river across from Sun Dance sits another large property, owned by Bob, a retired police officer from San Diego who trains seeing-eye dogs. Splitting the river into two streams is a densely forested peninsula that partially separates the two properties. This stretch of land extends 200 yards downstream and is owned by Jim, an architect from Butte who likes to build things. Ten years ago Jim built a water wheel connected to a covered wooden bridge that crosses the river.

Shortly after Alicia moved in she had two log footbridges built across Rock Creek. The bridges provided access from her property to Jim's peninsula. She stretched an electric fence across the river and put up a sign warning: "This is an electric fence." Soon Alicia's horses were walking across the bridges to the peninsula, stomping around, eating Jim's grass, and fouling the area with manure. The horses also attracted the attention of Bob's seeing-eye dogs, which interfered with the dogs' training. Bob called Jim, who called Alicia: "Those horses have to go." Alicia agreed to keep her horses off the peninsula.

In order to bring in hay for the horses, the men who worked for Alicia began using the road that runs past the six cabins. No one had ever used the road for access to Sun Dance Estates. In fact, everybody thought the road stopped at Jim's cabin. But suddenly truck tracks could be followed from the bridge all the way past the six cabins up to and into the Sun Dance property. The tires of the trucks crushed wildflowers and the knee-high prairie grass that had once nearly covered the old road. The Sun Dance people were also using the old road as a trail for their horses. Clumps of horse manure appeared alongside the Indian paintbrush growing in the road.

Folks started complaining: "Why don't they use their own bridge!" "They are wrecking our bridge!" Skip James, the retired doctor next to us, suggested that we start driving through Alicia's property: "We need to go up to her and ask for the keys to her back gate. We can form a caravan of cars and pickups and drive from one bridge to the next. We can go in shifts." "I'll help organize the project," I said.

The protest project never got off the ground, but Alicia's people eventually stopped using the community bridge as much. All seemed well and good until Frank, the horseshoer who lived next to Jim, began to see horse manure in the river. He came over to me one afternoon when I was fishing off the big rock near our cabin. He pointed to clumps of stained straw and debris along the edge of the river, and then pointed upstream: "They are cleaning out the horse barn and throwing the straw and manure in the river. Smell it?" "Dammit. Good grief," I said. "Who do those people think they are anyway? What can we do?" I asked.

Frank, who speaks very little but wears a big black cowboy hat, replied, "We can stop 'em from ridin' their horses up this way if you agree to put a No Trespassing sign on the old Pear property. That way they won't have any place to ride the horses, 'cause they are shut off from up above by them rocks." I agreed. Frank continued, "Maybe you can talk to somebody in town about them throwing manure in the river. Go to the courthouse." I said we would.

So we did. They sent us to the county commissioner's office. Dan Farley said, "Oh, you folks live downriver from those Sun Dance people. I heard about them. Bob Nichols has been in complaining about their horses bothering his dogs. What are they doing now?"

My wife began, "They seem to be cleaning out the horse stalls and throwing the straw and manure in the river."

"Have you seen them do this?" Farley asked.

"No," I said, "but there is manure and straw in the river, and it was not there before."

"How do you know it is not coming from someplace farther upstream?"

"I don't," I said, "but it started appearing after they moved in with their five horses. Seems pretty clear to me."

"What do you think happens on the ranches in this valley?" he asked. "Don't you suppose their manure gets into the river too? There is nothing we can do about it. There were thirty-five new families who moved into this valley last year, and ten of them have horses. Am I supposed to go out and check on each one of them? I can't do that. But it is illegal to pollute a Montana river. Maybe you can have some luck with the Montana Water Commission. Here is their telephone number."

Not hopeful, we left the commissioner's office and returned to our cabin. I put in a call to the water people. As we drove back to the cabin I recalled Edward Abbey's complaints about cattle and the West, how cattle have ruined the range and the rivers: "The whole American West stinks of cattle. Along every flowing stream, around every seep and spring and water hole and well, you'll find acres and acres of what range management specialists call sacrifice areas, . . . [p]laces where the earth is . . . denuded of forage— except maybe for some cacti . . . or maybe a few mutilated trees" (Abbey 1994, 150; see also Stuebner 1999, 8). Abbey's solution to the cattle problem also came to mind, "I suggest that, in order to improve the range, we open a hunting season on cattle" (1994, 153). Maybe we could shoot Alicia's horses. But that seemed too cruel. Maybe she could just move, or board her horses on a ranch, as Frank proposed.

Alicia had turned her stretch of Rock Creek into one of Abbey's sacrifice areas. Her men had trimmed back all the underbrush near the river. The previously dark and shaded river now opened to partial, and in places full, sun. This trimming gave her horses free access to the entire riverbank. Within weeks they had crushed and destroyed all of the ground-level vegetation beneath the trees that were next to the water. The riverbank started to crumble. The once crystal-clear river became clouded, muddy, and dirty. In front of each of the new footbridges Alicia's men brought in boulders and large rocks. The new rocks altered the flow of the water and disturbed the old trout pools that had been hidden in the shade. Horse manure appeared on the edges of the river. The manure transformed the banks of the river into a breeding ground for mosquitoes and flies. These flies competed with the mayfly hatches that danced and dove on the surface of the water in the early evening.

Trout fishing went to hell. Every time I crossed over into Alicia's property, a horse came up to me. If I got near the water, a horse stuck its head over my shoulder, and flies and mosquitoes swarmed around my head. My old trout pools had disappeared. Gone were the days when I could throw a line in the water and pull out a brook trout for breakfast. Two summers earlier I had made this part of the river a sacred place.

At that time the guest house had been rented to a family from Portland, Oregon. They had two teenage children, Mark and Leigh, and a big sheepdog named Rufus. I taught Mark and Leigh how to catch brook trout in the stream. Rufus and I became friends. Often I'd catch a trout, and it would jump out of the river with a force that would cause my fishing line to become caught on a tree limb extending out over the water. When this happened, Rufus would jump up on my shoulder and try to take a bite out of the trout as it dangled back and forth in the air over my head. In the process, Rufus would get trout blood smeared on his face and dirt on my shirt. My warm memories of fishing this pristine stretch of Rock Creek with Mark, Leigh, and Rufus have been ruined by the presence of Alicia and her horses.

It took two days to get through to the water commission people. The man I spoke with was anxious for details but slow to act. "When did this pollution start?" he asked. "Can anyone else confirm what you have seen? We will be in that area next week. I'll see what I can do. We sure appreciate your calling, but unless we see someone in the act, we can't do much."

I gave him Bob's name and phone number. Two days later we left for the summer. In early September I got an e-mail note from Skip James. He said:

> Trying to deal with the people who bought the Sun Dance property isn't going anywhere. The Montana Water Control people in Helena tell me that they cannot enforce any change other than in court, and that eyewitness or photographic proof would be required. Talking with the owners is pointless, because the man Alicia lives with is a nut. (He has 130 mounted specimens of animals he has slaughtered, including a full-sized hippo.)... The fact that they have five horses on a place unfit for one is not relevant so long as the animals are well-fed and not mistreated. The horse urine and excrement filters into Rock Creek, but a specific source can't be proven: too many horses along the creek upstream.... There isn't much we can do other than prevent them from riding across our property. With your permission, I will plant a No Trespassing sign at the foot of the trail they use to get up the hill.... [I]f we refuse to permit them to cross our property, they'll have to use the YBRA bridge. Won't change the horse problem, but we won't have to look

at it.... [E]veryone is angry. *Sic transit gloria mundi*: So passes away the glory of the world. See you at Christmas. Skip.

When we returned at Christmastime I walked up the lane to Alicia's electric fence and looked in at her horses. They seemed undernourished to me. But maybe I wanted to see that. They looked too thin. These were sad lonesome horses with nowhere to go. They were fenced in by a partially frozen river on one side and a rock cliff on the other. There were mounds of steaming manure and straw along the banks of the river.

On Christmas Day we walked up the canyon, past Alicia's estate. Inside the great hall somebody played Christmas music. The sound of Frank Sinatra singing "White Christmas" came from the outside speakers located on the deck around the sunken swimming pool. Near her bridge, in a snowbank next to the river, between two pine trees, loomed a large, elk-sized animal. The animal seemed poised in midstep, virtually immobile. At first I thought it was a frozen, dead, bloated horse. The next morning the animal still stood there in the same bizarre position.

That afternoon my wife met with a seamstress in town, Mrs. Smith, to talk about finishing a quilting project. She told Mrs. Smith where we lived. The seamstress said she knew Alicia. In fact, she was making living room curtains for her, but things had gotten complicated. Alicia had to pick out a new fabric because her Jake did not like the wild animal pattern she had first selected.

My wife told Mrs. Smith about the animal we had seen near the river. Mrs. Smith said Jake had stuffed a bull elk and placed it next to the river. He wanted people to think they had elk on their property.

Somehow this all seemed fitting. A stuffed bull elk at one end of the estate, starving live horses on the other. Artificial nature, preserved wildlife, the hunter's bounty on display for the world to see; no pollution here.

I fantasized that Jake would kill and stuff the five starving horses on the back end of the property. Maybe Edward Abbey had gotten to me. Jake and I would place the horses near the river, next to the rock cliffs, even beside one of the trout pools where I used to fish with Rufus. I could go and sit on a rock and pretend that a stuffed horse was nuzzling my neck. I'd have my little spot of pure nature all to myself, no real horses to bother me. Maybe Jake was onto something.

In looking back at my grandfather's photo, I imagine he would take delight in my having found my place along a river that runs into the Yellowstone. So it is with his imagined regret that I share something sad about this little piece of Rock Creek history. This "something" perhaps reveals more about me and my relationship to Grandpa, and to the natural world, than it does about Rock Creek, Montana, or even about the West, for that matter. To trace the history of a river, or "a raindrop, as John Muir would have done, is also to trace the history of the soul" (Ehrlich 1998, 72). When Rufus left, he took a little bit of the soul of Rock Creek with him. Alicia and her horses have made the river a less sacred place. In turn, our performances, our efforts to enact narratives of the self, become less sacred as well.

CODA

I am not suggesting we emulate native peoples—in this case, the Navajo.
We can't. We are not Navajo. Besides, their traditional stories don't work
for us. It's like drinking another man's medicine. Their stories hold meaning
for us only as examples. They can teach us what is possible. We must create
and find our own stories, our own myths.

(TERRY TEMPEST WILLIAMS 1984, 3, 5)

Sacagawea is our mother. She is the first gene pair of the American DNA.

(ALEXIE 2002)

In struggling to find my own place in Yellowstone, I learned that it, like
the postmodern West itself, exists only as a multiplicity of conflicting
symbols, distorted pictures, memories, plundered sites, and romantic myths
(Doyle 2007). Two themes are central to this romantic mythology: Native
Americans as iconic representations of the Wild West, and Yellowstone as a
site of self-realization. In the last decade these two themes were folded into
a series of cultural performances, including the bicentennial celebrations
of Lewis and Clark, historical reenactments of Sacagawea's life, twenty-first-
century museum exhibits honoring nineteenth-century representations
of Yellowstone, new essays on Crazy Mule's maps, last dances for Chief
Illiniwek and other pretend Indians. I have attempted to write my way into
and alongside these cultural formations, reading them from the standpoint
of personal memory and family history.

THE BOTH/AND DILEMMA

It is no longer enough to criticize the old myths. We need performance events and public ceremonies that honor countermemories of grief and loss, a politics of possibility which can turn history around. These performances move in two directions at the same time, attempting to unravel the knot that links postmodern selfhood with idealized versions of Native Americans and the landscapes of the West. The knot connects consumption and criticism. It asks: Can I be a consumer and critic of the West at the same time? How do I balance these two identities? Laurel Richardson calls this the "both/and dilemma."[1]

The consumption/cultural critic dilemma bleeds into a second one involving Native Americans. I seek a politics of representation that does two things at the same time: it recognizes the brutal U.S. colonization of Indian nations, but it does not naively idealize Native Americans (Cook-Lynn 2007). Confronting this version of the both/and dilemma requires that I avoid statements and representations that essentialize American Indians. Unfortunately, I have frequently slipped into the Hollywood black hole. I have written about celluloid Indians from my childhood. I have taken many of the Indian myths at face value. I have written as if contemporary Native Americans were cut from a single cloth.

But nothing can escape the politics of representation. A new set of narratives and performance ethics concerning consumption, criticism, and Native Americans is required. This ethic would be based on dialogue, on authentic representation. It would draw audiences and performers into interactive relationships. It would attempt to avoid the four ethical pitfalls identified by Dwight Conquergood (1985)—namely, "the Custodian's Rip-Off," "the Enthusiast's Infatuation," "the Curator's Exhibitionism," and "the Skeptic's Cop-Out" (1985, 4).[2] Conquergood sets a high standard. He demands that we move from the spaces of tourism, consumption, trophy collection, cultural voyeurism, and cultural critic. He challenges us to be vulnerable participants in our own performance narratives. He encourages an empowering performance ethic framed by care, love, hope, and mutual respect. I have only partially succeeded in realizing this ethic in the plays and autoethnographic narratives that constitute the core of this book. Too often I bordered on cyncism.

LIVING IN THE POSTMODERN WEST

If I want to follow Conquergood, there are several ways for me to live in the postmodern West: tourist, spectator, cynic, skeptic, enthusiast, collector, consumer, curator, custodian, property owner, anthropologist, sociologist, father, husband, son, grandfather, fisherman, conservationist, preservationist, tree hugger, cultural critic. These identities all involve consumption. In consuming the postmodern West, I foster an identity that brushes up against the selfsame romantic myths that operated when Thomas Moran painted *Grand Canyon of the Yellowstone*. I imagine myself as a free, natural, romantic, democratic self anchored in the western wilderness experience.

But at one level this is pure, self-serving myth. After all, I'm like fellow Illinoisan Ronald Reagan. He loved his West and his ranch and his horses. Like Reagan, I'm just a guy from Illinois (and Iowa) who found his way to that place where the northern Rocky Mountains are so high they disappear into white clouds, and the sky turns soft orange, purple, and deep blue at nighttime (Doyle 2007, 27).

As a performer of these postmodern western identities, I am mindful of my complicit relationship with this very space along Rock Creek that my wife and I call ours. We participate in the Red Lodge economy. We encourage managed growth and good conservation practices in Red Lodge by giving money to the Beartooth Conservation Alliance. We shop at the Beartooth IGA, buy tools, bug spray, and household items at the Red Lodge True Value hardware store. Even though we own property, out of habit I buy an out-of-state fishing license every year. We pay local persons to stain our deck and care for our log cabin. We are Friends of the Red Lodge Carnegie Library. We contribute books to their annual book sale. We volunteered when they computerized the library holdings. We hire two local women to clean the cabin. We bought a gas-guzzling 1997 Ford Explorer from the local Chevrolet dealer, who voted for George Bush in 2000 and 2004. With our neighbors next door, we bought the lot across the road from our two cabins. We explored giving it to the Nature Conservancy and thus placing it in trust for the public good. The conservancy doesn't take gifts as small as our less-than-one-acre lot. So we pay our taxes on the lot and hire another neighbor to spray for knapweed and other noxious plants that grow across the road.

So here is one version of my both/and dilemma. This is the "holier-than-thou" version. How can I talk myself into believing that my investments and engagements are any different—any less destructive—than Alicia's? I am consuming nature, commodifying my consumption experience, selling that experience in my books and in articles. I am using the experiences, documents, and texts of others to craft a book. How does this differ from what the U.S. government did when it took land from Native Americans to use for its own purposes? Whose political or land ethic is operating here (Leopold 1949)?

I seek a space between "both/and" and "and." I want to be culturally and environmentally sensitive, I want to know that this "wild country" is available to me, and I want to be part of this "geography of hope" (Stegner 1980, 153). But I don't want to engage in consumption practices that leave scars on the earth. I value our cabin, but I know that trees were cut down to build it right on the edge of Rock Creek.

Everywhere I look it is possible to see the traces and histories of previous both/and performances: dirt roads slashed into the side of Mount Maurice; a logging road above our cabin that leads to scenes of erosion; satellite dishes and power company poles on the West Bench that mar the skyline; ski slopes cut through old-growth forest on Rock Creek Mountain; ugly condos going up along Rock Creek; mile-deep collapsing mine shafts 3 miles south of town at Bear Creek; water pollution in town caused by runoff from a resort; hill-sized mounds of sledge and a crumbling dam across Rock Creek that are reminders of what the mining industry did to the river and town. We are hip-deep in this Red Lodge landscape.

NATIVE AMERICANS

Nor do I want to engage in consumption performances that idealize Native Americans, turning them into fancy dancers, drummers, ex-army scouts, hunters, trappers, basket and blanket weavers, jewelers, alcoholics, welfare recipients, novelists, or major league baseball players. Some precontact Native Americans were horse raiders, slaveholders, militarily aggressive groups, and misogynist societies (see Calloway 2003). Some postcontact American Indians were also slaveholders, horse thieves, trappers, and army scouts. And Hollywood continues to hire non–Native Americans to perform these essentialized identities. Today there are Native Americans who are assimilated and nonassimilated, colonized and noncolonized.

There are Native Americans who are cultural custodians, enthusiasts, curators, and skeptics. There are traditionalists, pseudotraditionalists, and modernists, and some who live in trailer homes on reservations, drive SUVs, and eat takeout pizza. We are all—white and Native American—part of this same tarnished space.

But remember, the American West was stolen from Native Americans. The reservations are a direct result of the Indian wars of resistance to the nineteenth- and twentieth-century colonial efforts to seize native lands and resources. At this level the story of the West is not a story of native self-determination, sovereignty, and indigenousness. It is a story of theft, genocide, violence, and tyranny (Cook-Lynn 2007, 95). What kind of postmodern self anchors itself in this cultural space?

COUNTERNARRATIVES

So I return to an angry Edward Abbey (1984, 1994), an even angrier Elizabeth Cook-Lynn (2007), and the poetry of Terry Tempest Williams (2001). If Elizabeth Cook-Lynn is right—that is, history does repeat itself (2007, 210)—then how do we create the conditions for a new history?[3] I don't want to endorse Abbey and shoot all the cows and shut down the ranchers. I don't necessarily want to retreat to the canyons of southern Utah and hang out in Moab. I'm not inclined to talk my wife into selling our cabin and giving the money to the Hardin-Crow public school system.

Williams says we need intellectual humility and political courage in the days ahead:

> We need humility to say we may not know enough to intrude on these wildlands with our desire for more timber, more coal, more housing, and development.... We will need political courage to say we need to honor and protect all the wilderness that is left on this continent to balance all the wilderness we have destroyed; we need wilderness for the health of our communities and for the health of the communities we acknowledge to exist beyond our species. We will need both intellectual humility and political courage to say...we made...mistake[s]...and let us take down with humility what we once built with pride.
>
> (WILLIAMS 2001, 181–82)

It is not enough to admit mistakes. Substitute Native Americans for wilderness in Williams's text. We need Native Americans, just as we need the wilderness, just as we need African Americans, Hispanic Americans, queer Americans, Anglo-Americans. We need an inclusive but separatist cultural narrative, a narrative that gives room and history to everyone. Political courage is required. Political courage means caring and...staying with an idea long enough, being rooted in a place deeply enough, and telling the story widely enough to those who will listen, until it is recognized as wisdom—wisdom reflected back to society through the rejuvenation and well-being of the next generation.

(WILLIAMS 2001, 182)

It means telling this history in our public schools and elsewhere so it becomes part of our national consciousness. It means creating a new narrative, a new politics of representation, new ways of resolving—and hopefully erasing the both/and dilemma.

Outside our cabin along Rock Creek, all around us the natural world enacts itself. We are spectators to this world. C. L. Rawlins echoes our relationship with nature: "I could tell you about a place.... If you wakened there, you would hear a light wind, brushing downslope like a hand on a bare shoulder.... In the calm, a bird calls, is answered, calls again. The stream treads a staircase of boulders. At the corner of your eye, a doe and fawn step into the meadow and lower their heads" (1994, 389). And "somewhere lawless animals cross boundaries without a blink" (Rawlins 1994, 395).

I watch in wonder as a huge moose teaches her young calves how to jump over a dilapidated barb-wire fence which is alongside the trout pool near the dam on the lower falls of Rock Creek. The moose and her young navigate this space shaped by humans, making it their own.

Richard Nelson reminds me that while "moving through nature [I am]...never truly alone" (1983, 14). It is midday. I am outside Silver Gate, Montana, knee-deep in the Soda Butte River, fishing for a huge brown trout. Having crossed the line into Yellowstone National Park, I am nervous. I do not have a park fishing permit. I turn around at the sound of a noise behind me. There on a sandy spit of land reaching out into the river stand four deer—a young buck, two smaller does, and a fawn. The deer stare wide-eyed at me, as if I had walked into their backyard. I leave as quietly as possible. I brush against velvet-textured wild moss flowers. I look back at the doe. She seems to spank her young fawn with a forehoof (see Senior 1997, 335).

INDIGENOUS MODELS OF DEMOCRACY

It is painful to accept that Lewis and Clark practiced a form of democracy that was racist and genocidal. But it is possible to use the Lewis and Clark and Thomas Jefferson narratives as an occasion for reimagining indigenous human rights. Repeating earlier arguments, borrowed from Williams (1997, 62–67), Jefferson's theory of democracy, as implemented by Lewis and Clark, can be taken up by indigenous peoples in their claims for the inalienable rights of self-governance and sovereign authority over their own lands.

Timothy Begaye (2008) does just this. He demonstrates that Native Americans implemented a form of democracy that emphasized inclusion and the free and full participation of all members of a society in civic discourse, regardless of social or political status, gender, ethnicity, or race. He elaborates this model with examples drawn from the forms of democracy that were employed by the Iroquois Confederacy, the Cherokees, the Mississippi Choctaw, the White Mountain Apaches, and the Navajo Nation.

The architects of American democracy subverted this full-inclusion model. The Jeffersonian model of democracy that Lewis and Clark carried west denied citizenship and full sovereignty rights to Native Americans, African Americans, and women. Today there is a pressing need to return full sovereignty to all Native Americans. Their indigenous models of democracy should be allowed to flourish under full federal financial sponsorship.

Begaye closes with this note: "In a truly legitimate democratic society, the discussion of democracy...would be irrelevant because everyone would be free to participate and express themselves regarding the welfare of the community." Sadly, this has not been the case for Native Americans in the United States.

A RIVER HORSE

William Least Heat-Moon (1999) also turns Lewis and Clark performances and celebrations on their heads. He did his own version of the expedition of the Corps of Discovery, sailing a small boat named Nikawa ("river horse" in Osage) from New York harbor, down the Ohio and Mississippi rivers, up the Missouri River, and down the Columbia River to the Pacific Ocean. This river horse journey offers an alternative First Nations' account of the Lewis and Clark river journey. Heat-Moon reads Native Americans directly into his story and in the process challenges the official 2003–2005 versions of the Lewis and Clark myth. He imagines a new set of tellings, some quite humorous, that can become part of public consciousness.

As they headed up the Missouri River, through Sioux Country, he and his small crew spent a night at the Fort Randall Casino and Hotel, in Wagner, South Dakota, where they also gambled and played the slot machines. At breakfast the next day:

> A young Yankton waitress needled us about our losses (but for the Professor who had won twenty dollars) at the slot machines the night before. Pilotis said, "Consider the money reparation." And she said: "You've got a long way to go then."…Our relationship with the Yanktons was recapitulated, if reworked, history: the night before, when the Professor began his winning streak, several Indian employees gathered around the slot machine, the thing gleaming like a campfire, while he dropped in coins like Clark tossing out twists of tobacco and ribbons.…[A] young Yankton asked where we'd come from, Pilotis answered, and she said, "Are you redoing Lewis and Clark here?"…I said yes because it's the best water route west. She shook her head, "I mean, are you reliving a little of the history?" Until that evening, I would have said no.
>
> (HEAT-MOON 1999, 264–65)

Casinos, Native Americans, gambling, Indians, Yankton waitresses: Who's losing to whom? Whose history? Whose expedition?

At one level, the subject matter of this book has always been the land: parks, prairies, mountains, rivers, and canyons. Who owns the West? (Kittridge 1996). Whose West?

> "The question of the land and the law is the quintessential subject matter. Without the possession of land, there are no tribal nations and there is no concomitant relationship between colonials and indigenists."
>
> (COOK-LYNN 2007, 199)

We must start with the land. I started with the park, with Yellowstone, with "Indians in the Park." By ridding the park of Indians, the government erased the rights of tribal nations to this space, to this land, and in doing that forever altered the relationship between the government and the Indian nations.

To restore a Native American presence in the park, to stage reintegration ceremonies with Bannock natives in tribal dress, seems a charade (Nabokov and Loendorf 2004). How do you give back what should never have been taken in the first place?

Kittridge helps here. If we are ever going to get past these stories of loss and dispossession and violence:

> We need to invent a new story for ourselves,
> in which we live in a society that understands
> killing the natural world is a way of killing ourselves....
> We need a story in which the processes of communality
> and mutual responsibility are fundamental....
> [T]hen maybe we'll be able to decide,
> in some responsible way,. . .
> where to find the money to care for our poor
> and disoriented and our disabled and our dispossessed:...
> the Native Americans.
>
> (KITTRIDGE 1996, 142–43)

We need stories that lead us to better care for one another. We need stories that drive us to action, stories that honor difference, and value nonviolence, stories that model inclusion, love, care, hope, stories derived from childhood memories,

> stories that tell us why taking care,
> why compassion and the humane treatment
> of our fellows is more important
> than feathering our own nests.[P]
>
> (KITTRIDGE 1996, 167)

When I turned and saw that doe outside Yellowstone spank her young fawn with a forehoof, I knew I was in the presence of pure unconditional love, pure caring. I hoped that someday that I could learn to love that way.

There is a week in July on our deck over Rock Creek when the male and female flowers on the giant cottonwood become airborne on cottony structures, and the "air everywhere you turn is filled with cottonwood snow" (Doyle 2007, 27). When that happens you know what it is like to live along this roaring river in the shadows of the Beartooth Mountains. It "only happens when the sky is so blue you want to just stand there and laugh all day" (Doyle 2007, 27). And a week later, when the cottonwood flowers have turned to leaves, and the wind from the canyon stirs the air, the limbs and leaves on the giant cottonwood "rustle and quiver and shimmer and seem to sigh all day long" (Roosevelt 1888, 3). Then you are in the presence of something greater then yourself.

My narrative has turned on events that never happened. In the summer of 1952, when I was eleven, my grandfather did not take me to Yellowstone Park.

But I have followed my grandfather to this park. I have completed the journey he and I never took. I have completed this journey with my children and with my children's children. And today I attempt to find myself in ways that his Republican self might not like. The cabin on Rock Creek in the Beartooth Mountains has been a good place to begin the journey. It is 69 miles, give or take, from Yellowstone Park, and everybody needs a good place to start their search for their personal Yellowstone.

NOTES

Chapter 1

1. We started annual visits to Red Lodge and Yellowstone in 1988. As regular "seasonals," we now spend about six to eight weeks a year in the region.
2. I thank a postmodern archaeologist for this phrase.
3. From 1950 to 2005 there were more than 86 million visitors to the park.
4. This photograph was lost for many years, existing only in my memory. In the spring of 2006 my youngest daughter returned the photograph to me, saying her mother had come across it while cleaning out a closet. She wondered if I would want it! In it Grandfather is hatless, wearing dress pants and a white shirt open at the collar. He is looking straight into the camera, a wide sunny smile on his face. He is holding three large trout, two browns and a cutthroat. He stands in front of a white tent, next to a tall tree. The bumper of his car is barely visible at the lower left side of the picture. Next to this photograph was a small framed postcard reproduction of Thomas Moran's famous painting *The Grand Canyon of the Yellowstone.* In the top drawer of Grandpa's dresser were postcards of other scenes in the park, as well as a 1932 copy of the *Haynes Guide: Yellowstone National Park.* I discuss Moran's painting in Chapter 6, "Drawn to Yellowstone I."

Chapter 2

1. See Denzin (2002a) for an earlier version of this chapter. I thank Katherine E. Ryan, Kathy Charmaz, Patrick Jorgensen, and Laurel Richardson for their helpful comments.

2. Again, I present this as a layered text, a montage which moves among memories, events, history, and interpretations.
3. The use of *Indian* and *Native American* is problematic, as Michael Yellow Bird observes, because these are counterfeit, colonized, racist identities imposed by European Americans. He prefers, as do I, *First Nations* or *indigenous peoples* (2004, 47).
4. For the background of this fifty-five-year-old annual community event that celebrates ethnic history in Red Lodge see Lampi (1998, 79, 170–74), Olp (2000), and Christensen (2002).
5. Written in honor of the seventy-four miners killed in the Smith Mine Disaster of 1943 (Zuban and Owen 2000, 135–36). The Smith Mine was located in Washoe, five miles outside of Red Lodge.
6. The rodeo-riding members of the family (Turk, Alice, Bill, Marge, and Deb) have an entire wall devoted to their accomplishments in the Carbon County Peaks to Plains Museum (see Zuban and Owen 2000, 208–12).
7. There are hints of a Greek drama in this spectacle. The chief is not incurring the wrath or anger of the gods, but he is performing before a nearly all-white audience and refusing to defer to them.
8. See also the movie *Smoke Signals* (1998), based on Alexie's book. Alexie seems to be saying that indigenous peoples are trapped in a mythic western past that relives the racist ideologies that sustain the cowboy/Indian dichotomy. As long as First Nation persons replay this past, they will be trapped in the present (Alexie 1993, 22).
9. A rock-and-roll group from the 1970s. I thank Michael Elavsky and Robert Sloane for these lines and information.
10. The chief is an imaginary Native American, named after the native nations of Illinois and the long-disappeared Peoria tribe. His costume, made by Oglala Indians, reenacts imperialist nostalgic imagery associated with the nineteenth-century and early-twentieth-century Wild West shows of George Catlin and William Cody (see Reddin 1999; King and Springwood 2001, 51–52; also Welch 2000). There never was an Illiniwek Indian tribe (see King and Springwood 2001, 46). Of course Chief Haywood Big Day stepped into a part of this Wild West tradition on Montana Night in Red Lodge when he greeted Bill Greenough and smiled at Miss Montana.

Chapter 3

1. Of course First Nations peoples were everywhere present in the area called Yellowstone, long before it was discovered by white Americans. Crow, Blackfeet, Flathead, Sheepeaters, Bannock, Nez Perce, and Shoshone routinely traveled through the region, for ritual, economic, and political purposes. However, "It is no secret that banning American Indians and appropriating their lands were deemed necessary for the initial establishment and continued security of Yellowstone National Park" (Nabokov and Loendorf 2004, xi). I thank Mitch Allen for stressing this point.
2. In using the term *Indians* I am mindful once again of its racist legacies. By confronting the legacy directly, I hope to diminish its cultural power.
3. See also Hultkrantz (1979), who is credited with the contemporary version of the taboo geyser theory (see Nabokov and Loendorf 2004, 285).
4. See, for example, Hunsaker (2001, 2003), Clark and Edmonds (1979), Tinling (2001), Waldo (1978).

Chapter 4

1. This involves a reading of the Lewis and Clark journals and their various editions, starting with Biddle (1962/1814), moving to Coues (1965/1893), Thwaites (1904–1905), Jackson (1962), and Moulton (1983–2001; 2003). Other accounts include those of John Whitehouse, John Ordway, Patrick Gass, and Charles Floyd. On these supplemental journals see Slaughter 2003, 54; also Clarke 2002; on reading the various versions of the originals see the essays in Ronda 1998; also DeVoto 1997/1953; Jackson 1987; and Slaughter 2003, 47–64. In addition to these sources there is Ken Burns's 1997 documentary *Lewis and Clark: The Journey of the Corps of Discovery*; a Lewis and Clark newsletter, websites, and a "minor academic industry of conference proceedings, edited books, journal articles, and monographs written on the expedition" (Slaughter 2003, xiv).
2. Among the many other myths are those that read the men as gifted ethnographers and linguists, culturally sensitive frontier diplomats, models of multiculturalism in their dealings with Native Americans, as epic figures, as adventurers, heroes of a young nation, men who

overcame great obstacles to blaze a path through an uncharted frontier, and proto-ecologists who speak to us today (see Spence 2003 for a review).

3. I thank an anonymous reviewer for directing me to Wood's book, and for this quote.

4. To repeat, in 1796 the Yellowstone River was known as the Rock or Crow River. In 1797 it appeared on a map as *R. des Roches Jaunes*, or "River of the Yellow Stones"; in 1800 as the Rio Amarillo; in the late 1700s as the Elk; as the Crow or Yellow Rock in 1804; and the Yellow Stone in 1805 (see Jackson 1987, 122; also Coues 1965/1893, 283; DeVoto 1997/1953, 101).

5. I return to this story in Chapter 9.

6. I thank Shoshana Magnet for this example.

7. Jeffersonian constitutional democracy presumes that all white men are created equal, and that they have the natural, inalienable, self-determining rights of self-governance, life, liberty, the pursuit of happiness, the right to grant lands, and sovereign authority over those lands (Williams 1997, 57–58, 61). Jeffersonian democracy authorized the colonization of Native Americans.

Chapter 5

1. I take this title from McMurtry (2001, 157), who observes that Sacagawea's nickname, Janey, is used only once in the journals, on 23 November 1805, when Clark records the votes about where to construct a winter camp: "Janey in favour of a place where there is plenty of Potas" (Clark, in Moulton 2003, 243; see also note 14 below).

2. In 1950 Guthrie received the Pulitzer Prize for *The Way West*, the second novel in his historical series about the West. Guthrie also wrote the screenplay for *Shane*, a classic film about the Old West (Blew 1988, 685).

3. Her presence as a statue is also noteworthy, the three most prominent statues being Cooper's, dedicated in Portland in 1905; Crunelle's *Bird Woman*, dedicated in Bismarck, North Dakota, 1910; and Jackson's 1980 *Sacagawea*, which stands in the courtyard of the Buffalo Bill Historical Center in Cody, Wyoming. Jackson's "sculpture depicts a native woman who is connected to the earth" (Kessler1996, 179), while Crunelle's presents her as "a native mother . . . [with] a sleeping baby on her back" (Kessler 1996, 94). These statues celebrate the mythic West, a feminized,

indigenous frontier where native women helped white males "achieve the colonists' covenant to convert wilderness to sacred spaces" (Kessler 1996, 185; Kammen 1993, 28).

4. Guthrie also drew from the diaries and journals of nineteenth-century trappers (Garceau 2001, 151).

5. Stegner's "most Americans" should be qualified, to read "most white American males."

6. *Sacagawea Speaks beyond the Shining Mountains with Lewis and Clark* (Hunsaker 2001), for example, was present in the bookstores in Yellowstone Park, Billings, Cody, and Red Lodge, as were posters of her looking west, toward the mountains, holding her son, Jean Baptiste Charbonneau--Little Pompy.

7. As noted in Chapter 4, there are five original journals/diaries that form the basis of the so-called Lewis and Clark journals: those written by Lewis, Clark, Gass, Ordway, and Whitehouse. There are at least seven edited versions of these combined texts, those of Biddle (1962/1814), Coues (1965/1893), Thwaites (1904–1905), DeVoto (1997/1953), Jackson (1962), and Moulton (1983–2001).

8. This is Slaughter's count (2003, 102). Kessler's total is 193 (1996, 49). Of those he counts, Slaughter states that "only eleven are by name--ten times by one of the variant spellings of Sacajawea, and once as Janey. Only Lewis and Clark . . . ever name her. Lewis names her six times, Clark names her four times, plus once by the nickname Janey" (2003, 102). Kessler (1996, 48) notes that Clark comments on her more than forty-eight times, Lewis more than thirty-eight times, while the other journal writers (Ordway, Gass, Whitehouse) refer to her nineteen, nine, and eight times, respectively.

9. Like the Lewis and Clark story, Guthrie's story essentially begins as a mountain man, fur trader, Missouri River narrative, starting in St. Louis and progressing upriver through Native American territory to the Yellowstone River in Montana. Guthrie drew on the journals in writing *The Big Sky* (Garceau 2001, 123). Guthrie's major works--*The Big Sky*, *The Way West*, *These Thousand Hills*--were turned into Hollywood films: *The Big Sky* in 1952; *These Thousand Hills* in 1959, and *The Way West* in 196 7.   He worked on other films as well, including *Shane* (1953) and *The Kentuckian* (1955), but not on *Far Horizon* (1955), a film loosely based on Lewis and Clark's expedition, starring Donna Reed as Sacagawea, vying for the love of Charlton Heston and Fred MacMurray (D'Arc 2001, 86).

10. Teal Eye reappears in *Fair Land, Fair Land* (1982), the sixth book in Guthrie's saga. She has married Dick Summers.

11. There is a counterhistory about these events of 1620 and 1621 and that first Thanksgiving. By 1620, nearly annihilated by smallpox and the tactics of English warfare, which included setting fire to entire villages, the Wampanoags sought to form an alliance with the Plymouth community. Encouraged by Squanto, who spoke English, the Indians signed a treaty with the Pilgrims and celebrated by feasting and sharing food (Bradford in Wilson 1998, 111; Brandon 1974, 201). The Pilgrims would have none of this ritual sharing with the Indian "sauvages."

12. The appeal of her story is still strong. In 2005, *The New World*, directed by Terrence Malick and starring Colin Farrell, Christian Bale, and Q'Orianka Kilcher, offered yet another telling of her life and that of John Smith, played by Farrell.

13. Or, rather, the choice was made for her, as Charbonneau won her in a bet (Ambrose 1996, 187).

14. Of course this democratic gesture is only symbolic. York and Janey are only granted this power once. They are quickly returned to their servant identities in the expedition narrative.

15. Kessler (1996, 191–208) discusses counterhegemonic narratives that challenge this mythology, including Paula Gunn Allen's lengthy poem "The One Who Skins Cats," a rereading of the Sacagawea legend.

16. In contrast, Native American males are present under the foundational trope of Indian/white violence (Dickinson, Ott, and Aoki 2005, 97–98; also Slotkin 1992; Bartlett 1992).

17. Dedicated in 1981 and 1983, respectively. The historical center itself was formally dedicated in 1917.

18. Called the Smithsonian of the West (Dickinson, Ott, and Aoki 2005, 87), the center houses the Plains Indian Museum, the Cody Firearms Museum, the Draper Museum of Natural History, and the Whitney Gallery of Western Art (Bartlett 1992).

19. In 1980, 2-foot studio models of the statue sold for $15,000 apiece. In less than one day after the unveiling of the statue, Jackson recorded sales of just under $500,000 (Kessler 1996, 181). Jackson has produced more than eight hundred limited-edition sculptures depicting Sacagawea, reportedly now worth between $53,000 and $60,000 each (Kessler 1996, 181).

20. Little is gained by publishing new versions of her life when the narrative is entirely driven by the Lewis and Clark story line. Tellings such as those in Hunsaker (2001, 2003) commodify her story and reconnect it to the dominant historical narrative.

21. *Yellowstone Journal* describes itself as an independent journal dedicated to Yellowstone and geared to both visitors to and fans of the world's oldest national park (June 2005, 2).

22. And from other cultural mythologies as well, including her presence in the 2006 film *Night at the Museum*, in which she is alive and well, held captive, so to speak, in the Smithsonian Museum of Natural History. Teddy Roosevelt falls in love with her. She saves his life.

Chapter 6

1. I thank Laurel Richardson, Sara Delemont, Paul Atkinson, Li Xiong, James Salvo, Katherine E. Ryan, Grant Kien, Michael Giardina, and Kevin Dolan for their comments and assistance. I take the title "Drawn to Yellowstone" from Hassrick (2002), who was director of the Buffalo Bill Historical Center from 1976 to 1996.

2. *Grand Canyon of the Yellowstone* is a key painting of the nineteenth-century Rocky Mountain School, the successor to the Hudson River School, the school that produced "Great Pictures" (Wilkins 1998, 99).

3. There are least four figures in the painting. In the foreground, to the right of the three horses, are two persons, who Kinsey (1992, 44) interprets as William Henry Jackson, the famous photographer, and Moran himself, "seated with a sketchbook." In the middle ground are Ferdinand V. Hayden and a Native American.

4. In the summer of 2005 the newly opened Yellowstone Heritage and Research Center in Gardiner, Montana, made available the works of Thomas Moran that they had in their archives, including scraps from his diaries. Thus tourists were drawn to two versions of Yellowstone--the real park in the park archives and the represented park in the Buffalo Bill Historical Center.

5. Thomas Moran was born on 12 February 1837 in Bolton, England, the son of a hand-loom weaver. The family moved to Kensington, Pennsylvania, (near Philadelphia) in 1844. A talented young painter, Moran was influenced by the work of England's foremost landscape painter, J. M. W. Turner. Moran and his brother traveled to England in 1862 to study Turner's art (Wilkins 1998).

6. Horace Marden Albright was park superintendent from 1916 to 1929.

7. Gilder and Moran were neighbors and childhood friends. Gilder was editor-in-chief of *Century* Magazine (Hassrick 2002, 32).

8. American artist and pioneer photographer of the West (see Blair 2005).
9. Washburn was surveyor-general of the Montana Territory (Haines 1996a, 108).
10. These watercolors included *Great Springs of the Firehole River* (1871), *Lower Geyser Basin* (1873), and *Big Springs of Yellowstone Park* (1872).
11. At the urging of Cooke, who wanted to run a branch of his railroad through the park, Hayden surveyed the entire Yellowstone region (Haines 1996a, 153).
12. In 1865 and 1870 there were also discussions about making the region a park (see Schullery and Whittlesey 2003, 1–3).
13. There is confusion over whether or not Stevenson is in the painting. As indicated in note 3 above, there are at least four figures in the painting: Jackson, Moran, Hayden, and the Native American male (Kinsey 1992, 44). In Moran's 1871 engraving *Upper Falls of the Yellowstone, Wyoming*, published in *Scribner's Monthly*, May 1871, there are three figures looking into the canyon, and they may be Hayden, Stevenson, and Moran.
14. A method of colorization invented by Louis Prang involving the use of colored inks in lithography (Wilkins 1998, 97).

Chapter 7

1. As previously noted, the exhibit involved the work of more than twenty-eight artists, including move than fifty paintings, posters, and reproductions.
2. When asked about Native American artists and the park, the owner of the Yellowstone Gallery and Frameworks, which is on the edge of the park in Gardiner, Montana, stated, "To the best of my knowledge, there are no contemporary Native Americans painting Yellowstone. They are not known for their paintings of Yellowstone. Traditionally, their paintings focus on sacred objects, conflict, war, being one with nature, community rituals, animals, ceremonial dress, genre scenes, traditional life, idealized spaces" (interview, 11 July 2005).
3. The map appears deep into the online exhibit (which follows Hassrick's 2002 text), just after a reproduction of a William Henry Jackson photograph and before Thomas Moran's 1893 painting *Golden Gate, Yellowstone National Park*.
4. So named because its territory includes "the Yellowstone and Missouri river basin, from the Little Missouri to the Wind River Range and from

the Milk River south to the headwaters of the Bighorn and Powder rivers" (Sundstrom and Fredlund 1999, 47).

5. And, as established in Chapter 2, by 1872 there were no longer any Indians in the park. Catlin's dream was never realized.

6. However, in the Whitney Gallery of Western Art and the Plains Indian Museum, the BBHC was exhibiting the works of several contemporary Native American artists, including Earl Biss, Fritz Scholder, Oscar Howe, and T. C. Cannon. None of the Native American works involved representations of Yellowstone Park.

7. Following Hassrick, whose book was prominently displayed and was for sale at full price, the 2005 exhibit was divided into seven partially overlapping time periods: (1) Brushes with Discovery: 1830–70; (2) Railroad Art: 1870–90; (3) Tourist Guides: 1880–90; (4) Scenic Conservation: 1885–90; (5) Aesthetic Conservation: 1900–1925; (6) Steamy Angels and Vague Bears: 1920–40; and (7) The Modern View: 1980–present).

8. In 1890 Haynes managed to get himself named the park's official photographer (Hassrick 2002, 185). Haynes owned the Monida and Yellowstone Stage Company, which carried tourists from the Union Pacific lines into the park. Haynes sought but did not get permission to build a hotel at the site of Old Faithful geyser (Haines 1996b, 52). Instead, he received a share of the Wylie Permanent Camping Company profits.

9. Jay Cooke's Northern Pacific Railroad once again enters the picture, for it was involved as a silent partner in the construction of Old Faithful Inn (Haines 1996b, 119; Reinhart 2004, 6).

10. The *Haynes Guide* to the park, a product of the Haynes Picture Shops, was published and updated nearly every year from 1890 till 196   7. The Haynes business was established by F. Jay Haynes in1884, and it remained in the family until the fall of 1967, when Mrs. J. E. Haynes sold the business to Hamilton Stores, Inc. (Haines 1996a, 366–67).

11. He was thus part of the last phase of the American military and Indian wars of 1865–90.

12. This war involved a two-week skirmish in the park between Chief Joseph, with his band of six hundred Nez Perce, and at least three groups of tourists (see Haines 1996a, 219; also Janetski 2002, 69–82; Schullery, 1997, 105–106).

13. Before surrendering in April 1877, Crazy Mule was a hostage held in Fort Keogh. Upon surrender, he was recruited by General Nelson A. Miles.

14. On the origins and history of these two maps see Fredlund, Sundstrom, and Armstrong 1996, 5–10.
15. The wavy line is a pictographic convention often meaning holy or crazy (Fredlund, Sundstrom, and Armstrong 1996, 5).
16. The guide lists over a hundred geysers at ten sites throughout the park. Old Faithful is one of more than sixty geysers located at Upper Geyser Basin. According to the 1947 *Haynes Guide* (Haynes 1947, 87), "By measurement its height varies from 116 to 171 feet, the average interval is 66.3 minutes and the duration of each eruption 4 minutes. After dark one eruption is usually illuminated by a giant searchlight."
17. Haynes's photograph was the model for Daniel Chester French's famous 1923 marble sculpture *And the Sons of God Saw the Daughters of Men That They Were Fair*. French's composition was inspired "by the billowy monumental form of 'Old Faithful' geyser in eruption" (Hassrick 2002, 187). The dominant figure in the sculpture is an angel who seems to step from a cloud to embrace "an earthy female figure who reaches skyward from a rock; . . . the metaphor might be read as virginal Yellowstone surrendering to divinely guided man for his pleasure" (Hassrick 2002, 187).
18. It has undergone two restorations. The first was in 1980–83, the second, at a cost in excess of $22 million, was in 2004–2008.
19. Philip R. Goodwin (1882–1933) was a student of the Rhode Island School of Design, the Howard Pyle School, and the Art Students League of New York. His specialty was the outdoors, particularly hunting and fishing.
20. Carl Rungius (1869–1959) was America's leading wildlife painter, specializing in those moments, or predicaments, when a man confronts a potentially dangerous wild animal and the animal is aware of being seen (Gray and Harvey 1999, 3).
21. Bears, buffalo, deer, and horses are the most frequently represented animals in the *Drawn to Yellowstone* exhibit.
22. Remember the partially hidden brown bear in Moran's great painting. Bears have a complex history in myth and literature and popular culture. According to Shepard and Sanders (1985), bear myths and rituals center on the themes of renewal, the reincarnation of the soul, the symbolic replenishment of food, the passage of initiative, the renewal of clan power, symbols of bravery. Schullery (2002, 72) argues that between the years 1840 and 1900 bears (black, brown, grizzly) in western North America were symbols of evil wilderness. This changed with the conservation movement of the twentieth century, when all animals in

nature, especially bears, were regarded as all that is good and deserving of our protection.

23. As Alston Chase observes, as early as 1900 Yellowstone tourism "brought people who fed [primarily the black] bears, and people who produced garbage, which these opportunistic scavengers consumed. The white man, having destroyed the bears' original ecosystem, replaced it with another. Garbage made up to the bear the loss of spawning fish and drowning buffalo." The creation of the National Park Service in 1916 ushered in new attempts to lure tourists into the park, including bleachers around bear-feeding areas, where naturalists gave lectures on bear behavior (Chase 1986, 146). Garbage dumps at camp and hotel sites and automobiles acted as magnets for bears. The advent of driving in the park led to the "black-bear problem," for this "smaller and tamer species did the most damage to property [autos] and people" (Chase 1986, 146). The black bear is the species represented in the paintings of Mizen, Coe, and Caldwell. Garbage dumps in the park were closed by 1970 (Chase 1986, 146).

Chapter 8

1. This chapter reworks and extends materials originally written in 2002 and published in Denzin 2003b, 184–213. By the end of 2002, it appeared that the University of Illinois had found a way to retire Chief Illiniwek, its imaginary Indian chief who danced at halftime sporting events. Sadly, such was not the case: it took several lawsuits and the loss of a chancellor before the chief would be retired. It would seem that he danced for the last time on 21 February 2007.

2. According to Bogle (1994, 140–41), the Huck Finn fixation aligns a good white man who is an outcast with a trusty black man (also an outcast). The white man grows in stature through his association with the black man, who seems "to possess the soul the white man searches for" (Bogle 1994, 140).

3. The myth of cowboys and Indians lingers as a vital part of the heritage of the New West (see Deloria 1998). In magazines like *Cowboys and Indians*, *The True West*, and *Wildwest*, stories about Indian art, the violent Apaches, the Blackfoot and Cree wars, and "Tommy Lee Jones, Part Cowboy, Part Indian" can be read.

4. The Crow Indians, now confined to a reservation in eastern Montana, originally inhabited all of Carbon, Stillwater, and Yellowstone counties,

from the Beartooth Mountains on the west, to the Yellowstone River and North and South Dakota to the east, to the Clark's Fork of the Yellowstone River south to Wyoming (see Zuban and Owen 2000, 4–6).

5. I never intended to turn Red Lodge and its residents--a town and a community I love deeply--into a site of research. But the events discussed here seemed to require comment. It was as if these issues followed me from Champaign to Red Lodge.

6. I return to these lines from Cook-Lynn in Chapter 9.

Chapter 9

1. To repeat, I take this title, in part, from Schullery (1997). I thank Kathy Charmaz, Patricia Clough, Andy Fontana, Laurel Richardson, Christopher Schmitt, Rebecca Small, and Walt Harrington for their comments on earlier versions of this text.

2. See Cook-Lynn (1996; also 2001, 2007) The founding father of contemporary western literature and history, Stegner wrote twelve novels and seven nonfiction works, and he won numerous prestigious awards, including the Pulitzer Prize in 197   1.   He was a national figure in the environmental movement and a major historian of the West (see Benson 1996).

3. The grandfather I discuss is my mother's father.

4. My grandfather was Waldo William Townsley. John Townsley was a midcentury Yellowstone park superintendent (Schullery 1997, 160; 1994, 213; see also Everhart 1998, 164–65). John Townsley had a son named Forrest. When I was ten years old Grandma Townsley invited Uncle Forrest Townsley and Aunt Elizabeth to visit the farm. They came from Milwaukee. Aunt Elizabeth was an interior decorator. She decorated Grandma's living room. The Victorian walnut love seat she picked out in 1950 sits on our balcony today. In searching for Yellowstone, I claim my place in this version of Townsley family history.

5. Twenty-six tribes have histories with and in Yellowstone Park. The Nez Perce Trail has been designated as a National Historical Trail. The Bannocks have asked that the Bannock Trail be given the same designation (Christofferson 2007, 6).

6. This section reworks material in Denzin 2000b.

7. In November 2002 we bought the James's cabin and sold our first cabin to a family who remodeled it, giving it a log cabin exterior.

8. The name of the estate can be traced back to the late 1970s. At that time on Mount Maurice, the mountain directly above these cabins, there was a ski lodge named Sun Dance, so named because of the way the sun danced off the newly fallen snow. The owners of the estate took the name Sun Dance from the now-defunct ski lodge.
9. All names are pseudonyms.

Chapter 10

1. I steal this phrase from Laurel Richardson and thank her for raising the questions in this section.
2. Cultural custodians ransack their own pasts, looking for good stories to perform, often denigrating family members of cultural groups in the process. The enthusiast fails to become deeply involved in the cultural setting or narrative that he or she performs. The curator sensationalizes the other, staging performances that celebrate the exotic, the primitive, the abusive, violent other. The skeptic exercises detachment, distance, the cynic's viewpoint. He or she may ridicule or criticize the other.
3. She asserts that the terrors the world is now witnessing (in Iraq and elsewhere) may be the direct consequences of the events begun in America in past centuries. "Make no mistake: a holocaust happened here in our own lands and it continues here and elsewhere" (210).

References

1. This official tourist guide was written for and printed by the Northern Pacific Railroad. An appendix contains railroad rates and timetables.

REFERENCES

Abbey, Edward. 1994. "Something about Mac, Cows, Poker, Ranchers, Cowboys, Sex, and Power . . . and Almost Nothing about American Lit." Pp. 137–58 in D. Clow and D. Snow, eds., *Northern Lights: A Selection of New Writing from the American West*. New York: Vintage.

_____. 1984. "The Author's Preface to His Own Book." Pp. ix–xv in E. Abbey, *The Best of Edward Abbey*. San Francisco: Sierra Club.

Albers, Patricia. 1983. "Introduction: New Perspectives on Plains Indian Women." Pp. 1–28 in P. Albers and B. Medicine, eds., *The Hidden Half: Studies of Plains Indian Women*. Lanham, MD: University Press of America.

Alexie, Sherman. 2002. "What Sacagawea Means to Me." Viewpoint, *Time*, 8 July, 42. http://www.time.com/time/2002/lewis_clark/lprocon.html.

_____. 1995. *Reservation Blues*. New York: Grove.

_____. 1993. *Lone Ranger and Tonto Fistfight in Heaven*. New York: HarperCollins.

Allen, Paula Gunn. 1984. "The One Who Skins Cats." Pp. 10–24 in B. Brant, ed., *A Gathering of the Spirit: Writing and Art by North American Indian Women*. N.p.: Sinister Wisdom.

Alterman, Eric, and Mark Green. 2004. *The Book on Bush: How George W. (Mis)leads America*. New York: Viking.

Ambrose, Stephen. 2000. *Nothing Like It in the World: The Men Who Built the Transcontinental Railroad, 1863–1869*. New York: Simon & Schuster.

_____. 1996. *Undaunted Courage: Meriwether Lewis, Thomas Jefferson, and the Opening of the American West*. New York: Simon & Schuster.

Anderson, Nancy. 1997. "Catalogue, 1871–80: Breakthrough." Pp. 19–180 in Nancy Anderson, *Thomas Moran*, with contributions by Thomas P. Bruhn, Joni L. Kinsey, and Anne Morand. Washington, DC, and New Haven: National Gallery of Art and Yale University Press.

Aronowitz, Stanley. 1998. Introduction. Pp. 1–19 in Paulo Freire, *Pedagogy of Freedom: Ethics, Democracy, and Civic Courage*. Boulder: Roman & Littlefield.

Bagne, Mark, and Bob Richard. 2002. *Yellowstone Country: The Photographs of Jack Richard*. Cody, WY: Buffalo Bill Historical Center.

Bartlett, Richard A. 1992. *From Cody to the World: The First Seventy-Five Years of the Buffalo Bill Memorial Association*. Cody, WY: Buffalo Bill Historical Center.

_____. 1985. *Yellowstone: A Wilderness Besieged.* Tucson: University of Arizona Press.

Bears, Edwin C. 2005. Foreword. Pp. iv–xx in Thomas P. Lowry. *Venereal Disease and the Lewis and Clark Expedition.* Lincoln: University of Nebraska Press.

Beaumont, Shelley. 1997. "'Redskin' Mascot Up for a Vote." *Carbon County News,* 8 October: 1A–2A.

Begaye, Timothy. 2008. "Modern Democracy: The Complexities behind Appropriating Indigenous Models of Governance and Implementation." Pp. 745–60 in N. K. Denzin, Y. S. Lincoln, and L. Tuhiwai, eds., *Sage Handbook of Critical, Indigenous Methodologies.* Thousand Oaks, CA: Sage.

Benjamin, Walter.1999. *The Arcades Project.* Translated by Howard Eiland and Kevin McLaughlin. Cambridge: Belknap Press of Harvard University Press.

_____. 1983. "N Theoretics of Knowledge: Theory of Progress." *Philosophical Forum* 15.

_____. 1969. *Illuminations.* Translated by Harry Zohn. New York: Harcourt, Brace & World.

Benson, Jackson, J. 1996. *Wallace Stegner: His Life and Work.* New York: Penguin.

Berlo, Janet C., and Ruth B. Phillips. 1998. *Native North American Art.* New York: Oxford University Press.

Bevis, William W., and William E. Farr. 2001. Introduction. Pp. 1–8 in W. E. Farr and W. W. Bevis, eds., *Fifty Years after "The Big Sky": New Perspectives on the Fiction and Films of A. B. Guthrie Jr.* Helena: Montana Historical Society.

Biddle, Nicholas, ed. 1962. *History of the Expedition Under the Command of Captains Lewis and Clark, to the Sources of the Missouri, thence across the Rocky Mountains and down the River Columbia to the Pacific Ocean, performed during the years 1804-5-6, by order of the Government of the United States.* 2 vols., with an introduction by John Bakeless, and illustrated with watercolors and drawings by Carl Bodmer and other contemporary artists. New York: Heritage. (Reprint of 1814 edition, prepared for the Press by Paul Allen, 2 vols. Philadelphia: Bradford.)

Blair, Bob, ed. 2005. *William Henry Jackson's "The Pioneer Photographer."* Sante Fe: Museum of New Mexico. (With original text from the 1929 edition by William Henry Jackson in collaboration with Howard R. Driggs.)

Blevins, Winfred. 1989. *Roadside History of Yellowstone Park.* Missoula, MT: Mountain.

Blew, Mary Clearman. 2000. *Sister Coyote: Montana Stories.* New York: Lyons.

_____. 1999. *Bone Deep in Landscape: Writing, Reading, and Place.* Norman: University of Oklahoma Press.

_____. 1997. "The Exhausted West: A Last Look at Landscape." Pp. 173–84 in James P. Ronda, ed., *Thomas Jefferson and the Changing West: From Conquest to Conservation.* Albuquerque: University of New Mexico Press.

_____. 1994. *Balsamroot*. New York: Penguin.

_____. 1991. *All but the Waltz: A Memoir of Five Generations in the Life of a Montana Family*. New York: Penguin.

_____. 1990 *Runaway: A Collection of Stories*. Lewiston, ID: Confluence.

_____. 1988. "Frontier Dreams." Pp. 633–37 in W. Kittredge and A. Smith, eds., *The Last Best Place: A Montana Anthology*. Seattle: University of Washington Press.

_____. 1977. *Lambing Out and Other Stories*. Norman: Oklahoma University Press.

Boehme, Sarah E. 1997. *Whitney Gallery of Western Art*. Cody, WY: Buffalo Bill Historical Center.

Bogle, Donald. 1994. *Toms, Coons, Mulattoes, Mammies, and Bucks: An Interpretive History of Blacks in American Films*. 3d ed. New York: Continuum.

Book, Rick. 2003. *Sacagawea: The Making of a Legend*. Winnipeg: Heartland Associates.

Bosson, Howard. 1982. "Tall Tale Retold: The Influence of the Photographs of William Henry Jackson on the Passage of the Yellowstone Park Act of 1872." *Studies in Visual Communication* 8 (winter): 98–109.

Bowman, J. R. 1882. *The Pacific Tourist: J. R. Bowman's Illustrated Trans-Continental Guide of Travel from the Atlantic to the Pacific Ocean*. New York: J. R. Bowman.

Brandon, William. 1974. *The Last Americans: The Indian in American Culture*. New York: McGraw Hill.

Brautigan, Richard. 1967. *Trout Fishing in America: A Novel*. New York: Dell.

Brown, Dee. 1971. *Bury My Heart at Wounded Knee: An Indian History of the American West*. New York: Bantam.

Calloway, Colin G. 2003. *One Vast Winter Count: The Native American West before Lewis and Clark*. Lincoln: University of Nebraska Press.

Canaday, John.1961. *Mainstreams of Modern Art: David to Picasso*. New York: Simon & Schuster.

Catlin, George, 1880. *North American Indians: Being Letters and Notes on their Manners, Customs, and Conditions, Written during Eight Years' Travel amongst the Wildest Tribes in North America, 1832–1839*. Vol. 1. (Reprint, 1973, New York: Dover.)

Chambers, Frank. 1988. *Hayden and His Men: being a selection of 108 photographs by William Henry Jackson of the United States Geological and Geographical Survey of the Territories for the years 1870–1878, Ferdinand V. Hayden, Geologist in Charge*. Dillsburg, PA: Francis Paul Geoscience Literature.

Champaign-Urbana News-Gazette, ed. 2007. *Chief Illiniwek: A Tribute to an Illinois Tradition*. Champaign: Sports Publishing.

Chappel, Janet. 2002. *The Traveler's Yellowstone Treasures: Companion to the National Park*. Providence, RI: Granite Peak.

Chase, Alston. 2001. *In a Dark Wood: The Fight over Forests and the Myths of Nature.* New Brunswick, NJ: Transaction.

_____. 1986. *Playing God in Yellowstone: The Destruction of America's First National Park.* New York: Atlantic Monthly.

Christensen, Bonnie. 2002. *Red Lodge and the Mythic West: Coal Miners to Cowboys.* Lawrence: University of Kansas Press.

Christian, Shirley. 2004. *Before Lewis and Clark: The Story of the Chouteaus, the French Dynasty That Ruled America's Frontier.* New York: Farrar, Straus and Giroux.

Christians, Clifford G. 2005. "Ethics and Politics in Qualitative Research." Pp. 139-64 in N. K. Denzin and Y. S. Lincoln, eds., *Handbook of Qualitative Research,* 3d ed. Thousand Oaks, CA: Sage.

Christofferson, April. 2007. "Setting the Record Straight: Native Americans and Yellowstone, Past, Present, and Future." *Yellowstone Discovery* 22 (fall): 1–6.

Chittenden, Hiram Martin.1964. *The Yellowstone Park.* Edited and with an introduction by Richard A. Bartlett. Norman: University of Oklahoma Press. (Originally published 1895.)

Churchill, Ward. 1992. *Fantasies of the Master Race: Literature, Cinema, and the Colonization of American Indians.* Monroe, ME.: Common Courage.

Clark, Charles G. 2002. *The Men of the Lewis and Clark Expedition.* With an introduction by Dayton Duncan. Lincoln: University of Nebraska Press. (Originally published 1970.)

Clark, Ella E., and Margot Edmonds. 1979. *Sacagawea of the Lewis and Clark Expedition.* Los Angeles and Berkeley: University of California Press.

Conquergood, Dwight. 1998. "Beyond the Text: Toward a Performative Cultural Politics." Pp. 25–36 in S. J. Dailey, ed., *The Future of Performance Studies: Visions and Revisions.* Annandale, VA: National Communication Association.

_____. 1985. "Performing as a Moral Act: Ethical Dimensions of the Ethnography of Performance." *Literature in Performance* 5: 1–13.

Cook, Charles W. 1870. "The Valley of the Upper Yellowstone." *Western Monthly Magazine* 4 (July): 60–67.

Cook-Lynn, Elizabeth. 2007. *New Indians, Old Wars.* Urbana: University of Illinois Press.

_____. 2001. *Anti-Indianism in Modern America: A Voice from Tatekeya's Earth.* Urbana: University of Illinois Press.

_____. 1996. *Why I Can't Read Wallace Stegner and Other Essays.* Madison: University of Wisconsin Press.

Coues, Elliot, ed. 1965. *History of the Expedition under the Command of Lewis and Clark.* 3 vols. New York: Dover. (Reprint of 1893 Francis P. Harper 4-vol. ed.)

Cowan, Mrs. George. F. 1979. "Reminiscences of Pioneer Life: A Trip to the National Park in 1877--An Account of the Nez Perce Raid from a Woman's Standpoint-- Incidents and Accidents." Pp. 3–25 in Paul Schullery, ed., *Old Yellowstone Days*. Niwot: University Press of Colorado. (Originally published in *Wonderland* 12, March 1904.)

Crue, Cyd A. 2002. "White Racism/Redface Minstrels: Regimes of Power in Representation." Ph.D. diss., Department of Sociology, University of Illinois at Urbana-Champaign.

D'Arc, James V. 2001. "A. B. Guthrie Jr. in Hollywood: Variations on the Writing Experience." Pp. 73–103 in W. E. Farr and W. W. Bevis, eds., *Fifty Years after "The Big Sky": New Perspectives on the Fiction and Films of A. B. Guthrie Jr*. Helena: Montana Historical Society.

Davis, Susan G. 1997. *Spectacular Nature: Corporate Culture and the Sea World Experience*. Berkeley: University of California Press.

Davis, William T., ed. 1908. *Bradford's History of Plymouth Plantation: 1606–1646*. New York: Scribner's.

Deloria, Philip J. 2004. *Indians in Unexpected Places*. Lawrence: University of Kansas Press.

_____. 1998. *Playing Indian*. New Haven: Yale University Press.

Denzin, Norman K. 2008. "Drawn to Yellowstone: Jay Cooke's Railroad and Thomas Moran's *Grand Canyon of the Yellowstone*." *Qualitative Research* 8: forthcoming.

_____. 2007a. *Flags in the Window: Dispatches from the American War Zone*. New York: Peter Lang.

_____. 2007b. "Sacagawea's Nickname, or the Sacagawea Problem." *Qualitative Research* 7: 103–134.

_____. 2005a. "Emancipatory Discourses and the Politics of Interpretation." Pp. 933–58 in N. K. Denzin and Y. S. Lincoln, eds., *Handbook of Qualitative Research*, 3d ed. Thousand Oaks, CA: Sage.

_____. 2005b. "Indians in the Park." *Qualitative Research* 3: 9–33.

_____. 2004. "Remembering to Forget: Lewis and Clark and Native Americans in Yellowstone." *Communication and Critical/Cultural Studies* 1 (September): 219–49.

_____. 2003a. *Performing Ethnography: Critical Pedagogy and the Politics of Culture*. Thousand Oaks, CA: Sage.

_____. 2003b. "Redskins and Chiefs." *Cultural Studies/Critical Methodologies* 3: 262–80.

_____. 2002a. "Cowboys and Indians." *Symbolic Interaction* 25: 251–61.

_____. 2002b. *Reading Race: Hollywood and the Cinema of Racial Violence*. London: Sage.

_____. 2000a. "Rock Creek History." *Symbolic Interaction* 23: 71–8l.

Denzin, Norman K., and Yvonna S. Lincoln. 2003. "Introduction: 9/11 in American Culture." Pp. xiii–xxi in N. K. Denzin and Y. S. Lincoln, eds., *9/11 in American Culture*. Walnut Creek, CA: AltaMira.

_____. 2000b. "Searching for Yellowstone." *Symbolic Interaction* 26: 181–93.

DeVoto, Bernard. 1998. *Across the Wide Missouri*. New York: Houghton Mifflin. (Originally published 1947.)

_____, ed. 1997. *The Journals of Lewis and Clark*. New York: Houghton Mifflin. (Originally published 1953.)

_____. 1958. *The Course of Empire*. Boston: Houghton Mifflin.

_____. 1936. "Passage to India: From Christmas to Christmas with Lewis and Clark." *Saturday Review of Literature* 15 (December): 3–4, 20, 24, 28. (Reprinted in J. P. Ronda, ed., *Voyage of Discovery: Essays on the Lewis and Clark Expedition*, 89–100. Helena: Montana Historical Society, 1998.)

Dewey, John. 1927. *The Public and Its Problems*. New York: Henry Holt.

Dickinson, Greg, Brian L. Ott, and Eric Aoki. 2005. "Memory and Myth at the Buffalo Bill Museum." *Western Journal of Communication* 69 (April): 85–108.

Dominick, David. 1964. "The Sheepeaters." *Annals of Wyoming* 36 (2): 132–68.

Dorst, John D. 1999. *Looking West*. Philadelphia: University of Pennsylvania Press.

Dos Passos, John. 1937. *U.S.A.: I. The Forty-Second Parallel; II. Nineteen Nineteen; III. The Big Money*. New York: Modern Library.

Doyle, Brian. 2007. "What's It Like to Live in the West? *High Country News* 39 (1 October): 27.

Du Bois, W. E. B. 1969. *Darkwater: Voices from within the Veil*. New York: Schocken. (Originally published 1920.)

_____. 1989. *The Souls of Black Folk*. New York: Bantam (Originally published 1903.)

Duncan, Dayton. 2002. Introduction to the Bison Books Edition. Pp. v–xix in Charles G. Clarke, *The Men of the Lewis and Clark Expedition*. Lincoln: University of Nebraska Press. (Original Clarke book published 1970.)

Dye, Eva Emery. 1902. *The Conquest: The True Story of Lewis and Clark*. Chicago: C. McClung.

Dylan, Bob. 2004. *Chronicles*. Vol. 1. New York: Simon & Schuster.

Ebert, Roger. 2001a. "New Thoughts on the Chief." *Daily Illini* (University of Illinois at Urbana-Champaign), 20 March: 8.

_____. 2001b. "Noble Spirit More Than Just a Mascot." *Daily Illini* (University of Illinois at Urbana-Champaign), 7 March: 10.

Ehrlich, Gretel. 1988. "River History." Pp. 69–72 in W. Kittridge, ed., *Montana Spaces: Essays in Celebration of Montana*. New York: Lyons & Burford.

Ellison, Ralph. 1996. "A Coupla Scalped Indians." Pp. 63–81 in R. Ellison, *Flying Home*. New York: Vintage. (Originally published 1956 in *New World Writing*.)

Emerson, Ralph Waldo. 1836. *Nature*. Boston: J. Monroe.

Erdrich, Louise. 1993. *Love Medicine*. New York: HarperCollins.

Everhart, Bill. 1998. *Take Down the Flag and Feed the Horses*. Urbana: University of Illinois Press.

Fanselow, Julie. 1998. *Traveling the Lewis and Clark Trail*. Helena, MT: Falcon.

Farabee, Charles R. "Butch," Jr. 2003. *National Park Ranger: An American Icon*. Lanham, MD: Roberts Rinehart.

Farnell, Brenda. 1998. "Retire the Chief." *Anthropology Newsletter* 39 (4): 1, 4.

Farr, William E., and William W. Bevis, eds. 2001. Introduction. Pp. 1–8 in W. E. Farr and W. W. Bevis, eds., *Fifty Years after "The Big Sky": New Perspectives on the Fiction and Films of A. B. Guthrie Jr.* Helena: Montana Historical Society.

Fenn, Elizabeth A. 2001. *Pox Americana: The Great Smallpox Epidemic of 1775–82*. New York: Hill and Wang.

Fiedler, Leslie. 1988. "The Montana Face." Pp. 744–52 in W. Kittredge and A. Smith, eds., *The Last Best Place: A Montana Anthology*. Seattle: University of Washington Press.

———. 1971a. "Montana, or the End of Jean-Jacques Rousseau." Pp. 133–41 in *The Collected Essays of Leslie Fiedler*, vol. 1. New York: Stein and Day. (Originally published in December 1949 *Partisan Review* as "Montana.")

———. 1971b. "Montana: P.S." Pp. 331–36 in *The Collected Essays of Leslie Fiedler*, vol. 2. New York: Stein and Day.

———. 1971c. "Montana: P.P.S." Pp. 337–42 in *The Collected Essays of Leslie Fiedler*, vol. 2. New York: Stein and Day.

Fifer, Barbara, and Vicky Soderberg. 2001. *Along the Trail with Lewis and Clark*. 2d ed. Helena, MT: Farcountry.

Finch, Robert, and John Elder, eds. 1990. *The Norton Reader of Nature Writing*. New York: Norton.

Fitzgerald, F. Scott. 1925. *The Great Gatsby*. New York: Scribner's.

Fitzgerald, Mary. 2007. Letter to Editor: "Rethinking Our Mascot." *Carbon County News*, 4 October: 4.

Foley, Douglas E. 1995. *The Heartland Chronicles*. Philadelphia: University of Pennsylvania Press.

Fradin, Judith Bloom, and Dennis Brindell Fradin. 2002. *Who Was Sacagawea?* New York: Grossett & Dunlap.

Franscell, Ron. 2002. "Smallpox 'Holocaust' Haunts Indians." *Denver Post*, 13 October: A1.

Fredlund, Glen, Linea Sundstrom, and Rebecca Armstrong. 1996. "Crazy Mule's Maps of the Upper Missouri, 1877–80." *Plains Anthropologist* 41 (155): 5–27.

Freire, Paulo. 2001. *Pedagogy of the Oppressed*. Thirtieth anniversary edition, with an introduction by Donaldo Macedo. New York: Continuum.

Freire, Paulo. 1999. *Pedagogy of Hope*. New York: Continuum. (Originally published 1992.)

_____. 1998. *Pedagogy of Freedom: Ethics, Democracy, and Civic Courage*. Translated by Patrick Clarke, foreword by Donaldo Macedo, introduction by Stanley Aronowitz. Boulder, CO: Roman & Littlefield.

Fulsang, Deborah. 2003. "Beyond Blankets." *Globe and Mail*, 11 October: L1, L5.

Garceau. Dee. 2001. "Meditations on Women in *The Big Sky*." Pp. 119–56 in W. E. Farr and W. W. Bevis, eds., *Fifty Years after "The Big Sky": New Perspectives on the Fiction and Films of A. B. Guthrie Jr*. Helena: Montana Historical Society.

Gilman, Carolyn. 2003. *Lewis and Clark across the Divide*. With an introduction by James P. Ronda. Washington, DC: Smithsonian Books in association with Missouri Historical Society.

Goddard, Donald. 1980. "Shaped from Earth, Immortalized in Bronze: Sculptor Harry Jackson's *Sacagawea*." *The American West* 17 (March/April): 14–15, 56.

Goodall, Harold Lloyd, Jr. 2006. *A Need to Know: The Clandestine History of a CIA Family*. Walnut Creek, CA: Left Coast.

Graetz, Rick. 1997. "Sojurn to the Sky: The Beartooth Highway." *Montana Magazine*, July/August: 18–26.

Grandy, Sandy. 2000. "American Indian Identity and Intellectualism: The Quest for a New Red Pedagogy." *Qualitative Studies in Education* 13: 343–60.

Gray, Lyle C., and Eleanor Jones Harvey. 1999. "Carl Rungius in Context." *Antiques* (November): 1–3.

Green, Rayna. 1975. "The Pocahontas Perplex: The Image of Indian Women in American Culture." *Massachusetts Review* 16 (autumn): 698–714.

Grossman, Elizabeth. 2003. *Adventuring along the Lewis and Clark Trail*. San Francisco: Sierra Club.

Guthrie, A. B., Jr. 1982. *Fair Land, Fair Land*. Boston: Houghton Mifflin.

_____. 1947. *The Big Sky*. New York: William Sloane.

Haines, Aubrey L. 1996a. *The Yellowstone Story: A History of Our First National Park*. Rev. ed. Vol. 1. Yellowstone National Park, WY: Yellowstone Association. (Originally published 1977.)

_____. 1996b. *The Yellowstone Story: A History of Our First National Park*. Rev. ed. Vol. 2. Yellowstone National Park, WY: Yellowstone Association. (Originally published 1977.)

_____. 1972. Foreword. Pp. vii–xxi in N. P. Langford, *The Discovery of Yellowstone Park*. Lincoln: University of Nebraska Press.

Hall, Brian. 2003. *I Should Be Extremely Happy in Your Company: A Novel of Lewis and Clark*. New York: Viking.

Hall, Stuart. 1997. "What Is This 'Black' in Black Popular Culture?" Pp. 123–34 in V. Smith, ed., *Representing Blackness: Issues in Film and Video*. New Brunswick, NJ: Rutgers University Press.

Harrington, Walt. 2002. *The Everlasting Stream*. New York: Atlantic Monthly.

Hartnett, Stephen. 2003. *Incarceration Nation: Investigative Prison Poems of Hope and Terror*. Walnut Creek, CA: AltaMira.

Hassrick, Peter H. 2005. "Artists in America's First National Park." *Points West* (magazine of the Buffalo Bill Historical Center, Cody, WY), spring: 15–18.

_____. 2002. *Drawn to Yellowstone: Artists in America's First National Park*. Seattle: University of Washington Press.

Hayden, Ferdinand V. 1876. *The Yellowstone National Park, and the Mountain Regions of Portions of Idaho, Nevada, Colorado, and Utah*. Illustrated by Chromolithographic Reproductions of Water-Color Sketches of Thomas Moran, Artist to the Expedition of 1871. Boston: L. Prang. (Reprint: Tulsa, OK: Gilcrease Museum Association, 1997.)

_____. 1872. "The Wonders of the West II: More about the Yellowstone." *Scribner's Monthly* 3 (February): 388–96.

Haynes, Jack Ellis. 1953. *Haynes Guide: Yellowstone National Park*. 54th rev. ed. Bozeman, MT: Haynes Studios.

_____. 1947. *Haynes Guide: Yellowstone National Park*. 49th rev. ed. Bozeman, MT: Haynes Studios.

Heat-Moon, William Least. 1999. *River Horse: A Voyage across America*. Boston: Houghton Mifflin.

Hill, William E. 2001. *Following Lewis and Clark's Track: The Story of the Corps of Discovery*. Independence, MO: Oregon-California Trails Association.

hooks, bell. 1999. *Remembered Rapture*. New York: Henry Holt.

Horton, Sidney. 2003. "Keeping Their Legacy Alive." Illustrations by Jack Molloy and John James Audubon. *Audubon* (March): 90–93.

Hosmer, James K. 1903. *History of the Expedition of Captains Lewis, and Clark, 1804-5-6*. 2 vols. Chicago: A. C. McClurg.

House, Marguerite. 2005. "Yellowstone Draws Artists." *Points West* (magazine of the Buffalo Bill Historical Center, Cody, WY), spring: 16.

Hoxie, Frederick E. 2006. "The Story from Indian Country: What We Learned from the Lewis and Clark Bicentennial." *Montana: The Magazine of Western History* 56 (autumn): 38–46.

Huhndorf, Shari M. 2001. *Going Native: Indians in the American Cultural Imagination*. Ithaca, NY: Cornell University Press.

Hultkrantz, Ake. 1979. "The Fear of Geysers among Indians in the Yellowstone Park Area. Pp. 33–45 in Leslie B. Davis, ed., *Life-ways of Intermontane and Plains Montana Indians*. Occasion Papers of the Museum of the Rockies, no. 1. Bozeman, MT: Museum of the Rockies.

Hunsaker, Joyce Badgley. 2003. *They Call Me Sacagawea*. Guilford, CT: Globe Pequot.

_____. 2001. *Sacagawea Speaks beyond the Shining Mountains with Lewis and Clark*. Guilford, CT: Globe Pequot.

Hyde, John. 1887. *Official Guide to the Yellowstone National Park: A Manual for Tourists, Being a Description of the Mammoth Hot Springs, The Geyser Basins, The Cataracts, the Canons, and Other Features of the New Wonderland*. Rev. ed. St. Paul: Northern News.[1]

Irving,Washington. 1977. *The Adventures of Captain Bonneville*. Edited and with an introduction by Robert A. Ross and Alan Sandy. Boston: Twayne. (Originally published 1837.)

_____. 1964. *Astoria, or Anecdotes of an Enterprise beyond the Rocky Mountains*. Edited and with an introduction by Edgeley W. Todd. Norman: University of Oklahoma Press. (Originally published 1836.)

Jackson, Donald. 1987. *Among Sleeping Giants: Occasional Pieces on Lewis and Clark*. Urbana: University of Illinois Press.

Jackson, Donald, ed. 1978. *Letters of the Lewis and Clark Expedition*. 2d. ed. 2 vols. Urbana: University of Illinois Press.

Jackson, Donald, ed. 1962. *Letters of the Lewis and Clark Expedition with Related Documents, 1783–1854*. Urbana: University of Illinois Press.

Jackson, William Henry. 1940. *Time Exposure: The Autobiography of William Henry Jackson*. New York: Putnam's.

Jackson, William Henry, and Howard R. Diggs. 1929. *Pioneer Photographer: Rocky Mountain Adventures with a Camera*. Yonkers-on-Hudson, NY: World.

Janetski, Joel C. 2002. *Indians in Yellowstone National Park*. Rev. ed. Salt Lake City: University of Utah Press.

Jefferson, Thomas. 1807. "To William Henry Jackson." Pp. 344–45 in A. A. Lipscomb and A. E. Bergh, eds., *Writings of Thomas Jefferson*, vol. 2, Washington, DC, 1903–1904. Quoted in Mark Spence. 2003. "Historical Commentary: The Unnatural History of the Lewis and Clark Bicentennial." *Montana: The Magazine of Western History* 53 (summer): 60.

_____. 1803. "To Andrew Jackson, 16 February 1803." P. 357 in A. A. Lipscomb and A. E. Bergh, eds., *Writings of Thomas Jefferson*, vol. 10. Washington, DC, 1903–1904. Quoted in Mark Spence. 2003. "Historical Commentary: The Unnatural History of the Lewis and Clark Bicentennial." *Montana: The Magazine of Western History* 53 (summer): 59.

_____. 1785. *Notes on the State of Virginia*. Edited by William Peden. New York: Norton, 1972.

_____. 1776. The Declaration of Independence, A Transcription in Congress, July 4, 1776.

Josephson, Matthew. 1962. *The Robber Barons: The Great American Capitalists, 1861–1901*. New York: Harcourt, Brace & World.

Kammen, Michael. 1993. "The Problem of American Exceptionalism: A Reconsideration." *American Quarterly* 45 (March): 1–33.

Kessler, Donna J. 1996. *The Making of Sacagawea: A Euro-American Legend*. Tuscaloosa and London: University of Alabama Press.

Kimmelman, Michael. 2006. Art Review: "American Idyll: Homer, Church, and Moran: Sharp-eyed Guides to the Dawn of Tourism." *New York Times*, 19 May: B29, B32.

King, C. Richard, and Charles Fruehling Springwood. 2001. *Beyond the Cheers: Race as Spectacle in College Sport*. Albany: State University of New York Press.

Kinsey, Joni Louise. 2006. E-mail correspondence with Norman K. Denzin: Moran Painting. 31 January.

_____. 1997. "Moran and the Art of Publishing." Pp. 300–321 in N. Anderson, ed., *Thomas Moran*. New Haven and Washington, DC: Yale University Press and National Gallery of Art.

_____. 1992. *Thomas Moran and the Surveying of the American West*. Washington, DC: Smithsonian Institution.

Kittridge, William. 2000. *The Nature of Generosity*. New York: Knopf.

_____. 1999. *Taking Care*. Minneapolis: Milkwood Editions.

_____, ed. 1997. *The Portable Western Reader*. New York: Penguin.

_____. 1996. *Who Owns the West?* San Francisco: Murray House.

_____. 1992. *Hole in the Sky: A Memoir*. New York: Vintage.

_____. 1987. *Owning It All*. San Francisco: Murray House.

Kittridge, William, and Annick Smith, eds. 1988. *The Last Best Place: A Montana Anthology*. Seattle: University of Washington Press.

Lampi, Leona. 1998. *At the Foot of the Beartooth Mountains*. Coeur d'Alene, ID: Bookage.

Langford, Nathaniel Pitt. 1972. *The Discovery of Yellowstone Park*. Lincoln: University of Nebraska Press. (Originally published 1905.)

_____. 1871. "The Wonders of the Yellowstone." *Scribner's Monthly* 2 (May): 1–17; (June): 113–28.

Lear, Jonathan. 2006. *Radical Hope: Ethics in the Face of Cultural Devastation*. Cambridge: Harvard University Press.

Leopold, Aldo. 1949. *A Sand County Almanac: And Sketches Here and There*. New York: Oxford University Press.

Lewis, Meriwether.1808. "Essay on an Indian Policy." Pp. 1215–43 in Elliott Coues, ed., *History of the Expedition under the Command of Lewis and Clark*, 3 vols. New York: Dover Publications, 1965. (Reprint of 1893 Francis P. Harper 4-vol. ed.)

———. 1806. "Letter: [Clark] Lewis to Hugh Henry, 20 July 1806." Pp. 309–313 in Donald Jackson, ed., *Letters of the Lewis and Clark Expedition with Related Documents, 1783–1854*. Urbana: University of Illinois Press, 1962.

———. 1803. "Memorandum on Packing and Summary of Purchases, 30 June 1803." Pp. 92–99 in Donald Jackson, ed., *Letters of the Lewis and Clark Expedition with Related Documents, 1783–1854*. Urbana: University of Illinois Press, 1962.

Liljeblad, Sven. 1959. "Indian Peoples of Idaho." Pp. 29–59 in M. D. Beal and M. W. Wells, eds., *History of Idaho*. New York: Lewis Historical Publishing.

Limerick, Patricia Nelson. 2001. "Seeing and Being Seen: Tourism in the American West." Pp. 39–58 in D. M. Wrobel, and P. T. Long, eds., *Seeing and Being Seen: Tourism in the American West*. Lawrence: University of Kansas Press.

———. 2000. *Something in the Soil: Legacies and Reckonings in the New West*. New York: Norton.

———. 1997. "Explaining Ourselves: Jefferson, History, and the Changing West." Pp. 185–94 in J. P. Ronda, ed., *Thomas Jefferson and the Changing West: From Conquest to Conservation*. Albuquerque: University of New Mexico Press.

Loendorf, Lawrence L, and Nancy Medaris Stone. 2006. *Mountain Spirit: The Sheep Eater Indians of Yellowstone*. Salt Lake City: University of Utah Press.

Lowry, Thomas P. 2005. *Venereal Disease and the Lewis and Clark Expedition*. Lincoln: University of Nebraska Press.

Lubetkin, M. John. 2006. *Jay Cooke's Gamble: The Northern Pacific Railroad, the Sioux, and the Panic of 1873*. Norman: University of Oklahoma Press.

Madison, S. Soyini. 2005. *Critical Ethnography*. Thousand Oaks, CA: Sage.

———. 1999. "Performing Theory/Embodied Writing." *Text and Performance Quarterly* 19: 107–124.

Mailer, Norman. 2003. "Only in America." *New York Review of Books* 50 (27 March): 49–53.

Mayor, Adrienne. 1995. "The Nessus Shirt in the New World: Smallpox Blankets in History and Legend." *Journal of American Folklore* 108 (winter): 54–77.

McMurtry, Larry. 2001. *Sacagawea's Nickname: Essays on the American West*. New York: New York Review of Books.

———. 1999. *Walter Benjamin at the Dairy Queen: Reflections at Sixty and Beyond*. New York: Simon & Schuster.

Metcalf, Ben. 2002. "Wooden Dollar: The Undiscovered Sacajawea." *Harper's* 305 (December): 59–63.

Miller, Arthur. 1949. *Death of a Salesman*. New York: Viking.

Mills, Enos A. 1915. *Rocky Mountain Wonderland*. New York: Doubleday, Page.

Mills, C. Wright. 1959. *The Sociological Imagination*. New York: Oxford University Press.

Monaghan, Peter. 2002. "At 100, the Western Still Spurs Scholars." *Chronicle of Higher Education* 13 (December): A12–A14.

Moran, Thomas. 1871. "Thomas Moran's Yellowstone Diary." Yellowstone National Park: National Park Service, 22 December 2004: http:/www.nps.gov/yell/historyculture//thomasmoransdiary.htm.

Morand, Anne. 1996. "The Artistic Side of the Trip." Pp. 11–100 in A. Morand, *Thomas Moran: The Field Sketches, 1856–1923*. Norman: University of Oklahoma Press.

Moulton, Gary, ed. 2003. *The Lewis and Clark Expedition, An American Epic of Discovery: The Abridgement of the Definitive Nebraska Edition Meriwether Lewis and William Clark, and Members of the Corps of Discovery*. Lincoln: University of Nebraska Press.

———. 1983–2001. *The Journals of the Lewis and Clark Expedition*. 13 vols. Lincoln: University of Nebraska Press.

Muir, John. 1979. "The Yellowstone National Park." Pp. 39–74 in Paul Schullery, ed., *Old Yellowstone Days*. Niwot: University Press of Colorado. (Originally published 1898 in *Atlantic Monthly*; reprinted in J. Muir, *Our National Parks*, 1901.)

———. 1901. *Our National Parks*. New York: Houghton Mifflin.

Nabokov, Peter. 2006. *Where the Lighting Strikes: The Lives of American Indian Sacred Places*. New York: Penguin.

Nabokov, Peter, and Lawrence Loendorf. 2004. *Restoring a Presence: Americans and Yellowstone National Park*. Norman: University of Oklahoma Press.

Nagel, Joanne. 2001. Racial, Ethnic, and National Boundaries: Sexual Intersections and Symbolic Interactions." *Symbolic Interaction* 24: 123–39.

Nash, Roderick. 1982. *Wilderness and the American Mind*. 3d ed. New Haven: Yale University Press.

National Gallery of Art. 1997. "Thomas Moran." http/www.nga.gov/feature/moran/new11.shtm.

Nelson, Richard. 1983. *Make Prayers to the Raven: A Koyukon View of the Northern Forest*. Chicago: University of Chicago Press.

Newman, Peter C. 1989. *Empire of the Bay: An Illustrated History of Hudson's Bay Company*. New York: Viking Penguin.

New York Times. 2003. Editorial: "The Land of Lewis and Clark." *New York Times*, 10 August: 10.

Norris, Philetus W. 1880. *Annual Report of the Superintendent of the Yellowstone National Park to the Secretary of the Interior, Year 1880*. Washington, DC: U.S. Government Printing Office.

Norton, Henry J. 1873. *Wonder-Land Illustrated: Or Horseback Rides through the Yellowstone National Park*. Virginia City, NV: No publisher.

Oberholtzer, Ellis Paxson. 1907. *Jay Cooke: Financier of the Civil War*. Vol. 2. Philadelphia: George W. Jacobs.

Olp, Susan. 2000. "Montana Day Joins the Fiftieth Festival of Nations." *Billings Gazette*, 8 August: 2A–2B.

Orvis Company. 2003. *Men's Clothing Holiday 2003 Catalog*. Vol. 1. Manchester, VT: Orvis Company.

Persons, Stow. 1958. *American Minds: A History of Ideas*. New York: Henry Holt.

Pomeroy, Earl. 1957. *In Search of the Golden West: The Tourist in Western America*. Lincoln: University of Nebraska Press.

Prochaska, David. 2001. "At Home in Illinois: Presence of Chief Illiniwek." Pp. 157–88 in C. R. King and C. F. Springwood, eds., *Team Spirits: The Native American Mascots Controversy*. Lincoln: University of Nebraska Press.

Pyne, Stephen J. 1998. *How the Canyon Became Grand*. New York: Viking.

Rawlins, C. L. 1994. "The Meadow at the Corner of Your Eye." Pp. 389–95 in D. Clow and D. Snow, eds., *Northern Lights: A Selection of New Writing from the American West*. New York: Vintage.

Reddin, Paul. 1999. *Wild West Shows*. Urbana: University of Illinois Press.

Reinhart, Karen Wildung. 2004. "Old Faithful Inn: Centennial of a Beloved Landmark." *Yellowstone Science* 12 (spring): 5–22.

Richarsdson, Heather Cox. 2007. *West from Appomattox: The Reconstruction of America after the Civil War*. New Haven: Yale University Press.

Richardson, Laurel. 2001. "Poetic Representation of Interviews." Pp. 877–92 in J. F. Gubrium and J. A. Holstein, eds., *Handbook of Interview Research*. Thousand Oaks, CA: Sage.

———. 2000. "Writing: A Method of Inquiry." Pp. 923–48 in N. K. Denzin and Y. S. Lincoln, eds., *Handbook of Qualitative Research*, 2d ed. Thousand Oaks, CA: Sage.

Ring, Ray. 2001. "Bad Moon Rising: The Waning of Montana's Once-Mighty Progressive Coalition." *High Country News* 33 (17 December): 1, 10–13.

Ronda, James P., ed. 1998. *Voyages of Discovery: Essays on the Lewis and Clark Expedition*. Helena: Montana Historical Society.

———, ed. 1997. Introduction. *Thomas Jefferson and the Changing West: From Conquest to Conservation*. Albuquerque: University of New Mexico Press

———. 1984. *Lewis and Clark among the Indians*. Lincoln: University of Nebraska Press.

Roosevelt, Theodore. 1888. *Ranch Life and the Hunting Trail*. New York: Scribner's.

Rothman, Hal K. 1998. *Devil's Bargain: Tourism in the Twentieth-Century American West*. Lawrence: University of Kansas Press.

Rowland, Della. 1989. *The Story of Sacajawea: Guide to Lewis and Clark*. New York: Bantam Doubleday.

Runte, Alfred. 1998. *Trains of Discovery: Western Railroads and the National Parks*. 4th ed. Niwot, CO: Roberts Rinehart.

Runte, Alfred. 1997. *National Parks: The American Experience*. 3d ed. Lincoln: University of Nebraska Press. (Originally published 1979.)

Ruskin, John. 1847. *Modern Painters*. 5 vols. New York: Wiley.

Sanders, Jeffrey. 2000. Review of *Indian Country, God's Country: Native Americans and the National Parks* by Philip Burnham. *American Indian Culture and Research Journal* 24 (4): 198.

Saunders, Richard L. 2003. "Yellowstone in Fictional Literature: Themes and Ideas." Pp. ix–xv in R. L. Saunders, ed., *A Yellowstone Reader: The National Park in Folklore, Popular Fiction, and Verse*. Salt Lake City: University of Utah Press.

Schullery, Paul. 2002. *Lewis and Clark among the Grizzlies*. Helena, MT: Globe Pequot.

_____. 2001. "Privations and Inconveniences:" Early Tourism in Yellowstone Park." Pp. 227–47 in D. M. Wrobel, and P. T. Long, eds., *Seeing and Being Seen: Tourism in the American West*. Lawrence: University of Kansas Press.

_____. 1997. *Searching for Yellowstone: Ecology and Wonder in the Last Wilderness*. Boston: Houghton Mifflin.

_____. 1994. *Mountain Time: A Yellowstone Memoir*. Boulder, CO: Roberts Rinehart.

_____, ed. 1979a. *Old Yellowstone Days*. Niwot: University Press of Colorado.

_____. 1979b. "Introduction: 1: Mrs. George Cowan, 1877." Pp. 1–2 in Paul Schullery, ed., 1979a.

_____. 1979c. "Introduction: 4: Owen Wister, 1887." Pp. 65–66 in Paul Schullery, ed., 1979a.

Schullery, Paul, and Lee Whittlesey. 2003. *Myth and History in the Creation of Yellowstone National Park*. Lincoln: University of Nebraska Press.

Senior, Dawn. 1997. "Never Alone." Pp. 335–36 in L. Hasselstrom, G. Collier, and N. Curtis, eds., *Leaning into the Wind: Women Write from the Heart of the West*. New York: Houghton Mifflin.

Shaffer, Marguerite S. 2001. *See America First: Tourism and National Identity, 1880–1940*. Washington, DC: Smithsonian Institution.

Sheldon, G. W. 1879. *American Painters*. New York: Appleton.

Shepard, Paul, and Barry Sanders. 1985. *The Sacred Paw: The Bear in Nature, Myth, and Literature*. New York: Viking.

Shepard, Sam 1981. *True West*. Pp. 1–60 in *Sam Shepard: Seven Plays*. New York: Bantam.

Silliman, Eugene Lee. 2003. Introduction. Pp. 1–29 in E. L. Silliman, ed., *A Ride to the Infernal Regions: Yellowstone's First Tourists* by Calvin C. Clawson. Helena, MT.: Riverbend.

Slaughter, Thomas P. 2003. *Exploring Lewis and Clark: Reflections on Men and Wilderness*. New York: Knopf.

Slotkin, Richard. 1992. *Gunfighter Nation: The Myth of the Frontier in Twentieth-Century America*. New York: Atheneum.

Smith, Anna Deavere. 2004. *House Arrest and Piano*. New York: Anchor.

_____. 2000. *Talk to Me: Listening between the Lines*. New York: Random House.

_____. 1994. *Twilight: Los Angeles, 1992*. New York: Doubleday.

_____. 1993. *Fires in the Mirror*. New York: Doubleday.

Smith, Diane. 1999. *Letters from Yellowstone*. New York: Penguin.

Smith, Linda Tuhiwai. 1999. *Decolonizing Methodologies: Research and Indigenous Peoples*. Dunedin, New Zealand: University of Otago Press.

Smith, Valerie, ed. 1997. Introduction. Pp. 1–12 in *Representing Blackness: Issues in film and Video*. New Brunswick, NJ: Rutgers University Press.

Spence, Mark. 2003. "Historical Commentary: The Unnatural History of the Lewis and Clark Bicentennial." *Montana: The Magazine of Western History* 53 (summer): 56–63.

_____. 1999. *Dispossessing the Wilderness: Indian Removal and the Making of the National Parks*. New York: Oxford University Press.

Spindel, Carol. 2000. *Dancing at Halftime: Sports and the Controversy over American Indian Mascots*. New York: New York University Press.

Stegner, Wallace. 1992. *Where the Bluebird Sings to the Lemonade Springs: Living and Writing in the West*. New York: Random House.

_____. 1983. "The Best Idea We Ever Had." *Wilderness* 46 (spring): 4.

_____. 1980. *The Sound of Mountain Water*. New York: Penguin.

_____. 1979. *Recapitulation*. New York: Doubleday.

_____. 1965. Foreword. Pp. vii–xii in A. B. Guthrie Jr., *The Big Sky*. Sentry ed. Boston: Houghton Mifflin.

_____. 1962. *Wolf Willow: A History, a Story, and a Memory of the Last Plains Frontier*. New York: Viking.

_____. 1954. *Beyond the Hundredth Meridian: John Wesley Powell and the Second Opening of the West*. With an introduction by Bernard DeVoto. New York: Penguin.

_____. 1943. *The Big Rock Candy Mountain*. New York: Doubleday.

Stein, Roger. 1967. *John Ruskin and Aesthetic Thought in America: 1840–1900*. Cambridge: Harvard University Press.

Strong, William E. 1876. *A Trip to the Yellowstone National Park in July, August, and September, 1875*. Edited by Richard Bartlett. Norman: University of Oklahoma Press.

Stuebner, Stephen. 1999. "Jon Marvel vs. the Marlboro Man." *High Country News*, 2 August: 1, 8–9.

Sundstrom, Linea, and Glen Fredlund. 1999. "The Crazy Mule Maps: A Northern Cheyenne's View of Montana and Western Dakota in 1878." *Montana: The Magazine of Western History* 49 (spring): 46–57.

Sutter, Paul S. 2002. *Driven Wild: How the Fight against Automobiles Launched the Modern Wilderness Movement*. Foreword by William Cronon. Seattle: University of Washington Press.

Sutton, Ann, and Myron Sutton.1972. *Yellowstone: A Century of the Wilderness Idea*. New York: Macmillan.

Taibo, Pacio Ignacio II. 2003. *Returning as Shadows*. Translated by Ezra E. Fitz. New York: St. Martin's.

Taylor, Alan. 2001. *American Colonies: The Settling of North America*. New York: Viking Penguin.

Taylor, Charles. 2007. "A Different Kind of Courage": review of Jonathan Lear, *Radical Hope: Ethics in the Face of Cultural Devastation*. *New York Review of Books* 54 (April): 4–8.

Thoreau, Henry David. 1982. *The Portable Thoreau* Edited by Carl Bode. New York: Penguin.

———. 1854. *Walden: Or Life in the Woods*. Boston: Ticknor and Fields.

Thwaites, Reuben Gold, ed. 1904–1905. *Original Journals of the Lewis and Clark Expedition*. New York: Arno reprint, 1969. (Original publisher: Washington, DC: Government Printing Office, 1904, reprinted from the Annual Report of the American Historical Association for year 1903, vol. 1, 105–129).

Tinling, Marion. 2001. *Sacagawea's Son: The Life of Jean Baptiste Charbonneau*. Missoula, MT: Mountain.

Tompkins, Jane. 1992. *West of Everything: The Inner Life of Westerns*. New York: Oxford University Press.

Trachtenberg. Alan. 2004. *Shades of Hiawatha: Staging Indians, Making Americans, 1880–1930*. New York: Hill and Wang.

Trumbull, Walter. 1871. "The Washburn Yellowstone Expedition, No. II." *Overland Monthly* 6 (June): 496.

Turner, Erin H. 2003. *It Happened on the Lewis and Clark Expedition*. Helena, MT: Globe Pequot.

Turner, Frederick Jackson. 1920. *The Frontier in American History*. New York: Holt, Rinehart and Winston.

Turner, Victor. 1986a. "Dewey, Dilthey, and Drama: An Essay in the Anthropology of Experience." Pp. 33–44 in V. M. Turner and E. M. Bruner, eds., *The Anthropology of Experience*. Urbana: University of Illinois Press.

———. 1986b. *The Anthropology of Performance*. New York: Performing Arts Journal.

———. 1982. *From Ritual to Theatre*. New York: Performing Arts Journal.

Ulmer, Gregory. 1989. *Teletheory: Grammatology in the Age of Video*. New York: Routledge.

Updike, John. 2006. "Love of Fact": review of *Treasures from Olana: Landscapes by Frederic Edwin Church*, exhibition at the National Academy Museum, New York, 9 February–30 April 2006. *New York Review of Books* 53 (23 March): 8, 10.

Utley, Robert M. 1997. *A Life Wild and Perilous: Mountain Men and the Paths to the Pacific*. New York: Henry Holt.

Vogel, Virgil J. 1972. *This Country Was Ours: A Documentary History of the American Indian*. New York: Harper & Row.

Volmann, William T. 2005. "Lewis and Clark on the Edge." *New York Times* Op-Ed (20 November): 12.

Waite, Thorton. 1997. *Yellowstone Branch of the Union Pacific: Route of the Yellowstone Special*. Columbia, MO: Bruggenjohann/Reese.

Waitley, Douglas. 1998. *William Henry Jackson: Framing the Frontier*. Missoula, MT.: Mountain.

Waldman, Carl. 1985. *Atlas of the North American Indian*. New York: Facts on File.

Waldo, Anna Lee. 1978. *Sacajawea*. New York: Avon.

Walker, Dale L. 2003. "York's Story." Pp. 47-66 in D. L. Walker, ed., *Westward: A Fictional History of the American West*. New York: Forge.

Wallace, Anthony F. C. 1999. *Jefferson and the Indians: The Tragic Fate of the First Americans*. Cambridge: Belknap Press of Harvard University Press.

Wallace, Anthony F. C. 1997. "'The Obtaining :Lands': Thomas Jefferson and the Native Americans." Pp. 25–42 in J. P. Ronda, ed., *Thomas Jefferson and the Changing West: From Conquest to Conservation*. Albuquerque: University of New Mexico Press.

Warren, Louis S. 2005. *Buffalo Bill's America: William Cody and the Wild West Show*. New York: Knopf.

Weems, Mary 2002. *I Speak from the Wound That Is My Mouth*. New York: Peter Lang.

Welch, James. 2000. *The Heartsong of Charging Elk*. New York: Doubleday.

Whitman, Walt. 1982. *Complete Poetry and Collected Prose*. New York: Library of America.

Whittlesey, Lee H. 2007. "The Nez Perce in Yellowstone in 1877." *Montana: The Magazine of Western History* 57 (spring): 48–55.

Whittlesey, Lee H. 2006. "A Brief Look at Moran Point and Artist Point and Their Association with Thomas Moran and William Henry Jackson." *Yellowstone Science* 14 (fall): 7–12.

Whittlesey, Lee H. 2003. *A Yellowstone Album: A Photographic Celebration of the First National Park*. Boulder, CO: Roberts Rinehart.

Whittlesey, Lee H. 1988, *Yellowstone Place Names*. Helena: Montana Historical Society.

Wilkins, Thurman. 1998. *Thomas Moran: Artist of the Mountains*. 2d ed., rev. and enlarged (1st ed. 1966). Norman: University of Oklahoma Press.

Williams, Raymond. 1980. *The City and the Country*. New York: Oxford University Press.

Williams, Robert A., Jr. 1997. "Thomas Jefferson: Indigenous American Storyteller." Pp. 43–74 in J. P. Ronda, ed., *Thomas Jefferson and the Changing West: From Conquest to Conservation*. Albuquerque: University of New Mexico Press.

Williams, Terry Tempest. 2001. *Red: Passion and Patience in the Desert*. New York: Pantheon.

_____. 2000. *Leap*. New York: Vintage.

_____. 1984. *Pieces of White Shell: A Journey to Navajoland*. Albuquerque: University of New Mexico Press.

Wilson, James. 1998. *The Earth Shall Weep: A History of Native America*. New York: Atlantic Monthly.

Wilton, Andrew, and Tim Barringer. 2002. *American Sublime: Landscape Painting in the United States, 1820–1880*. Princeton, NJ: Princeton University Press.

Wingate, George W. 1999. *Through the Yellowstone Park on Horseback*. With an introduction by Gordon B. Dodds. Moscow: University of Idaho Press. (Originally published 1886.)

Wister, Owen. 1936. "Old Yellowstone Days." *Harper's Monthly Magazine*, March: 474.

_____. 1902. *The Virginian: A Horseman of the Plains*. New York: Penguin.

Wolfrom, Anna. 1918. *Sacajawea: The Indian Princess, The Indian Girl Who Piloted the Lewis and Clark Expedition across the Rocky Mountains. A Play in Three Acts*. Kansas City: Burton.

Wood, Paul. 2001. "Chief Furor Leaves Boy Ostracized." *News-Gazette*, 11 March: A1, B6.

Wood, W. Raymond. 2003. *Prologue to Lewis and Clark: The Mackay and Evans Expedition*. Tulsa: University of Oklahoma Press.

Worster, Donald. 2001. *A River Running West: The Life of John Wesley Powell*. New York: Oxford University Press.

Wrobel, David M., and Patrick T. Long, eds. 2001. *Seeing and Being Seen: Tourism in the American West*. Foreword by Earl Pomeroy. Lawrence: University of Kansas Press.

Yellow Bird, Michael. 2004. "Cowboys and Indians: Toys of Genocide, Icons of American Colonization." *Wicazo Sa Review* 19 (fall):33–38.

Yellowstone Association. 2000. *Yellowstone: The Official Guided to Touring America's First National Park*. Yellowstone National Park, WY: Yellowstone Association.

Yellowstone Association Institute. 2003. Summer Calendar of Courses. Yellowstone National Park, WY: Yellowstone Association Institute.

Yellowstone Journal. 2005. Vol. 12 (June).

Yellowstone National Park. 2002. "Windows into Wonderland: The Influence of Art on Yellowstone." http://www.windowsintowonderland.org/art/parttwo/art11. htm.

Zinn, Howard. 2003. *A People's History of the United States: 1492–Present.* New York: HarperCollins. (Originally published 1980.)

Zuban, Shirley, and Harry J. Owen, eds. 2000. *Red Lodge: Saga of a Western Area Revisited*: Billings, MT: Frontier.

FILMOGRAPHY

Bury My Heart at Wounded Knee. 2007. HBO Films, a Wolf Films/Traveler's Rest Films Production: Screenplay: Daniel Giat; Director: Yves Simoneau; Cast: Aidan Quinn, Adam Beach, August Schellenberg, Eric Schweig, J. K. Simmons, Wes Studi, Colm Feore, Gordon Tootoosis, Anna Paquin, Fred Dalton Thompson.

Good Night and Good Luck. 2005. Warner Brothers. Director: George Clooney.

INDEX

ABOUT THE AUTHOR

Norman K. Denzin is Distinguished Professor of Communications, College of Communications Scholar, and Research Professor of Communications, Sociology, and Humanities at the University of Illinois, Urbana-Champaign. One of the world's foremost authorities on qualitative research and cultural criticism, Denzin is the author or editor of more than two dozen books, including *Reading Race*; *Performance Ethnography*; *The Cinematic Society*; *The Voyeur's Gaze*; *Flags at the Window: Dispatches from the American War Zone*; *Images of Postmodern Society*; *The Recovering Alcoholic*; and *The Alcoholic Self*. He is past editor of *The Sociological Quarterly*, coeditor (with Yvonna S. Lincoln) of three editions of the landmark *Handbook of Qualitative Research*, coeditor (with Michael D. Giardina) of three plenary volumes from the first three International Congresses of Qualitative Inquiry, coeditor (with Lincoln) of the methods journal *Qualitative Inquiry*, founding editor of *Cultural Studies/Critical Methodologies* and *International Review of Qualitative Research*, series editor of *Studies in Symbolic Interaction*, and *Cultural Critique* series editor for Peter Lang Publishing.